Power in Congress

Power in Congress

Who Has It

How They Got It

How They Use It

Congressional Quarterly Inc., 1414 22nd St., N.W., Washington, D.C. 20037

Congressional Quarterly Inc.

Congressional Quarterly Inc., an editorial research service and publishing company, serves clients in the fields of news, education, business, and government. It combines specific coverage of Congress, government, and politics by Congressional Quarterly with the more general subject range of an affiliated service, Editorial Research Reports.

Congressional Quarterly publishes the *Congressional Quarterly Weekly Report* and a variety of books, including college political science textbooks under the CQ Press imprint and public affairs paperbacks on developing issues and events. CQ also publishes information directories and reference books on the federal government, national elections, and politics, including the *Guide to Congress*, the *Guide to the U.S. Supreme Court*, the *Guide to U.S. Elections,* and *Politics in America*. The *CQ Almanac*, a compendium of legislation for one session of Congress, is published each year. *Congress and the Nation*, a record of government for a presidential term, is published every four years.

CQ publishes *The Congressional Monitor*, a daily report on current and future activities of congressional committees, and several newsletters including *Congressional Insight*, a weekly analysis of congressional action, and *Campaign Practices Reports*, a semimonthly update on campaign laws.

The online delivery of CQ's Washington Alert Service provides clients with immediate access to Congressional Quarterly's institutional information and expertise.

Printed in the United States of America

Library of Congress Cataloging-in-Publication Data

Power in Congress—who has it, how they got it, how they use it.

Includes index.

1. United States. Congress—Leadership. 2. United States. Congress—Committees. I. Congressional Quarterly, inc.
JK1067.P68 1987 328.73'076 87-9219
ISBN 0-87187-436-9

Editor: Tracy White.
Contributors: Jacqueline Calmes, Nadine Cohodas, Joseph A. Davis, Alan Ehrenhalt, Stephen Gettinger, Rob Gurwitt, Janet Hook, Pat Towell, Tom Watson.
Cover: Richard A. Pottern.
Graphics: pp. 6, 23, 49, 50, 59, 77 - Ken Heinen; pp. 12, 31, 38, 45, 52, 53, 75 - Sue Klemens; p. 15 - Marty LaVor © 1986; p. 26 - *South Bend Tribune;* p. 48 - *U.S. News & World Report*/Chick Harrity; pp. 55, 81, 106 - Stan Barouh; pp. 61, 86 - Brad Markel; p. 66 - Bruce Katz; p. 69 - Lana Harris; pp. 74, 95 - Teresa Zabala; p. 88 - *The Washington Post*/James K. W. Atherton; p. 91 - NYT Pictures; pp. 104, 105 - National Portrait Gallery, Smithsonian Institution.
Indexer: Bernice Eisen.

Table of Contents

Power in Congress

Introduction

Somewhere in the American political system there are bound to be people who have power and know it.

It is hard to imagine a Supreme Court justice unaware of the importance of his or her role as one of nine ultimate authorities on the meaning of the Constitution. It is equally difficult to conceive of a Federal Reserve chairman who is unable to grasp the effect he or she can have on the nation's economy.

But self-conscious power is an extreme rarity among the people who hold key positions in American political life. Government at all levels is populated by highly placed people who work hard to accumulate influence but who are convinced that the real power resides with someone else.

Thus we have governors who lament their dependence on Washington; cabinet secretaries who complain about the inertia of the departments that they run; members of Congress who feel that only the administration can do much about the federal deficit; and members of the administration who feel that only Congress can do anything about it.

Nearly anywhere one looks in politics these days, power remains an elusive commodity. It is never quite clear who has it, how they got it, or how they use it.

Heights of House Powerlessness

What is true of politics in general is true of Congress in particular. In the Senate and House of the 1980s, with old-fashioned autocracy out of fashion, nearly everyone is free to latch on to at least a share of influence over some committee or some subject. But a Congress in which power is shared is one in which most of the players spend much of their time wondering why their shares are not larger.

It may not come as much of a surprise that freshman House members, in what is supposed to be an era of equality, still complain that they are too far down the totem pole to have much impact on the problems they spent their first campaigns promising earnestly to solve. But it is interesting how far up the totem pole the feelings of powerlessness can reach.

Chairmen of House committees that are used to spending money and creating programs complain that their function in life has been all but obliterated by the tyranny of the Budget Committee, with its fixation on cutting spending and reducing deficits. But members of the Budget Committee, far from seeing themselves as tyrants, are frustrated by their inability to make a noticeable dent in the deficit during the full decade the budget process has been in operation.

House Republicans, after more than a quarter-century under the yoke of minority status, often talk of an arrogant and power-hungry Democratic majority that has made their lives, in the words of GOP leader Robert H. Michel of Illinois, "discouraging and debilitating."

But the man whose power most frustrates them, Speaker Jim Wright of Texas, does not take much comfort in his freedom to dominate Republicans—he is worried that a decline in the power of Congress as a whole has limited his ability to govern the institution the way Speakers like the late Sam Rayburn did in years gone by.

"If I had been free to choose a time in the last twenty-five years to become Speaker," Wright said shortly before taking over, "I wouldn't have chosen this moment. I'm coming to the office at a time when Congress is circumscribed."

Most members of Congress would willingly change places with Wright, of course, but wherever they are in the hierarchy of Capitol Hill, they tend to voice similar frustrations about the powerlessness of what is supposed to be a powerful place. Democrats and Republicans, junior and senior members alike, insist that they are not in it for the power—if power was all they wanted, they would be doing something else.

"For all practical purposes," said a four-term House Democrat, "power doesn't keep people here. They come, they realize they don't have it. But they don't want to switch to something else. There are only ten or fifteen people here who have real power as a result of their positions."

One gets an oddly similar answer from a top Democratic leader—somebody who would merit an automatic place on the first member's list of ten or fifteen powerful people. "It isn't often a sense of power that's important to us," he insisted. "A hell of a lot of state legislators have more power than most of us do." His theory is that members of Congress remain in office term after term because they have an intense desire to be at the center of events, even if their personal ability to influence those events is limited.

There is evidence for that point of view in the growing demand for seats on two House committees that have relatively little tangible influence on public policy. The Budget Committee not only has been unable to tame the deficit, but also produces a budget resolution that the rest of Congress often ignores as the crucial spending decisions are made piece by piece over the course of the year. The Foreign Affairs Committee possesses little legislative responsibility of any kind; the job of its members is largely to comment on foreign policy decisions made by the executive branch.

At a time when deficits and foreign policy controversies dominate the news, committees like Budget and Foreign Affairs are the center of attention and excitement. That may or may not be power, but for many members of the House, it seems to be fun.

Limits on Senate Power

Senators cannot complain of powerlessness in quite the same way House members can. Each one of them serves on a variety of committees broad enough to allow unregulated grazing over the legislative spectrum, and whatever a senator is not able to bring up in committee, he or she can introduce on the floor, where it does not even have to be germane to the subject under discussion.

But in recent years, senators have worried about power in a different way. The more freedom they acquire as individuals, the more paralyzed their institution seems to become.

The right to filibuster, reserved a generation ago for the civil rights question and a handful of other historically divisive issues, is now used with virtual impunity on dozens of less important subjects. A handful of intransigent senators—one, if he or she is determined enough—can prevent the passage of any bill that does not have the sixty votes required to force the filibuster to a close. More commonly, especially in the crucial last few weeks of a session, a senator can use the threat of filibuster to prevent the leadership from bringing legislation to the floor at all.

It is this problem that has led numerous senators to lament in recent years, especially as sessions trudge awkwardly to an end, that they feel mired in futility as they serve in what are supposed to be positions of national influence. "Unless we recognize that things are out of control and procedures have to be changed," Democrat Dale Bumpers of Arkansas said during the 98th Congress, "we'll never be an effective legislative body again."

Since then, that has emerged as an increasingly common sentiment. But when it comes to expressing Senate frustrations, the champion has been Barry Goldwater, who retired in 1986 after thirty years as a Republican senator from Arizona. "If this is the world's greatest deliberative body," he told a colleague one day in 1982, "I'd hate to see the world's worst."

Two years later, as the Senate met in a Saturday session forced by a filibuster, he told his colleagues on the floor that they were "beginning to look like a bunch of jackasses." Malcolm Wallop, his GOP colleague from Wyoming, consoled him by pointing out that the condition had existed for some time.

And in May of 1986, when Republican leaders gave in to a Democratic filibuster and agreed to postpone a key vote on President Ronald Reagan's proposed Saudi arms sale, Goldwater told them bluntly that they—the majority party—were losing effective control of the institution. "We are supposed to run this place," he said, "but I am beginning to think we do not."

Few are as blunt as Goldwater, but most members of the House and Senate seem to feel the way he does at least a few times during a standard congressional session. There remain some traditional conservatives, like former Republican representative Barber B. Conable of New York, who point out that the legislative branch was designed to impede government power, not to facilitate it. "Congress is working the way it is supposed to work," Conable used to enjoy saying, "which is not very well."

Power Exercised

Fortunately, however, at least for those of a more activist bent than Conable, there is a significant gap between what members of Congress say and what they are able to accomplish.

The 99th Congress, which adjourned in October 1986 after as frustrating an end-of-session marathon as any in recent years, did after all rewrite the nation's immigration laws and overhaul the Internal Revenue Code virtually from scratch. Both were legislative projects of immense complexity, involving too many powerful societal forces even to count, and neither one developed a significant constituency among the American people. But both were achieved.

Cynics who consider those broad accomplishments flukes should at least think about the skill with which individual members of Congress accumulate and use power every day, year in and year out. Some of those individuals and their methods are detailed in the pages that follow.

They include such diverse members as Democratic representative Henry A. Waxman of California, who accomplished the piecemeal enactment of a new national health program for children during six years of retrenchment for just such programs under the Reagan administration; Republican representative Edward R. Madigan of Illinois, Waxman's sometime-adversary on the House Energy and Commerce Committee, who influences dozens of public policy questions in every Congress while GOP colleagues bemoan their powerlessness as members of the minority; Republican senator Phil Gramm of Texas, who arrived in Congress in 1979, helped rewrite the federal budget in 1981, and successfully promoted a dramatic spending reduction initiative as a newly elected senator four years later, all without benefit of the personal popularity usually considered essential for success of that sort; and Democratic senator Bill Bradley of New Jersey, whose sheer determination and intellectual persistence managed to keep tax revision alive at a time when dozens of members of more obvious political skill were announcing its demise.

Other power-related topics examined in these pages include the influence of the leadership in the House and Senate, the constant power of some committees and the cyclical power of most of the others, the difficulties of state delegation power, and the role the media play in portraying and, perhaps, boosting the power of members.

A long look at these subjects suggests that the real story of power in Congress is not the frustration most members feel about its absence, but the amount that a few people are able to do in an institution that often seems designed to block them at every turn.

1

The Hill Leaders

Less than three months passed between the end of the 99th Congress and the start of the historic 100th, but in that time the nation's political ground had convulsed. About all that remained stable were the leadership teams that members of both parties, in both chambers, chose to guide them.

In 1986 a foreign-policy scandal threatened to paralyze President Reagan's administration in its final two years, and to preoccupy Congress. And for the first time in his presidency, Congress was entirely in Democrats' hands after heavier-than-expected losses in the November 1986 elections cost Republicans control of the Senate.

The upheaval in government contrasted with the continuity that marked the House and Senate leadership elections late in 1986. Despite growing emphasis on leaders' public appeal and their role as national party spokesmen, members in each chamber remained loyal to those who, for the most part, had made it up the leadership ladder the traditional way—as insiders, appealing to their small circle of party colleagues.

The 100th Congress marks the institution's bicentennial. But the history of selecting leaders does not go back nearly so far as 1789; the process and every office except Speaker, which was created in the Constitution, evolved only in this century, and particularly in the postwar years.

Following is a look at those offices, the members who hold them, and the power they wield as Congress heads into its third century.

House Leaders

In the House all top Democratic offices but one changed hands in the reshuffling after Speaker Thomas P. O'Neill, Jr., of Massachusetts retired. Yet the result was less a changing of the guard than a promotion of the existing one.

Jim Wright of Texas, majority leader throughout O'Neill's ten-year speakership, succeeded him without opposition. Likewise, Thomas S. Foley of Washington rose unchallenged from the number three Democratic post of majority whip, the leadership's chief vote-counter, to take Wright's old job as majority leader.

The new whip, Tony Coelho of California, is former chairman of the fund-raising Democratic Congressional Campaign Committee (DCCC). Coelho easily defeated two rivals in the only contest of the December

In electing a Speaker, Democrats have hewed to a longstanding pattern of succession. Jim Wright of Texas became the eleventh in a row to advance from party floor leader to House Speaker.

1986 House leadership elections.

Richard A. Gephardt of Missouri won an uncontested second term as Democratic Caucus chairman. The leadership then chose David E. Bonior of Michigan from among seven deputy whips to be chief deputy whip, and named Beryl Anthony, Jr., of Arkansas to be DCCC chairman.

In electing a Speaker, Democrats hewed to a longstanding pattern of succession. Of the fifteen Speakers in this century, Wright became the twelfth—and the eleventh in a row since 1925—to advance from the post of party floor leader.

But the 1986 leadership elections were notable in that Democrats not only adhered to what Congress scholar Robert L. Peabody has called an "automatic escalator" from leader to Speaker, but they also took action that could cement a third step, from whip to leader.

That already is a trend, though not so old as the leader-to-Speaker pattern. Of the six Democratic floor leaders since 1949, Foley is the fifth to move up from whip. The exception was Wright; he was a deputy whip in 1976 when he beat the majority whip and two others to become leader.

Electing the Whip

In 1986, for the first time, the whip was elected rather than hand-picked by the leadership. "Having the whip elected rather than appointed gives the whip even more glow in climbing the leadership ladder. You've got a pretty strong endorsement behind you, having been elected by the majority of your caucus," said former Speaker Carl Albert of Oklahoma (1947-1977). Albert, like Speaker John McCormack (1928-1971) of Massachusetts before him and O'Neill after him, held all three top offices.

But Coelho pointed out that he must win members' approval every two years, unlike an appointive whip. And Morris K. Udall of Arizona predicted, "It's going to invite takers-on."

That kind of attention on the entry-level whip's job, some observers suggest, will distract would-be competitors for the top two spots.

Lynne P. Brown, an expert on congressional leadership at New York University who watched the Democrats' caucus from the House gallery, said, "What struck me was the top two slots going completely uncontested. Perhaps making the whip elective siphoned off some of the competitive spirit that otherwise may have been focused at the top offices. It's been an easy climb from majority leader to Speaker, but openings for majority leader have usually been contested."

Senate Democrats and Republicans in both chambers long have elected whips, who are their number two leaders. But for

House Democrats, who have controlled the chamber and picked the Speaker for most of this century, the whip is third in line behind the Speaker and majority leader. Those two appointed the whip to ensure loyalty.

Making the office elective was a concession to junior members. Since the 1970s, they had demanded a voice in picking the officer who seemed to be in line for Speaker.

Also, they said the whip should act as a liaison officer between them and the leaders, not merely the leaders' enforcer and intelligence agent. "It democratized the process," said third-term member Richard J. Durbin of Illinois.

"I guess I think a good case can be made that the pattern of succession has solidified, that the whip is an heir apparent, so there is a good case for election," Brown said. "At the same time, you have to decide, who are the followers?"

Senior Democrat Dan Rostenkowski of Illinois, who was considered for whip in 1971 and 1981, said of elections, "I think that was the biggest mistake we made. It should not be a popularity contest. The whip was the workhorse who looked at you as a member and pointed out your frailties, who could say, 'If this vote's a matter of philosophy or if your election hinges on it, go ahead and take a walk. But you're just being cantankerous. . . .' Now the whip has to massage members.

"The guys that have to watch the whip are the majority leader and the Speaker. The whip has no obligation to them, because he's elected."

As Coelho's case illustrated, electing the whip also can cost members a geographically balanced leadership.

Traditionally, the Speaker and leader named their lieutenant from a region other than theirs. Since Wright, Foley, and Coelho are all from west of the Mississippi River, the leaders have filled other, lower posts with members from east of that divide.

Up the Democrats' Escalator

House Democrats have been able to all but institutionalize their lines of succession because of the long time they have been the majority—fifty-two of the past fifty-six years.

Peabody first suggested more than a decade ago that the process had become like an escalator. Now, he said, "I don't know if it's a good thing; it can be argued that it eliminates competition at all levels." But, he added, "It allows the House to get on with business." Transitions, like the one between the 99th and 100th Congresses, are smooth.

Wright likes the process: "The best thing that can be said for it is, it works. Congress needs to be led by people who understand the institution and the problems, and who have seen Congress grapple with things, succeed, and fail."

Among the critics are two members who have been frustrated by the system. "It's a good thing if you're the majority leader," quipped Rostenkowski, who in the previous two years had considered running for Speaker but decided he could not muster the votes to overcome Wright.

Udall, who led an unsuccessful revolt of young Democrats against Speaker McCormack in 1969 and lost the majority leadership to Whip Hale Boggs of Louisiana in 1971, said, "It would be hard to do, but there ought to be some rules to make it harder [for leaders to advance].

"I was chiding Wright and Coelho this fall—we talk so much about the rights of the unborn; what about the rights of the unelected? Thirty to forty new Democrats come here in December, saying, 'We're glad to be here and decide on our leaders.' And

Elected Whip Tony Coelho: . . .

For years, House Democratic reformers argued that the rank and file, not party leaders, should pick the majority whip because that job had become the first step on an escalator to the speakership.

Members finally got their chance December 8, 1986, when for the first time the whip was elected rather than appointed. But their choice of Tony Coelho of California to be House Democrats' third-ranking leader, chief vote-counter, and floor manager was like most other internal House elections. It turned on the candidates' personal relations with their colleagues, not on some forward-looking concern for who might be Speaker by the twenty-first century.

"I think each election stands on its own," said Doug Barnard, Jr., of Georgia, a Coelho supporter. "When you win the confidence of the majority of sitting members, it's evidence of the esteem you are held in at that time. I don't think it's any guarantee of passage." Coelho agreed. "The whip will be elected every two years," he said. "If members aren't satisfied, they can make a change."

In modern times, however, that has rarely happened; only death or defeat at the polls back home have knocked climbers from the Democratic leadership ladder.

Both former Speaker Thomas P. O'Neill, Jr., of Massachusetts (1977-1986) and his predecessor, Carl Albert of Oklahoma (1947-1977), rose to the top after serving as whip and majority leader. Majority Leader Hale Boggs of Louisiana (1941-1943, 1947-1973) was reaching for the last of the three steps when he was killed in a 1972 plane crash in Alaska.

Majority Whip John Brademas of Indiana (1959-1981) was defeated for reelection to Congress in 1980, but his successor, Thomas S. Foley of Washington, now has been elected majority leader and is widely considered heir apparent to Jim Wright of Texas. Of recent leaders, only Wright skipped the whip's job on his way up; he became majority leader in 1976, beating the incumbent whip, John McFall of California, and three other rivals.

Money and Kindness

Coelho's springboard onto this ladder was a job once held by O'Neill—chairmanship of the Democratic Congressional Campaign Committee (DCCC), the party's fund-raising arm for House campaigns. Even his rivals for whip praised Coelho for modernizing and enriching the DCCC in the six years since the Democrats' 1980 losses.

When a leadership reshuffling loomed after O'Neill announced his retirement in 1985, and House Democrats changed their rules to make the whip an elective post, Coelho was the front-runner from the start. He never lost that status against as many as five rivals, and easily defeated the only two who stayed in the race to the end. The vote, by secret ballot, was 167 for Coelho, 78 for Charles B. Rangel, N.Y., and 15 for W. G. "Bill" Hefner, N.C.

"Money, whether we like it or not, is a pretty powerful tool," Hefner said, referring to Coelho's advantage as DCCC chairman. "He was the man who signed the checks," Rangel said.

. . . Harvesting the Fruits of His Labor

In particular, Coelho drew support among younger members elected and reelected with his help. As John D. Dingell, Mich., noted in a speech nominating Coelho, three-fourths of House Democrats have been elected since 1978, and "all can point to what Tony has done to see that they're here."

But junior members more often cited his visits to their districts or other personal favors rather than DCCC contributions. "I was good friends with him when I first ran in 1982," said Ronald D. Coleman of Texas. "He came to the district—stood with me in the plaza in El Paso."

"The 1982 class was almost raised by Tony," said another member of that class, Jim Cooper of Tennessee. "What matters when you come here is who's been nice to you, who's helped you out on all the petty day-to-day issues."

Barbara B. Kennelly, Conn., said that when she arrived in Congress after a special election in 1982, only Coelho paid much attention. "That kindness that Tony showed me then I will never forget," she said.

Coelho has kept in touch regularly with the mother of Richard H. Lehman, Calif., since the time in 1973 when Lehman's seventeen-year-old brother Charlie was killed in an auto accident en route to work at the district office of Rep. B. F. Sisk, D-Calif. (1955-1979). Coelho ran Sisk's Washington office. "That tells you something about Tony," Lehman said. "He has a caring, sensitive side to him that gets lost when people just think of the numbers man."

Starting Early

Coelho also benefited from early groundwork that won numerous commitments. One supporter, W. J. "Billy" Tauzin, La., said, "Rangel called me and asked for support and I said, 'Charlie, would you ask a fellow to break his word?' I'd committed to Coelho way back."

Hefner said that when he began campaigning "lots of new members, especially southerners, said they'd committed to Tony already."

Among those who backed his rivals, Coelho won promises of support if their chosen candidates dropped out—as three eventually did. "I was first committed to Bill Alexander [Ark.] because of a close, personal relationship we'd had since I came, but I was heavily approached during that time by Coelho," Barnard said. "When Alexander dropped out, I gave him my commitment."

In the final months, however, Rangel seemed a threat. He argued strongly that the leadership should be balanced geographically, and that with Coelho as whip it would be composed only of members from west of the Mississippi.

Coelho's efforts to blunt that pitch were reflected in the five speakers he chose to nominate him during the December 1986 Democratic caucus. These supporters represented all regions, and each stressed that Coelho was "a national Democrat" whose DCCC work had made him familiar with all members' districts and constituent pressures.

we in effect say to them, 'Sorry, friend, it's too late. You have this guy who once was picked by some long-forgotten Speaker to be assistant whip and here he is.' You permit the past generation to pick the leaders of the future."

Critics have suggested the escalator advances leaders who are wrong for the times when they finally reach the top.

Wright came to the House just two years after O'Neill, in 1955. For both men, Sam Rayburn of Texas (1913-1961) was their first example of a Speaker—a benevolent autocrat with power so centralized he was said to run the House out of his hip pocket.

As Brown said of O'Neill, "When he came of political age, the House was tremendously hierarchical." But O'Neill became Speaker in 1977, two years after junior Democrats forced democratizing changes, and "the style of his reign was one of inclusiveness. . . . He did what all leaders do—the style depends on the situation you find yourself in if you want to stay leader."

Wright's Style

Similarly, while observers expect Wright to strengthen the Speaker's office, no one anticipates an attempt to turn back the clock.

Immediately after his election by the caucus, Wright outlined a legislative program and appointed allies to the deputy whips' organization and to the Steering and Policy Committee that makes Democrats' committee assignments. He also indicated that he would revive Steering and Policy's policy-making role.

"The new Speaker has enormous leeway and has shown he plans to use it," political scientist Nelson W. Polsby, a visiting professor at Harvard University, said.

Wright oversees work on major legislation, directing the various committee chairmen to play their parts in turn and speedily. Three bills that he shepherded through the House in 1986—aimed at terrorism, illegal drugs, and the trade deficit—"are valid models for [dealing with] important national problems," he said. "If several committees are involved, there needs to be some coherence."

"Jim Wright obviously intends to influence legislation," Udall said. Peabody predicted Wright "is going to be the exception" to his finding that leaders rarely get involved in legislative substance. "The question is to what extent he can do that without stepping on chairmen's toes." Wright's response: "Bring 'em in and make 'em part of the team."

Another risk is getting too far ahead of your followers. Some say Wright did just that on the day of his election, when he said that deficit reduction might require delaying cuts in income tax rates, which were the linchpin of the 1986 tax code overhaul.

Wright needs his followers. Junior members dominate the 258-member Democratic Caucus. Moreover, changes of the recent past, particularly the dilution of chairmen's power and the revival of the caucus as a policy voice, have enhanced their impact.

"The only way to lead now is by consensus," said Buddy MacKay of Florida, elected in 1982. It is his sanguine view that anyone can succeed with a good idea and a coalition; to that end, he and others are active in caucuses on the budget and trade. Leaders, he said, "are going to lead where the followers want to go."

That is not to say the Speaker is powerless. In fact, the democratizing changes since the 1970s were mostly at committee chairmen's expense. The Speaker was given new control over floor action and committee assignments through his power to pick members of the Rules and Steering and Policy committees.

"When it comes to the Speaker's power, the big thing is the ability to name the Rules Committee," said Gary Hymel, former aide to Boggs and O'Neill, now chief lobbyist for Hill and Knowlton. Rules sets the terms under which nearly every House bill is debated. *(See Chapter 4.)*

"The Speaker is more powerful today than any time since the revolt against Joe Cannon," Polsby said.

In the 1910 reaction against the tyrannical Joseph G. Cannon of Illinois, the Speaker was stripped of the Rules chairmanship and the power to make committee assignments. The office declined for years afterward, while the position of majority leader developed and gained in stature.

Wright's Leadership Team

In viewing the Wright era, it is essential to assess the roles of others on his leadership team.

Foley is widely esteemed as a coalition builder, a bridge both between Democratic factions and to the Republicans. As a whip since 1981, he seemed tailored to British prime minister Benjamin Disraeli's nineteenth-century remark that the job required someone with "consummate knowledge of human nature, the most amiable flexibility, and complete self-control."

In a majority leader, however, some members initially seemed to want someone more partisan. Foley's chances of advancing to that post were at first uncertain. But his work through the 99th Congress, particularly on the budget and in opposition to Reagan's request to arm Nicaraguan rebels, solidified his support, especially among junior members.

As Wright self-deprecatingly conceded after his election, the deliberate and even-tempered Foley complements his own rash, hot-tempered inclinations.

"Tom is cautious; he's unlikely to go off on any bongo crusades," Udall said. "He balances nicely with Jim Wright, who is gung-ho lots of the time, sees a problem and wants to solve it this afternoon."

Foley's link to junior Democrats, which can alert him—and has—to restiveness brewing among them, recalls his own days as a reform-minded member; he backed Udall in both his bids against established leaders.

But it is Coelho whom many younger members consider their direct link to the leadership. The question is how well he will relate to his fellow leaders, especially Wright.

Around the time of the 1984 elections, Coelho was an organizer, along with Gephardt and the late Gillis Long of Louisiana, then-chairman of the Democratic Caucus, of a group that met periodically to discuss the future of the House and the party—and how both might be improved without O'Neill or Wright as national spokesman. Though Coelho and Gephardt insisted afterward that the meetings were meant only as constructive forums, others describe them in terms of a "conspiracy" or "revolution."

Little came of the sessions. O'Neill suspected Coelho as the instigator, sources say, but Wright's attitude is not clear. One insider said Wright views Coelho as one of perhaps two members "capable of leading a rebellion." The other is Rostenkowski.

Wright and Rostenkowski

That Wright and Rostenkowski are depicted as rivals is ironic, since Rostenkowski managed Wright's upset victory for majority leader a decade ago. But since that time, associates say, a chill has set in as each man correctly perceived the other as the chief rival for a common life's ambition—the speakership. It is compounded, they say, by Wright's seeming anxiety about Rostenkowski's ambitions and Rostenkowski's refusal to disavow them. "I can't conceive of any member of Congress *not* wanting to be

In 1986 Tony Coelho, D-Calif., became the House's first elected whip. Unlike an appointive whip, the elected whip must win members' approval every two years.

Speaker," Rostenkowski said in an interview.

Despite more than twenty-eight years in the House, watching others climb the leadership ladder with hardly a fall, he has not given up hope of breaking in out of line, insiders say. So he helped Wright in 1976 and then in 1981, though he was in line for the whip's job, opted instead to be chairman of Ways and Means, never believing that he might be putting the top rung out of reach. He freely acknowledges that he had considered challenging Wright for the speakership.

Asked what had happened between them, he said, "Nothing. . . . I just think I could have been a better Speaker. I'm not saying he won't be a good Speaker. I like Jim Wright. He's my friend."

For Rostenkowski, the disappointment of not being Speaker is exacerbated by a firm belief that he would be if not for Carl Albert. The breach between them dates to 1968; Albert, then majority leader, was presiding at the riotous Democratic Convention in Chicago, and Rostenkowski, at the command of Mayor Richard J. Daley and President Lyndon Johnson, wrested the gavel to take control.

In 1970, when Albert opened his bid to succeed McCormack as Speaker the coming January, Rostenkowski withheld Illinois members' letter of support, at Daley's urging. Meanwhile, he worked hard for Bogg's election as majority leader, and Boggs planned to name him whip.

"When Boggs suggested Rostenkowski for whip, I just vetoed it," Albert recalled. "I said, 'It's got to be somebody who supports me.' "

For Rostenkowski, it was a double loss; days before he had been defeated for a third term as caucus chairman. Albert tapped O'Neill; two years later, O'Neill became majority leader when a plane carrying Boggs disappeared in Alaska, and by 1977 he had succeeded Albert as Speaker.

Rostenkowski takes credit for Wright's victory in the 1976 majority leadership race from start to finish.

"I talked him into running," he said, took him to Chicago to meet Daley and, with the mayor, lined up support of other big-city members, traded vote-counting intelligence with rival Phillip Burton of California, and devised the strategy for a second-ballot victory.

On the final vote, Rostenkowski said, he persuaded Thomas L. Ashley of Ohio (1955-1981) to switch his support from Burton to Wright. Wright won by a single vote.

Whether Wright and Rostenkowski are rivals is of more than academic interest; any tax or trade bill Wright might favor must come from Rostenkowski's committee.

"As someone who has worked long and hard with Danny, and who has watched Wright over many years, I would be very cautious in describing them as rivals," former Rostenkowski aide James C. Healey said. "I think they'll work very well together. The press makes more of personal feuds than there is."

Wright denies there is a feud.

Rostenkowski said, "We won't always agree," and, insofar as he harbors ambitions to be Speaker, "I am a rival." But, like Healey, he suggested reporters exaggerate: "They want to see a fight up here."

Republican Leaders

While Democrats are easing into a new era of leadership, House Republicans are headed for the fourth Congress by the same team.

Once again, Robert H. Michel of Illinois is minority leader; Trent Lott of Mississippi, minority whip; Jack F. Kemp of New York, conference chairman; and Dick Cheney of Wyoming, the Policy Committee chairman. Guy Vander Jagt of Michigan is in his thirteenth year as head of the National Republican Congressional Committee, fund-raiser for House GOP candidates.

The only newcomer is Edward R. Madigan of Illinois, Lott's choice as chief deputy whip. The appointment seemed to defy the norms of congressional leadership selection. Madigan is older than most lower-echelon leaders. He does nothing for geographic balance, coming from the same state as Michel and Lynn Martin, the conference vice chairman. And Madigan already is something of a leadership veteran as ranking member of the Agriculture Committee. *(See pp. 50-51.)*

Continuity—the 1980s evidence notwithstanding—is not as much a leadership tradition for House Republicans as it is for Democrats. While no House Democratic leader has been unseated in modern times, two Republicans have. Charles Halleck of Indiana (1935-1969) ousted Joseph W. Martin, Jr., of Massachusetts (1925-1967) as minority leader in 1959, and Halleck in turn was defeated by Gerald R. Ford of Michigan in 1965.

Polsby attributes Republicans' greater restiveness to two factors. They lose more elections, which provokes survivors to seek change; the heavy electoral losses in 1958 and 1964 were partly responsible for Martin's and Halleck's ousters.

Also, Republicans have a larger proportion of ambitious junior members because party elders tend to move to higher office or retire early, frustrated by life in the minority and without hope of a committee chairmanship.

In addition, a minority leader has none of the Speaker's powers over lower-level leadership posts, committee staffing and assignments, or the floor fate of members' bills, so he cannot compel allegiance like the Democrats' leader. Absent such inside benefits, political ideology has played more of a role.

It is a measure of Michel's ability that he has survived in the Reagan years, given the 1982 election losses, his members' jealousy of Senate Republicans for their majority status and influence at the White House, and the increasing activism of his members on both the left and right.

The threat was always greater on the right, with junior conservatives urging confrontation with Democrats. With what he calls "gentle persuasion," Michel has balanced their demands against those of moderates in the party. Having maintained his lines to Democrats, he is able to win victories that would be impossible without their votes.

"It takes a genius to get unity and shared purpose out of such a group, and Bob Michel has done it time and time again," Henry J. Hyde of Illinois said in nominating Michel.

In his acceptance speech, Michel displayed a feisty new style—but one geared more toward fellow Republicans in the Senate and the administration than House Democrats. "With the loss of the Senate, we have a new and important role to play," he said. "We intend to be heard and heeded. . . . It is precisely at a time like this that the president needs congressional leadership on the Hill." Michel expressed regret about the Senate loss, but relief that House Republicans now could act without always deferring to a GOP majority there.

Senate Leaders

In the Senate the Democratic and Republican leaders remain the same, but their roles changed dramatically as Democrats reclaimed the majority they had held for twenty-six years before 1980.

Majority life is nothing new to the Democratic leaders. The top three—Majority Leader Robert C. Byrd of West Virginia, Majority Whip Alan Cranston of California, and Conference Secretary Daniel K. Inouye of Hawaii—all have served for ten years, the first four in the majority.

Though Republicans were in control six years, their leadership team led only for the last two. Robert Dole of Kansas is minority leader; Alan K. Simpson of Wyoming assistant minority leader; and John H. Chafee of Rhode Island, conference chairman.

Both parties have new chairmen for their campaign fund-raising arms: John Kerry of Massachusetts at the Democratic Senatorial Campaign Committee and Rudy Boschwitz of Minnesota at the National Republican Senatorial Committee.

The offices of leader and whip (the latter known as assistant leader on the GOP side) are of more recent vintage than House offices. In the House the Speaker had evolved from a ceremonial presiding officer to a power center by the Civil War, a minority leader was in place to counter the Speaker by the 1880s, and majority leaders were taking some floor-management duties from committee chairmen after the turn of the century.

But the Senate had no central authority, and committee chairmen continued to control floor action, until the leader and whip jobs evolved in 1911-1913. Peabody, in his book *Leadership in Congress*, attributes the Senate's late start to the weaker party loyalties of its members and their characteristic individualism—traits that continue to separate House members and senators.

Since the Senate offices took hold, Byrd is the eleventh Democratic floor leader and Dole the fifteenth Republican leader. In the 100th Congress, facing off across the Senate's center aisle, as they did in the 99th Congress, almost everything except the position of their desks has changed.

Byrd: Majority Rules

Byrd is no longer just the protector of the minority; he occasionally must be the impartial representative of all senators, on the floor and against the House and the administration. His party cannot devote most of its efforts to objecting to GOP initiatives as it did in the minority; it must enact legislation of its own.

To legislate, Byrd needs votes, and here he has an edge over his Republican predecessors as majority leader, Dole and Howard H. Baker, Jr., of Tennessee (1967-1985, majority leader 1981-1985). His party has a fifty-four to forty-six margin of control, larger than either GOP leader enjoyed.

But it is smaller than the Democrats' margin during Byrd's earlier stint as majority leader. He must hold his own troops and, on occasion, attract enough Republicans to offset defectors.

Senate Majority Leader Robert C. Byrd of West Virginia must be the impartial representative of all senators, on the floor and against the House and the administration.

Though criticized as a poor party spokesman, Byrd draws strength among colleagues for his willingness to let those with expertise articulate policy. On the Senate floor, he is the foremost expert on rules and procedure.

But the mandate to govern is not limited to the Senate. With Democrats also controlling the House, Byrd and Wright share responsibility for proposing legislative alternatives to Reagan's policies and then steering them through both chambers and onto the president's desk. That is especially critical as the two parties position for the 1988 presidential election.

Both Byrd, who did not get along well with O'Neill, and Wright have repeatedly pledged to cooperate.

In December 1986 Byrd told a Democratic audience, "This Speaker and this majority leader are going to work closer together than this country has seen the Senate and House work together since the days when Lyndon Johnson was leader of the Senate and Sam Rayburn was leader of the House." Texas Democrats Johnson and Rayburn led concurrently, 1955-1961.

Dole: Minority Campaigns

Dole, meanwhile, no longer has to answer for the Senate's record of achievement. He is freer to attack the other party.

At the same time, observers say, too acerbic an approach could revive the damaging "hatchet man" reputation of his unsuccessful campaign as President Ford's running mate in 1976—just as Dole is revving up his expected 1988 campaign for the presidency. And if Reagan or the Republican senators hope to have any impact on legislation, Dole must work with Senate Democrats.

Polsby said both Dole and Michel are constrained by their obligation to coordinate strategy with the White House. Now that is a greater burden. A president's influence in Congress typically wanes in his final two years, but Reagan has been further hobbled by the 1986 Iran arms scandal.

Meanwhile, Dole is increasingly preoccupied with his presidential campaign. *(See pages 21-29.)* A full-scale campaign requires that Dole be repeatedly absent during most or all of the two-year Congress. It will be harder to schedule campaign appearances around Senate business because, as minority leader, Dole loses the critical power over what legislation the Senate debates, and when.

Dole also has less power than Byrd within party circles, and that is true regardless of who heads the majority. A Democratic leader also chairs the party's conference, which is the Senate Democrats' caucus, its policy committee, and the Steering Committee that makes committee assignments.

Efficiency of Household Appliances . . .

On February 5, 1987, the Senate faced its first head-on test of party strength in the 100th Congress. The issue was who runs the Senate.

By the time it was over, a new precedent had been set under Senate rules and Senate Majority Leader Robert C. Byrd, D-W.Va., had chastised Vice President George Bush for a ruling he made as the Senate's presiding officer.

The power of the minority in Congress is the power to delay, and Republicans, as the new minority, were reminding the Democrats they held it. The Democrats, in turn, set about reminding the Republicans that they held the power of moving a bill.

But the GOP pulled out Bush as their hole card—giving them some sway over rulings of the chair and the recognition of members.

To add to the tension, both Minority Leader Robert Dole of Kansas and Phil Gramm, R-Texas, claimed they had been denied recognition by the chair—an offense of the first magnitude under Senate rules and tradition—when a Democrat was presiding.

The immediate fuss was over a bill setting energy efficiency standards for household appliances and some fairly obscure points of order under Senate rules.

The flap began when Gramm sought to prevent Byrd from calling up the appliance bill. President Reagan pocket-vetoed a virtually identical measure late in 1986, and the White House still opposed the bill on the grounds that it intruded on the free market.

Gramm, whose antiregulatory philosophy matches that of Reagan, had asked leaders of both parties for a delay in taking up the bill. Gramm said he wanted to give the administration time to come up with a compromise offer, to educate his colleagues on the issues, and to avoid another veto and override battle.

Byrd, however, decided to proceed. "As the majority leader of the Senate, I have a responsibility to try to keep the Senate moving and to act on the calendar," he said.

Under Senate rules, a motion to proceed to a bill is nondebatable during "morning business" (usually the first two hours of a legislative day, devoted to routine matters). Byrd hoped to make a motion to proceed during morning business.

Gramm, meanwhile, tried to delay the motion to proceed for two hours, so he could filibuster it. He tried to do that by forcing a time-consuming series of quorum calls and challenging Byrd's motion to dispense with the reading of the *Journal* of the previous day.

Dole must share those powers under Republicans' decentralized system. Separate leaders chair the conference (Chafee), policy committee (William L. Armstrong of Colorado), and Committee on Committees (Paul S. Trible, Jr., of Virginia).

For both Dole and Byrd, however, real day-to-day power rests on their powers of persuasion, their ability to wring concessions from independent members. Asked what power a GOP leader has, former assistant majority leader Ted Stevens of Alaska quickly answered, "Whatever he earns."

"The days of the strong Lyndon Johnson and Everett Dirksen-type leaders are gone," said William F. Hildenbrand, former top aide to minority leaders Hugh Scott of Pennsylvania and Baker, and secretary of the Senate from 1981-1985. Dirksen of

... Sets Off Senate Power Skirmish

In a 1986 resolution authorizing live TV coverage of floor proceedings, the Senate approved a couple of rules changes designed to avoid monotonous delays and unseemly filibusters. In one such change, it made undebatable the motion to approve the *Journal*, so that it does not have to be read. Gramm could not delay that motion with debate, so he had to use quorum calls and related procedures.

After more than an hour of seeing senators called repeatedly to the floor, only to hear Gramm suggest that a quorum was not present, Byrd, widely recognized as a master parliamentarian, counterattacked.

Byrd made a point of order that a second quorum call, once a quorum has already been established, on a motion to approve the *Journal* is dilatory and therefore out of order. Harry Reid, D-Nev., who was presiding at the time, submitted that point of order to the Senate, which sustained it 51-38, largely along party lines.

Before that vote was taken, pandemonium erupted on the floor—with Gramm trying to stop the vote with repeated protests that a quorum was not present. Reid said that the purpose of the roll call was to decide whether such a quorum call was in order and ordered the clerk to go ahead calling the roll.

Dole at that point appealed the ruling of the chair, although he did not specify which ruling. Reid answered that a roll call was in progress, although the calling of names by the clerk had not actually begun. This was when Dole said Reid failed to recognize him.

Dole, as the roll call began, was heard to say, "Get the vice president."

The vice president rushed over to the Senate from the White House, and was in the chair when the roll call ended. He proceeded to Gramm's quorum call and approval of the *Journal*. By that time, however, the two-hour period was over, and Gramm had won a tactical victory for the day.

Byrd said the Senate had set a precedent by sustaining his point of order, and that Bush had failed to recognize that precedent when he proceeded to Gramm's last quorum call. Bush, however, insisted he had done nothing wrong.

The timing of the bill's consideration was ultimately settled for a later date.

Illinois, GOP minority leader from 1959-1969, and Johnson represent for each party the leaders who, by force of personality and legislative skill, gained unprecedented power over colleagues.

"Members in those days allowed that to happen because it was considered part of the institution," Hildenbrand said. "Members today don't care about the institution and the traditions of the Senate like the members thirty years ago did. They are looking out for themselves, and their party."

Insiders on Top

Concern for party was the reason two Democrats in as many Congresses gave for seeking to unseat Byrd. Lawton Chiles of Florida failed in December 1984 after a one-week campaign. In 1986 J. Bennett

Johnston of Louisiana campaigned for about six months but withdrew the week before the November 20 elections caucus.

Chiles and Johnston voiced the disgruntlement of moderate-to-conservative Democrats that the national party and its leaders did not convey a vibrant, middle-of-the-road image that appealed to voters, especially in the South. The complaints paralleled those directed against O'Neill in the House during Reagan's first term.

The two senators' failure to convert such dissatisfaction into a successful coup illustrates a central fact about leaders in both chambers, including Byrd. Leaders reach the top after years of spending time on the floor, mastering parliamentary rules and constantly doing favors for members. A challenger who comes in at the final act, exhorting members to think beyond personal relationships, generally is doomed to fail.

Polsby first contrasted the successful "inside strategy" with what he called the "outside strategy" in 1962, in an analysis of Albert's victory for majority leader. Albert, the insider, easily defeated Richard Bolling of Missouri, who had mobilized national interest groups behind an issue-oriented campaign.

Polsby, observing leadership races twenty-five years later, said, "On average, I would bet on the inside strategy." Brown agreed: "There is lip service to picking leaders who can forge policy and carry it to the people, but . . . an inside strategy is still what wins elections."

Post-Byrd, Post-Dole

In 1986, during the time Byrd was lining up support to withstand Johnston's challenge, reports circulated that he had told senators he would serve only one more term if elected. Byrd later refused to confirm or deny the reports.

In any case, members and observers have begun speculating about successors to both Byrd and Dole, in the event that Dole's presidential bid causes him to step down. What feeds speculation is the fact that neither party in the Senate has developed a pattern of succession as predictable as that of House Democrats.

"In general, you wouldn't expect that, given the fact you are working with smaller numbers," Polsby said. "Members' personal idiosyncracies are more obvious."

"Senators often tend to see these positions [leader and assistant leader] in terms of different positions to be filled by different kinds of people," Norman J. Ornstein, an expert on Congress at the American Enterprise Institute, said. "The characteristics you want in a whip—on the floor a lot, counting votes, immersed in the process, juggling schedules for ninety-nine other prima donnas—are not necessarily the traits you want in a leader."

An example is Stevens. During eight years as assistant GOP floor leader, his intense and sometimes hot-tempered style was well-suited to enforcing party discipline and "whipping" members for votes. But it was widely considered a liability when he ran for majority leader in a five-man field in 1984. Even so, he only narrowly lost to Dole on the last ballot.

From 1910 until after World War II, five whips had a chance to move up to leader and only one, a Republican, succeeded. Since 1947, however, all four Democratic whips who had a chance to move up did so—Scott Lucas of Illinois, Johnson, Mike Mansfield of Montana, and Byrd. But that is not to say whips always advance. For some, a vacancy in the leader's job never came. Others were ousted as whip before it could.

Russell B. Long of Louisiana, who declined to seek reelection in 1986 after thirty-eight years in the Senate, served two terms before his 1969 loss to Edward M. Kennedy of Massachusetts, who in turn lost to Byrd in 1971.

Senate Republicans have had less success at following a line of succession. Of six whips since World War II who had the opportunity to become the Republican floor leader, half have failed.

That includes the last two: Stevens in 1984 and Robert Griffin of Michigan, who lost the minority leadership race to Howard Baker eight years earlier. "On our side, I don't think there is a concept of succession," Stevens said. "We just don't seem to develop that."

The reasons appear similar to those on the House Republican side: youth, ideological differences, and, after so long in the minority, a lack of institutional perks to parcel out.

"We seem to have more of a philosophical problem on the Republican side than the Democrats have," Hildenbrand said, referring to the constant ideological tension between the party's conservative and liberal wings. In addition, he said, "We have younger people without institutional memories or loyalties to the seniority system."

As proof of Republicans' lack of a leadership ladder, Simpson is not considered heir apparent to Dole just because he is number two. But he is widely seen as a prospective candidate.

"If Dole leaves, it's a wide-open fight," Hildenbrand said. "I do not see Republicans just rolling over and saying, 'Al, you're the leader.' "

Stevens certainly would not. Asked if Simpson is heir apparent, he replied, "I think I am. I'm the one who only missed it by two votes" in 1984.

The Democrats' second-in-command, Cranston, is said to have little chance of moving to the leader's office after Byrd leaves it, if he tries. He is said to be too old and too liberal.

Favored instead is Inouye, the third-ranking leader. He is one of the most popular members within the Senate but, after twenty-four years there, one of the least known outside it. He has had to sacrifice some of his preference for behind-the-scenes work in the 100th Congress, however. Thirteen years after gaining exposure on the Senate Watergate Committee, Inouye heads the select committee investigating the Iran-contra affair.

Inouye may be the front-runner, but many observers expect a contest to replace Byrd when he leaves office. On both sides, then, a few Democrats and Republicans are maneuvering for some future leadership election. Beyond the evidence that insiders finish first, there seems to be no formula for success.

"I've never been able to figure out how a guy gets to be leader," Hildenbrand said. "There are so many factors that go into it, no one up there can tell you how the leadership is finally chosen."

2

Leaders With Portfolio

Robert Dole: Senate Minority Leader

Just before the Labor Day recess in 1986, as senators were plodding through yet another late-night session, some weary reporters in the Senate press room momentarily ignored the proceedings to watch a television game show.

At one point, three contestants were asked to identify President Gerald R. Ford's running mate in 1976. One wrongly answered Nelson Rockefeller. The others did not even guess.

The reporters snickered. The correct name belonged not to some figure from politics past, but to the man running the show just yards away—Senate Republican Leader Robert Dole of Kansas.

A decade after the 1976 campaign, Dole was laboring to become so well-known, and liked, that by 1988 he would once again be on the national Republican ticket—this time as the presidential nominee.

To that end, he may have been glad if voters had largely forgotten his role in the 1976 loss, one that tarred him long afterward as a "hatchet man."

Dole's role as the Senate's leader in the 99th Congress, which put him center stage once proceedings were televised live nationwide, was the one he hoped would carry him into the White House.

But it was a role of multiple, sometimes conflicting, personas. Dole had to be the statesmanlike head of Congress's upper chamber, yet a partisan promoter of fellow Republicans seeking reelection. He had to protect the institutional rights of the legislative branch, yet serve as chief Capitol Hill lobbyist for a Republican president.

All the while, Dole had to advance his own interests and identity if he were to rise above the crowd competing for his party's 1988 nomination.

Conflicting Ambitions?

Since Dole's role as Senate minority leader in the 100th Congress lasts from January 1987 through 1988, the question of whether Dole can be both leader and presidential candidate loomed larger than it did in 1984, when Dole beat four rivals for the leadership job.

His predecessor, Republican Howard H. Baker, Jr., of Tennessee, said it couldn't be done. Dole's closest contender for leader in 1984, Ted Stevens of Alaska, said it shouldn't be.

"His ambition is to be president; my only ambition is to be the Republican leader," Stevens said.

But Dole's leadership has stilled most colleagues' doubts.

In the 99th Congress, with a thin 53-47 Republican majority, he averted major losses and engineered several significant victories.

Among the latter were a comprehensive overhaul of the tax code, a law relaxing gun controls, approval of a long-stalled genocide treaty, which Jewish groups had wanted, and approval of President Reagan's Saudi arms sale, which Jewish groups had opposed, and passage of military aid to Nicaraguan rebels.

"Bob Dole has performed way beyond what even his supporters expected," said Pete V. Domenici of New Mexico, another Republican who had sought the leadership position.

"He's turned out to be the best leader we could have," said Minnesota Republican Dave Durenberger.

There are critics, however. "You can't do the two jobs," said Lowell P. Weicker, Jr., a Republican from Connecticut. "It is very difficult to run for president and [also] be the catalyst around which all points of view come together in the [Republican] party."

Weicker saw "a clear-cut choosing of being Bob Dole the candidate, not the catalyst." One result, he said, is "unabated contentiousness on the Senate floor. Everybody is at each other's throat all the time."

"It's just chaos," said a Senate Republican who asked to be unnamed. "You hear more and more the idea of, 'When is he going to decide what he is going to be? Is he going to be a presidential candidate, or the president's man, or the Senate's man?' "

Dole, of course, saw no problems. His various roles, he said, "all run together. . . . First I want to be a good senator. Then I want to be a good . . . leader. If you can fulfill those two things, the other things just fall into place."

Loss of Senate Control

For his wit, intelligence, command, and hustle, Dole is by all accounts one of the Senate's most effective members. And apart from the questions about his ability to be both leader and presidential candidate, criticisms of his leadership are few.

Speaking of his tenure as Senate majority leader, some committee chairmen said Dole held matters too close to his vest; while Baker had conducted weekly meetings with them, Dole called the chairmen together infrequently.

Some Republicans agree with Durenberger, who said, "Dole is not a good vote-counter. . . . That's a repeated problem."

In explaining the lapses, these members said Republicans often weren't forced to commit to how they would vote, and Dole lacked his predecessor's sources in Democrats' ranks. "Howard Baker could get a feel for the Democratic side that I know Dole does not have," said one source.

Dole's defenders disputed the contention. "What has he lost?" asked Rudy Boschwitz of Minnesota. "He wins."

"The acid test is performance and he's had some close calls, but he hasn't dropped one yet," said former senator Charles McC. Mathias, Jr., R-Md.

Whether Dole's success as a senator and leader can translate into a winning presidential campaign depended in part on the fall 1986 elections.

Dole won reelection for a fourth term as a Kansas senator. Republicans as a whole, however, did not fare as well. They lost their majority status in the November elections, putting the Democrats in power. Dole, thus, was demoted to minority leader.

That, said Kentucky Democrat Wendell H. Ford, is a less visible post from which to run for president, particularly against Vice President George Bush, the GOP front-runner.

Stevens argued that Dole, as minority leader, would find it harder to juggle campaign travels and Senate GOP business since he no longer controlled the Senate schedule.

But Nancy Landon Kassebaum, Dole's Republican colleague from Kansas, said, "I've always thought he would be better off as minority leader, because then he could criticize [Democrats' failures] and have more time to be away from the Senate."

Dole struggled hard to retain Senate power. In 1986, as a *Republican* leader in an election year, colleagues had expected him to orchestrate floor action in ways that advanced the candidacies of the eighteen other Republican senators who sought reelection. Dole complied.

"Dole is always looking at the political consequences to our incumbents," said Thomas C. Griscom, executive director of the National Republican Senatorial Committee. "That's important when we're fighting for our political survival."

Democrats, predictably, chafed. "You can't say it's never been done before, but he's using the Senate for Republican reelection campaigns, and it's being done more frequently and blatantly than ever before," charged George J. Mitchell of Maine, chairman of the Democratic Senatorial Campaign Committee.

When the Senate debated a measure to raise the federal debt limit, Dole accommodated numerous requests from Republican colleagues wanting to offer unrelated amendments that could help their reelection bids.

Oil-state member Don Nickles of Oklahoma won adoption of his proposal to repeal the so-called windfall profits tax on petroleum. Paula Hawkins of Florida, home to many retirees, passed an amendment to assure cost-of-living hikes for Social Security even if inflation remains low. Hawkins was defeated in her November bid for reelection.

Dole believes his dual roles as Senate Republican leader and presidential candidate are manageable: "If you're willing to give up your time, you can make it work."

In April Dole helped Charles E. Grassley, up for reelection in Iowa, with a rare gambit that allowed a floor vote on Grassley's bill making labor violence subject to federal anti-extortion penalties, though the bill had lost in committee. It was defeated as expected, but the attempt was important to business groups.

Dole's political antennae reached beyond the floor. When the Finance Committee voted in July 1986 to raise tobacco taxes to reduce the deficit, Dole lobbied panelists to reverse the decision, which imperiled tobacco-state Republican James T. Broyhill of North Carolina. He failed, narrowly. Broyhill later lost his seat to Democrat Terry Sanford.

As the Senate impresario, Dole could use the floor for televised tributes to fellow Republicans. For instance, it was Dole who won Senate passage of a measure forcing the Reagan administration to let the Soviet Union buy subsidized U.S. grain. But he publicly gave credit to James Abdnor of South Dakota, whose Democratic rival, Rep. Thomas A. Daschle, was sponsor of a similar House bill promoting farm exports. Daschle defeated Abdnor in the November election.

As the grain flap showed, sometimes Dole's efforts for Republicans meant bucking their president.

Another example is the issue of sanctions aimed at South Africa's white-minority government. After loyally blocking action in 1985 on a bill Reagan opposed, in 1986 Dole expedited passage of an even tougher one. He rebuffed veto threats and, in an angry session at the White House, reportedly said the matter had become "a domestic civil rights issue."

Dole also tried to alleviate the political damage that Reagan's free-trade policies had caused Republicans in states that had lost businesses and jobs to foreign competition.

On weekends Dole continued his work for Republicans, making campaign appearances that raised their identity and his own. He taped political ads; in one he vouched for Hawkins's claim to be "the Senate's general in the war on drugs."

What the Democrats Think

Dole's partisanship was no surprise to Democrats. He is, after all, the man who charged in the 1976 campaign that the country's four armed conflicts in this century were "Democrat wars."

"Dole is considerably more partisan than Baker," Mitchell said. "But I don't state that as a criticism. Our system contemplates that."

Members of both parties say the Senate itself became a more partisan place while Dole was leader. Democrats had only recently overcome the 1980 shock of losing their longtime majority and were emboldened, Boschwitz said, "by the sweet smell of control in their nostrils."

Domenici likened the floor to an arena, where both sides seek political advantage: "Very rarely have you had an occasion where that was so controlling. It's in that atmosphere that Dole has to run this place."

The tension was exposed in August 1986 in an extraordinary argument between Dole and Democratic leader Robert C. Byrd of West Virginia. The exchange climaxed a two-week standoff between Democrats and Dole, who insisted that a vote on aid for Nicaraguan rebels, which most Democrats opposed, be linked to a vote for South Africa sanctions, which had bipartisan support.

What sparked Byrd's attack was Dole's charge that Byrd tried to "sneak" a South Africa amendment onto a pending defense bill. Byrd snapped that he had offered the amendment openly, and only after Dole tried to choke off debate on the bill in a way that would bar a South Africa amendment.

Then Byrd vented other complaints: "I have had enough of this business of having the majority leader stand here and act as a traffic cop on this floor. . . . He determines who will call up an amendment, when they will call up an amendment, and what will be in the amendment.

". . . While a senator may today be in a position to choke off the rights of another senator, the time will come when the worm will turn."

Dole defended his actions, and told Byrd, "I did not become the majority leader to lose."

Byrd subsequently declined to be interviewed about Dole, while Dole dismissed the incident as "nothing in the scheme of things."

That aside, Democrats generally praised Dole and, like Mitchell, excused some of his partisanship as part of the game.

"I think he's a good leader; I think he's effective. I have no difficulty working with him, because he respects my point of view," Metzenbaum said. "There are times when I've had to stand up against him and it rarely gets personal. Oh, there have been a few times when he's lost his cool. But don't we all?"

"Bob Dole has been fair and never broken his word to me," said Nebraska Democrat J. James Exon. "For a man with that many balls up in the air, all of which could come down any time, I think he's done a good job."

The Manion Fight

The Democrats say their side had no big complaints about Dole—until the fight in 1986 to confirm Daniel A. Manion, Reagan's nominee to be a federal appeals court judge.

"I think the handling of the Manion thing was deplorable," Mitchell said. "What it displayed about him was that he'll do just about anything to win."

Democrats called Manion unqualified, while Republicans said the conservative was being harassed on ideological grounds. He was finally confirmed July 23 when the Senate voted 49-50 against reconsidering an earlier, disputed 48-46 vote in Manion's favor.

Democrats had sought the first vote, calling Dole's bluff after he taunted them for stalling. He was taken by surprise. But in complicated maneuvering, the votes of three Manion opponents were "paired" by Dole with those of three absent Republicans who Dole said were for Manion, although he had not spoken with them. In effect, this canceled the "no" votes and produced a 47-47 tie.

Byrd then switched his vote to "yea" to avert Bush's tie-breaker and to be able to demand a second vote, as only those on the winning side can do. As it turned out, two of the three absent Republicans, Barry Goldwater of Arizona and Bob Packwood of Oregon, had not yet decided how to vote.

"It was poorly handled," said Kassebaum, a Manion foe who paired with Goldwater. "The one thing that was troubling in the whole issue was the pairing of votes. It bothered Goldwater. In the past, you always had to get the senator's approval."

Kassebaum does not blame either Dole or Dan Quayle, R-Ind., who pressed her to pair her vote with Goldwater. But she is critical that Senate leaders did not do a better job of counting votes, and were caught off guard.

Dole, in his defense, noted it was Quayle who arranged the Kassebaum-Goldwater pair and that Democrats waived his offer to contact Packwood, assuming Packwood would have voted for Manion.

On the second vote, Goldwater again was absent but allowed his vote to be paired with a Manion opponent. Packwood voted to reconsider the original approval of the nominee, indicating his opposition to Manion.

Metzenbaum, although a leading Manion opponent, said Dole "was just doing his job. I feel certain he did not intentionally misrepresent the facts."

But a Republican senator, a Dole admirer, said the Manion incident illustrates that Dole's political intuitiveness, usually a great asset, can backfire. "Manion is the

In 1986 Dole ran into criticism for the way he handled the vote to confirm federal appeals court judge nominee Daniel A. Manion.

best example there's been of Bob Dole flying by the seat of his pants," the senator said.

White House Lobbyist

The fact is, Manion was confirmed. So along with blame, Dole also gets the credit for scoring a major victory for the president. It was only one example of Dole effectively performing the role of White House lobbyist, and at a time when both Republicans and Democrats were increasingly inclined to snub the president despite his popularity.

When Dole was elected leader, one Senate Republican hailed the result as a "declaration of independence" from the White House. Still, pushing the president's program is part of the job when the leader is of the same party.

"While Dole clearly ran on the position that he was leader of the Senate first, and the president's man second, you have to recognize the reality of dealing with a very popular president like Reagan," Domenici said.

In his first days on the job, Dole sacrificed home-state interests to oppose a farm relief bill that Reagan later vetoed. A widely published photo showed farmers with a banner reading, "We're from Kansas. Bob Dole doesn't work for us, either."

"Sometimes I just have to marvel," Exon said. "How he in good conscience subscribes to these anti-agriculture policies of this administration and gets by with it in a farm state is a tribute to his agility."

Dole moved ingeniously in 1985 to block the earlier South Africa bill, averting a major slap at Reagan's foreign policy for the time. When opponents insisted on the bill's passage, after Dole had persuaded the president to order sanctions on his own, Dole had the bill locked in a safe.

Perhaps Dole's most frustrating work on Reagan's behalf involved the budget. In 1985 and 1986 he shelved the Senate Budget Committee's budget resolutions so he could forge changes acceptable to Reagan.

That contrasted with the defiance Dole voiced on his first day as leader. On January 3, 1985, he declared deficit reduction as Senate Republicans' top priority. They would break with tradition, he said then, and draft a budget without waiting for a Reagan package that was sure to be rejected.

But Dole was unable to craft a budget, and the Budget Committee's subsequent package had more funding for domestic programs and less for defense than Reagan would support.

Dole then brokered a compromise. With Reagan's approval and Bush's tie-breaking vote, on May 10 the Senate voted 50-49 for a fiscal 1986 budget freezing Social Security, holding defense to an inflation increase, and killing thirteen domestic programs.

Dole not only had Bush there for the 2 a.m. vote; he had California Republican Pete Wilson brought from a hospital by ambulance and gurney. "He has a certain flare which he uses to pull the chestnuts out of the fire," Mathias said of Dole.

But later, after a meeting of Dole, Reagan, and House Speaker Thomas P. O'Neill, Jr., D-Mass., Reagan reneged on his backing for a Social Security freeze when O'Neill agreed to support higher defense spending.

Until then, said former senator Mark Andrews, R-N.D., "Bob was making an honest, good-faith effort to get the White House to move." But as a party to the Reagan-O'Neill swap, "he left a lot of his troops hanging" with the politically dangerous vote on Social Security.

In 1986 the Budget Committee produced a bipartisan fiscal 1987 budget that again defied the president on defense, taxes, and domestic cuts. Dole scrapped it, too, partly in deference to the president but mostly because a majority of Republicans would not support it on the floor.

In 1985 Reagan's abandonment of the Senate's budget freezing Social Security was the first big setback for Dole's goal of being the leader who presided over significant deficit reduction. "A lot of people just sort of gave up after that," he said.

And in 1986 the president's goal—overhaul of the tax code—took over. "I hope we haven't backed off the budget," Dole said. "We haven't tried to do that."

For a long time Dole was a reluctant shepherd for Reagan's tax initiative, agreeing with most Republican senators that budget cutting was more important. But the historic result, which cleared Congress September 27, 1986, promised to rank as a major achievement of his leadership.

Unlike any predecessor, Dole is subject to administration pressure even at home—his wife is Transportation Secretary Elizabeth Hanford Dole. The link was obvious in 1986 when the Senate, to the vexation of many members, spent two weeks on a bill allowing her department to sell Conrail, the federal freight railroad. It passed, only to die in the House. But overall, Republicans were content with the balance Dole had struck.

"He is less the president's man than Howard Baker was," Stafford said. "Baker considered himself the president's spokesman in the Senate. Dole considers himself the Senate's spokesman to the president."

"I'm obviously loyal to the president," Dole said, citing a Congressional Quarterly study rating his 1985 presidential support at 92 percent, the Senate's highest score. "And that's how it should be. But on the other hand, my constituency is the Republican senators and not the White House. And they didn't elect me to try to run over the senators in favor of the White House or anybody else."

Wooing the Right

If managing Reagan's legislative portfolio was sometimes a problem, it also boosted Dole's stock among the pro-Reagan conservatives who will determine the party's nominee.

But his approaches to that group went beyond loyal service to Reagan, members said. "I don't think there's any doubt he's making a deliberate play to the right," Metzenbaum said.

"I don't know that he is reaching out to the conservatives, at least not gratuitously," said Republican senator Jesse Helms of North Carolina, a leader of the right. "I think that Bob is basically a conservative. . . . I don't see that there is any political adjustment to be made on Bob Dole's part."

That Dole's conservative credentials were questioned is a sign of the GOP's rightward tilt since 1976, when Ford tapped him partly to pacify Reagan's backers. Reagan reportedly cleared the choice.

Moreover, Dole was no recent convert to causes dear to conservative groups. A theme of his 1974 Senate campaign was support for a constitutional ban on abortions. Since 1961, his first year in Congress, Dole's voting record annually ranked high in conservative groups' ratings and at the bottom of liberal groups' lists.

"He has a legitimate claim on conservatives' support," Stafford said. "But some of them might not agree."

The most-often cited evidence of Dole's courtship of the conservative doubters were his forays into foreign policy, an area in which he had not been notably active before.

After Reagan ordered an attack on Libya in April 1986 to retaliate for alleged terrorism, leaders in both parties proposed designating members with whom the president should consult before future military actions. But Dole joined conservatives in sponsoring a bill freeing the president from existing restrictions on his war powers in cases of terrorism.

In 1986 Dole also pressured the administration for covert aid to rebels fighting leftist Angola. He led conservatives in urging Reagan to disown the 1979 strategic arms limitation treaty, SALT II, charging the Soviet Union with "blatantly violating" its limits.

Dole was a tireless advocate of Reagan's requests for aid to rebels battling the Marxist Nicaraguan government, calling them by Reagan's term—"freedom fighters."

On domestic issues, Dole pushed votes for a balanced budget, school prayer, and presidential power to veto items in appropriations bills. Though unsuccessful, conservatives applauded the effort.

But among antitax, supply-side conservatives, Dole remained suspect for his achievements as Finance Committee chairman, prior to becoming leader. When deficits climbed after 1981, he was instrumental in passing the largest peacetime tax increase in U.S. history in 1982 and, in 1984, another $50 billion tax bill.

For such efforts at deficit reduction, Dole was damned as "the tax collector for the welfare state" by conservative House Republican Newt Gingrich of Georgia, and the title was widely publicized.

Subsequently, Dole, as leader, privately lobbied for budgets that would not raise taxes significantly. At one point in 1985, a Democratic Senate source said, he reminded a budget group of Gingrich's censure. "He talked of taking the heat once and said he didn't want to do it again," this source recalled.

Several senators said Dole's actions that were perceived as self-promotions to the right often were a leader's attempts to represent his members.

Dole dismissed talk that he was moving to the right to curry conservative favor for a presidential bid.

"I've been voting here for twenty-some years. I don't think I've changed any," he said.

Durenberger noticed a rightward shift. But, he added, "Bob Dole is not going to sell himself out just to be president of the United States."

What Lies Ahead?

Dole's strategy of using the Senate leadership as a springboard to the presidency is a gamble that will test voters' recent bias against Washington insiders.

Former governors Ronald Reagan and Jimmy Carter both parlayed that bias into victory, and Reagan still rails against the government he now heads.

In contrast, Dole boasts a quarter-century in both chambers of Congress and a wife who heads a federal agency. "We're going back to the real world," he joked after the right-dominated 1984 GOP convention. "It's called Washington."

For the time Dole believes the dual roles are manageable. "If you're willing to give up your time, you can make it work," he said.

But, he added, "if it really got to be where I really had a good shot at the nomination, then I think I'd have to revisit the leadership question." Meanwhile, "I don't know why you'd give up something unless you know you're going to have something else."

Sam Nunn: The Careful Exercise of Power

When Sam Nunn, as a newly elected Democratic senator, first won a spot on the influential Armed Services Committee, some political observers back home in Georgia were dubious.

"The immediate concern, which Nunn obviously shares to some extent," a local newspaper reported, "is that the seemingly attractive committee assignment will turn out to be something of a political albatross which will earn the young senator few friends and make him a lot of enemies."

By 1986—thirteen years and many political battles later—Nunn had earned a different kind of assessment from the committee's crusty chairman, Barry Goldwater, an Arizona Republican. "We better come up with somebody," Goldwater said of the GOP, "or I'm going to support this guy for president. He's terrific."

Such praise, coming as the Senate approved Goldwater's pet project of reorganizing the Pentagon, is typical of his blunt hyperbole. But it also reflects the esteem in which most senators hold Nunn—now chairman of the Armed Services Committee. In an era of cosmetically tailored politicians, Nunn—with his light brown hair combed straight across a bald spot and his flat drawl—has become a power by the simple expedient of knowing what he is talking about.

Nothing testifies more eloquently to Nunn's personal dominance of Senate defense debates than the frustration of those critics—typically to his political left—whose loudest complaint is that he has not taken up their particular cause.

Some want him to lead a center-left coalition that would reshape President Reagan's defense program, which Nunn attacked for lacking strategic coherence.

On a partisan level, although Nunn supports Reagan more consistently than almost any other Senate Democrat, some party leaders see Nunn's prestige as an important political asset that could erase their party's image as being "weak" on defense.

But as Congress has become disaffected with Reagan's military buildup, some Capitol Hill aides and lobbyists complain that Nunn has been too hesitant to take on the tough ones. He has the talents of a brilliant legislative technician, they say, but has not shown the will to be a national political leader.

A New Role?

Some of these critics thought Nunn would be forced to take a tougher stance when the Senate took up Reagan's $5.4 billion budget request for research on an antimissile defense—the strategic defense initiative (SDI).

Nunn repeatedly brushed aside as a fantasy Reagan's conception of SDI as a nationwide shield. Moreover, in 1987, a year of severe budget austerity, funds spent on SDI meant less money for the improvements in conventional military forces that Nunn emphasized over the years.

On top of that, one influential critic thinks Nunn finally is showing the kind of national political ambition that will make him susceptible to pressure from more liberal Democrats.

In a wide-ranging interview early in June 1986, Nunn said he would speak out "more forcefully" on SDI. He did not tip his hand, but he rejected the position taken by forty-six senators—including some prominent centrists—who signed a letter calling for a $2 billion reduction in Reagan's request.

"I can agree with many things said in the letter," Nunn said, "but I cannot agree with the bottom line." It was incumbent on the critics to propose a coherent alternative to Reagan's program, Nunn insisted. "Just to cut $2 billion off of it or go to a 3 percent growth rate is not enough."

Some liberal arms control advocates disagreed with Nunn's belief that SDI had some value as "arms control leverage"—an incentive for hefty Soviet concessions in the Geneva arms talks in return for restraint of SDI. As a rule, liberal arms control advocates have rejected using weapons as bargaining chips.

The issue highlights a fundamental obstacle to any facile coalition between Nunn and more liberal Democratic leaders: On some of the most politically charged defense issues, Nunn simply does not agree with them.

Knowing His Stuff

The key to Nunn's influence is knowledge. "He knows more about the subject he talks about than anybody else by the time he starts talking about it," said Armed Services member Carl Levin, D-Mich.

Tales of Nunn's capacity for homework—more significantly, of his demand for prodigious amounts of it—are legion, a point of pride among his staff and of envy among aides to other senators. "Nunn wants to make sure he understands the issue the best he can," said a committee aide. "It isn't until he's comfortable that he's ready to move."

One example of many: Late in May 1986, Nunn took home one weekend a ring binder more than two inches thick containing detailed analyses of issues that might arise in the Armed Services Committee's markup of the fiscal 1987 defense authorization bill. He returned the book to aides the following Tuesday, extensively underlined and annotated with his characteristic marginal notes.

Aides tell of him routinely digesting thirty-page memos on complex issues. "He'll ask for a lot more information than we could possibly send to any other senator," said one.

By all accounts, he is an omnivorous reader, has an extraordinarily talented staff and maintains a wide circle of expert contacts within the defense community.

For all the help, it is Nunn's reputation for personal mastery of issues that makes the difference. Said one aide, in what may be the highest accolade a staffer can give to a member of Congress, "You never worry about him going to a meeting by himself."

Picking His Shots

Another component of Nunn's reputation for legislative success is that his proposals usually sound reassuringly moderate.

They are shaped by what his colleague Levin calls "the practicalities of power" on Capitol Hill: that a member can only work so many issues at one time with any competence; that he can go to his colleagues for a tough vote only so many times and can ask them to move only so far from their earlier positions; and that he can push a massive bureaucracy only so far. "He not only reaches conclusions about what's right, but about what's achievable," said Levin.

In addition to knowing what to go for, Nunn gets high marks for knowing when to go for it. "His real genius is to . . . wait for the right moment to come up with a solution after allowing the sides to play themselves out," said Armed Services member William S. Cohen, R-Maine.

At the same time, he sees limits in how far he can push the executive branch. "You don't just go and change 100 percent of the opinion" in the Pentagon, Nunn said. "You've got to find a fertile field to plant the seed in."

For change to take hold, Nunn contends, a substantial part of the military bureaucracy must see its military merit. "It's like the board of directors of a company," said one Senate aide. "You've got to focus the attention of management."

However, to some of his critics, Nunn's caution goes to the point of timidity. One Democratic aide derided his record of arriving at a position "so firmly in the center that it must have been fashioned by a compass."

And a GOP observer contrasted Nunn's careful, incremental approach with the sweeping deficit-reduction legislation driven through the Senate last year by Texas freshman Phil Gramm, R. The comparison is difficult to evaluate: None of Nunn's issues engages sentiments similar to Congress's fever to slice deficits.

Courting His Colleagues

A third facet of Nunn's method is a velvet touch in dealing with his colleagues: "When you come out of a battle with Sam Nunn—which he usually wins—there's no animosity," commented J. James Exon, D-Neb., another Armed Services member.

Nunn's capacity for prodigious amounts of homework leads to a personal mastery of issues that makes the difference.

"I listen to people and I hear what they're saying," said Nunn. But more importantly, people believe Nunn is willing to change his mind based on the merits of an argument. "He is seen as capable of listening to the evidence and coming up with a new conclusion," said one Pentagon official.

Moreover, he gains points for not using his expertise to demolish less knowledgeable political foes in debate. "I think he feels that in the long term, it's better to consider other peoples' arguments, feelings, and positions before he dominates an argument," said Levin. Another senator put the point less diplomatically: Nunn treats his colleagues' viewpoints with respect, "no matter how asinine they might be."

Nunn also has a reputation for scrupulous observance of his commitments: "You can take an IOU from Sam Nunn and carry it to the bank," said Senate Sergeant-at-Arms Ernest E. Garcia, from 1981 to 1985 the Pentagon's chief of Senate liaison.

Other Hats

Nunn sometimes expresses frustration that his reputation as a defense specialist obscures his work on the Governmental Affairs Permanent Subcommittee on Investigations, where Nunn has probed organized crime, drug traffic, labor racketeering, and the government's control of secret information.

Nunn's investigations led directly to legislation cracking down on criminal abuse of the workers' compensation program for longshoremen, and increasing penalties for union officials found guilty of corruption.

He also pushed for creation of a conservation "soil bank" to encourage farmers to remove from crop production easily eroded land. Nevertheless, it is his work on defense that gives Nunn his clout.

Getting Started

Even before his election in November 1972, Nunn had gotten Senate Democratic leaders to agree to assign him a seat on Armed Services, partly through the intercession of his great-uncle, Rep. Carl Vinson, D-Ga. (1914-1965), a former chairman of the House Armed Services Committee.

Late in September 1973 Nunn took his first step into the policy arena that would make his reputation: NATO strategy. The Senate was restive over the number of U.S. troops deployed in Europe, partly because the U.S. balance of payments was hurt by the day-to-day living expenses on the continent of more than 300,000 American soldiers and their dependents. By only six votes, the body turned down an amendment to the annual defense authorization bill by Majority Leader Mike Mansfield, D-Mont., that would have slashed the number of U.S. troops stationed in Europe.

In hopes of co-opting some of the sentiment behind Mansfield's move, Nunn and Henry M. Jackson, D-Wash., then proposed an amendment—adopted overwhelmingly—directing the president to seek reimbursement by the allies for a greater share of the cost of stationing U.S. troops in Europe.

In February 1974 Nunn took his first trip to Europe at the request of Armed Services Chairman John C. Stennis, D-Miss., partly in preparation for another showdown with Mansfield. According to Nunn, that trip laid the foundation of his thinking on the alliance. It also set the pattern for his workaholic approach to boning up on an issue. He and committee aide Francis J. Sullivan "probably spent a hundred hours talking to every expert within reach of Washington," according to Nunn.

The trip produced a report documenting the Armed Services panel's brief for preserving the status quo regarding deployments to Europe. But Nunn also used the report to challenge key elements of NATO military policy in central Europe. He charged that:

- NATO was planning on an unrealistically long warning time to prepare for an attack, and thus had many of its troops too far back from the East German frontier.
- The alliance was getting too little combat power out of the troops it deployed, partly because too few were assigned to combat jobs and partly because its combat units had too little ammunition stockpiled for wartime.
- Because of the deficiencies in its nonnuclear military posture, the alliance would be driven to an early decision to use nuclear weapons in case of a Soviet attack.

When the Senate took up the annual defense bill that July, Nunn first led the battle against Mansfield's new troop withdrawal amendment, beating it 44-46.

He then offered successfully his own package of NATO amendments intended to goad the Pentagon to: shift personnel into combat roles; develop a coherent policy on the deployment of short-range nuclear weapons; and increase the efficiency of NATO's collective defense effort by standardizing more of its equipment.

In the years since his first NATO report, those themes have remained high on Nunn's agenda. "That's one of the good things about NATO," Nunn quipped while recalling his early inquiries. "Once you learn the defects, you can be reasonably sure that that knowledge is not going to become outmoded any time soon."

In 1976 Nunn returned to Europe with Armed Services Republican Dewey F. Bartlett, R-Okla. (1973-1979). The resulting report underscored Nunn's earlier critique and publicized a fear held by some military analysts: that improved Soviet forces might carry out a blitzkrieg attack before NATO could mobilize its defenses. Observers credit Nunn's work in stimulating changes in U.S. and NATO planning.

Other Campaigns

Nunn has ranged over other defense issues. Among his major thrusts:

Manpower

As chairman of the Armed Services Subcommittee on Manpower and Personnel, Nunn subjected the all-volunteer Army to withering scrutiny in the late-1970s.

He opposed the all-volunteer force on philosophical grounds: It was dangerous to insulate middle-class youth from the obligation to serve. But he also contended that the all-volunteer policy simply was not working. The services were plagued with recruits who were undisciplined and very difficult to train.

In 1980 Nunn threatened to cut the Army's manpower on grounds that it could not recruit enough qualified men. Cohen and Levin fended off that effort, but the committee approved (and Congress enacted) stiff limits on the number of recruits who could be accepted without a high school diploma.

The combination of the higher recruiting standards, pay hikes pushed by Nunn and John W. Warner, R-Va., and a 1980 recession produced a dramatic turnaround in the Pentagon's manpower problems. Says one participant in the battle, "It was Nunn's criticism that strengthened the all-volunteer force and made it viable."

Nuclear Strategy

Nunn had begun in the mid-1970s to study nuclear arms issues, focusing on the "survivability" of the U.S. forces as a key to the stability of the nuclear balance.

Nunn had supported the Carter administration plan to shuffle MX missiles at random among dozens of armored underground launch sites as a means of forestalling a Soviet attack.

When Reagan dropped that approach, Nunn and Cohen blocked his alternatives on grounds that none of them would ensure the survival of the missiles as well as the rejected Carter scheme.

Early in 1983, with Reagan's request for MX funding under fire, Nunn, Cohen, Foreign Relations Committee Chairman Charles H. Percy, R-Ill. (1967-1985), and a group of centrist House Democrats used MX as a bargaining lever on Reagan.

Though Reagan planned to deploy the new missile in existing launch silos that were vulnerable to a Soviet attack, Nunn and his allies supported MX production in return for Reagan's adoption of both a strategic weapons program and an arms control agenda that—in Nunn's view—promoted strategic arms stability.

NATO Planning

NATO returned to the top of Nunn's agenda in 1984. He was unhappy that NATO was dawdling on certain improvements in combat readiness. So he offered an amendment to the fiscal 1985 defense authorization bill that would have trimmed U.S. troops in Europe by up to 90,000 over three years unless NATO began meeting its force improvement goals.

The amendment was rejected 55-41 after the administration lobbied intensely against it. One Nunn skeptic cites the amendment as an instance of political opportunism. But Nunn's boosters—including some of the Reagan officials who fought him—insist that the amendment was meant to goad the administration and the allies into action, and that it succeeded.

Pentagon Reorganization

Early in 1984, in one of his first statements as the Armed Services panel's senior Democrat, Nunn announced the crusade that led to his most recent legislative triumph. "We will not be able to get the most effective fighting force possible until we begin to make some fundamental changes in the structure of the Defense Department," he declared.

Several studies had proposed changes along the same lines: shifting power from the separate military services to the chairman of the Joint Chiefs of Staff, the combat commanders in chief, and other institutions intended to coordinate the services.

But then-chairman John Tower, R-Texas, blocked any such moves and Nunn bided his time until Tower retired at the end of 1984. Tower's successor, Goldwater, saw eye-to-eye with Nunn on the issue and the two began a long legislative campaign.

Despite numerous compromises with other committee members, the two insist that the core of their idea—shifting significant power to the cross-service institutions—survived intact. Over vehement opposition from the Navy and some other quarters in the Pentagon, the Senate adopted the bill May 7, 1986.

What's the Beef?

Nunn's critics concede that he brings to bear on the issues an unrivaled expertise and political savvy. Given all that clout, they contend, his net impact on policy is too marginal.

Some complain that Nunn focuses on technical questions of secondary importance while skirting broader national issues. One experienced arms control lobbyist cited his focus on Pentagon reorganization as an example. "I don't find that to be an issue of ethical or moral importance," she declared.

As an example of dodging a big one, on the other hand, the critics cite Nunn's refusal to join any of the efforts to slice SDI funds during Senate floor debate on the fiscal 1986 defense authorization bill.

Nunn had scathingly dismissed Reagan's goal of a nationwide defense that would render nuclear missiles "impotent and obsolete."

When the bill came to the Senate floor, SDI critics believed they had a shot at cutting the program from the $3 billion recommended by Senate Armed Services to $1.9 billion, if only Nunn would help. Nunn did not actively oppose the amendment, but he voted against it and the cutback was defeated handily.

What looks like a question of will from one angle, however, may seem a difference of view from another. Nunn sees Pentagon reorganization as the precondition to solving a raft of problems—for instance, devising a rational defense program that fits whatever budget level Congress will provide.

Nunn declares that timing was an important consideration in the 1985 SDI battle; he was giving priority to ending the MX battle with a cap on the number of deployed missiles. "I felt [1985] was the time to put the MX debate to bed; and I didn't think the time was right for a major debate on SDI," Nunn said.

A Democratic aide cited another factor: Nunn and other skeptics felt obligated not to oppose the committee's stance on SDI. "Nunn wasn't down there in the well defending the committee's position," said the aide, "but he felt committed."

Another complaint is that Nunn too readily compromises for the sake of increasing an already adequate majority—what one Democratic aide called "the seventy-eight-vote syndrome."

The focus of this criticism was Nunn's negotiation with the White House in 1985 to cap the number of MX missiles deployed in vulnerable silos at fifty instead of forty. Sources on both sides of the battle contend that the White House had exhausted its political capital in earlier MX fights and that Nunn could have prevailed at the lower figure, winning a majority of fewer than sixty votes, comprising Democrats and a handful of liberal Republicans.

Nunn rejected that analysis. The highest priority was to end the MX debate, he insisted. If a narrow and largely Democratic Senate majority had forced a forty-missile cap on the White House, he said, "we would have been fighting again [in 1986]."

But one Pentagon official saw a broader reason for Nunn's conciliatory conduct. "He knew he had us," said the source, adding: "He values the fact that he's respected from all quarters. He doesn't need to make an enemy."

Is He 'Democratic' Enough?

Nunn's position to the right of the Democratic mainstream shows up when senators are rated on their voting records. During 1985, by Congressional Quarterly's analysis, he supported Reagan on contested issues more often than any other Democrat and he tied for first place with Howell Heflin, Ala., in the frequency with which he supported conservative positions. "I don't think there is anyone who has as much respect on an issue and is as out of line with his party," said one liberal activist.

He heads the national security policy group within the Senate Democratic Conference. But one Democratic defense aide complained that he is trying to get the members to focus on complex technical questions rather than questions of political strategy. "It shouldn't be a seminar," the exasperated aide said. "It should be a political action group. . . . He's not trying to appeal to Democrats on hot issues. He's trying to recreate them in his own image, and it won't work."

To this charge, Nunn responded, "We have to have as little as possible of partisan politics in national security. There's always going to be some, but the purpose of leadership is to minimize that."

Coming from almost any other public figure, such a statement would be summarily dismissed. But there seems to be a remarkably broad consensus that Nunn really believes it. "I can't fault him for that," said Levin. "He just doesn't believe that there's a 'Democratic' defense policy."

Levin also sees Nunn as an important party asset in spite of the fact that he frequently differs with a majority of his fellow Democrats on issues. "He's done more than anyone else to improve the Democratic image on defense," Levin said, by demonstrating "that there's no difference between the two parties in their commitment to defense."

But that contribution to the party's image does not satisfy critics' complaint that Nunn does not stand with his party's majority on politically key questions.

"Nunn is recognized as the leading spokesman for his party on national defense," said one of the critics. "To fulfill that kind of role over an extended period, you cannot do it from the standpoint of being one of eight or ten Democratic votes" aligned with Republicans on a hot issue.

Nunn's Democratic affiliation has been virtually irrelevant to his rise to power in the Senate. But some who wish he would move toward the party's center of gravity think that may have changed, citing his newly demonstrated interest in partywide affairs.

In 1985 he joined then-Virginia governor Charles S. Robb and Rep. Richard A. Gephardt, Mo., to form the Democratic Leadership Council (DLC) with the avowed intention of moving the party toward the political mainstream.

At the same time, some Democratic operatives began touting Nunn as a potential vice presidential—perhaps even a presidential—nominee.

Nunn does not disclaim interest in a future party nomination. But he insists that he is not seeking it at this time and would not jeopardize his various legislative campaigns to move into the broader arena.

He does not want to go "sputtering around the country, spending two days a week in the Senate, seeing a lot of the things I'm working on come to nothing," he said. "If someone told me right now that I'd have to start running for president next month or not in the rest of my life," he would pass.

Bill Gray: Thriving on Paradox

Since he came to Congress in 1979, Pennsylvania Democrat William H. Gray III has built an auspicious career by confounding expectations.

Gray arrived as a minister with no experience in either party politics or public office. He quickly maneuvered his way onto some of the most sought-after House committees.

In 1984, while more experienced members wrestled to become chairman of the Budget Committee, Gray slipped in from behind to win the leadership post—without stepping on any toes.

Though he is a black urban liberal at a time when that combination is out of political fashion, Gray has won the enthusiastic support of conservative southerners for his running of the committee.

In 1986 Gray faced the straitjacket of the Gramm-Rudman-Hollings law, which he opposed. But he shepherded a budget resolution through the House that went Gramm-Rudman one better, promising to bring deficits almost $7 billion below the law's $144 billion target.

Thriving on apparent paradox makes Gray hard to pin down. It is apparent that he is popular with his colleagues, but they do not seem able to define or predict him. In interviews with dozens of members and staff, none could name an enemy he had made—but none offered a revealing anecdote, either.

"Bill is a very sophisticated dancer," said an admiring Mickey Leland, D-Texas. Summed up a House leadership aide, "He's a very complex guy."

Gray operates with a deft style that leaves no fingerprints. He loves to preach but hates to tell others exactly what to do. With the press, he is informal but not informative. He avoids confrontation, yet chairs one of the most partisan committees in Congress. Some Republicans see him as a puppet of the Democratic leadership, but Democrats say he has often tugged the leadership along behind him.

An ambitious man who focuses intently

on the task at hand, Gray still leaves Washington frequently to tend to the affairs of the Baptist church in Philadelphia that was founded by his grandfather.

Gray himself sees no incongruity in all of this. "I decided my career would be preaching and teaching," he said. "After all, every sermon isn't delivered from the pulpit."

As Budget Committee chairman since 1985, Gray has won the thanks of party leaders. "I think he's doing very well," said Majority Leader Thomas S. Foley, D-Wash. "The percentage by which this budget was adopted among Democrats was truly extraordinary." Foley was referring to the fiscal 1987 budget resolution adopted by a 245-179 vote. Democrats voted for the plan 228-19.

In the twelve-year history of the budget process, the only greater margin occurred in Gray's first year as chairman, when Democrats voted 234-15 in favor of the House budget.

The Democratic leadership is intensely concerned about defections on the budget, since it sees the document as a fundamental statement of political priorities. Under Gray's predecessors, Democrats frequently failed to support the budget. Leaders recall 1977 and 1982 with particular bitterness; in those years, the Budget Committee's resolutions were defeated on the floor due to massive Democratic defections. In 1981 and 1982 conservative Democrats united with Republicans to pass budgets geared to Ronald Reagan's priorities.

The hallmark of Gray's tenure as committee chairman, according to committee members and others, is his ability to forge consensus. "Bill has a capacity for conciliation," said Speaker Jim Wright, D-Texas. "He has almost infinite patience—a willingness to sit for long tedious hours while others extrude for the airwaves the ecstatics of their positions."

Contrast With Jones

Gray's style as Budget chairman is in marked contrast with his predecessor, James R. Jones, D-Okla. A relatively conservative Democrat with a strong independent streak, Jones frequently clashed with leaders and with the liberal wing of his party.

"Jones's problem was real obvious: Jones never had the trust of his own committee," said Lynn Martin, R-Ill., who served under both chairmen. "Jones had to keep proving that he was a liberal. Bill Gray doesn't have to prove that he's a liberal."

In the House the Budget Committee has always divided sharply along partisan lines, while the Senate Budget Committee has frequently searched for bipartisan agreement. House Democrats meet in closed caucuses to hammer out a budget draft before allowing Republicans to see it.

In his first years as chairman (1981-1982), Jones would consult with trusted colleagues and aides, develop his own budget proposals, and then sell hard his "chairman's mark" to his committee. Later, Democratic leaders gave Jones more direction to keep their members from rebelling.

Gray's approach is different. He walks into the first sessions not with a chairman's mark but with a blank sheet of paper. He shuts the door and keeps Democrats meeting together for long hours until they iron out their differences and produce their own budget. "It makes them work, makes them understand that if they fund this, they've got to cut that," said Gray.

Talk, Talk, and More Talk

Building a Democratic consensus on the budget in 1986 was not easy. "I couldn't be Budget chairman. I don't have the patience," said Wright.

Several Democrats said they were oc-

Gray has found congregations in his Philadelphia church and on Capitol Hill: "After all, every sermon isn't delivered from the pulpit."

casionally frustrated by Gray's refusal to provide guidance when the committee seemed stuck.

"We finally reached the point where no one wanted to talk," said panel member Buddy MacKay, D-Fla. "I would have speeded it up. But maybe letting us get to the point of being worn out was part of his psychology."

Gray exhibited remarkable skill at avoiding and managing conflict, several members said. Gray's approach "is that of a lover, not a fighter," said Vic Fazio, D-Calif., a member of Budget.

"He's careful not to leave people personally threatened by the fact that they're on the losing side of an argument," said MacKay.

One technique Gray used, MacKay said, was to stop an argument and move to another issue when it became clear that a member was going to have to back down. When the panel resumed deliberations the next day, the decision was treated as if it had already been made.

When the panel's Democrats finally did come together on a plan, it was one in which they had pride of authorship, and one they went out and enthusiastically sold to a somewhat reluctant party leadership.

After it was over, members said they could point to almost no area of the budget that had Gray's personal stamp on it, but they suspected that the final document was what Gray wanted all along.

"He knows the direction he wants to go and very gently and subtly gets there with the members thinking they arrived at it themselves," said committee member Charles E. Schumer, D-N.Y.

Conservative Support

Some of Gray's most enthusiastic fans come from the conservative wing of his party. Charles W. Stenholm, a Texas Democrat who is not on the Budget Committee but who helped lead the 1981 revolt against the party leadership in favor of Reagan's economic program, said: "I can't think of anybody we could have elected as Budget chairman who could have done better—and I think I can speak for the conservative wing of Democrats."

Marvin Leath, D-Texas, a conservative who has played an important role on the committee in brokering agreement on defense spending, said Gray won his support because he was fair. The House resolution included $285 billion for defense, compared with the Senate's $301 billion and the administration's request for $320 billion. Leath said that cuts in domestic programs were equally deep.

"He's willing to lay his personal priorities on the deck and chop them along with others he thinks ought to be chopped," said Leath.

In 1985, at the start of his chairmanship, party leaders helped Gray's cause by adding Leath and other conservatives to the committee to broaden its base and make it better reflect the Democratic Caucus.

Preaching and Teaching

Watching Gray preach on a steamy summer Sunday in Philadelphia is like watching a man unchained, in comparison with his demeanor on the air-conditioned House floor.

He alternately shouts and whispers, quotes spirituals and modern theologians, shifts topics effortlessly from South Africa to the Bible. The arms of his black gown wave freely as he raises his hands to make a point.

Gray builds to a crescendo, then stands back and mops his brow as the congregation sends up a volley of "amens."

Some members believe the key to Gray was his background and continuing role as a minister. He preaches at Bright Hope Baptist Church two to three times a month, does most weddings and funerals there, and actively takes care of church affairs.

Former representative Bob Edgar, D-Pa., whose district adjoined Gray's, is a Methodist minister who entered Drew Theological Seminary two years after Gray. Edgar said that seminary training in preaching and counseling helped develop Gray's techniques. "He has the ability to read body language, to speak clearly, and to compromise with people of different philosophies," Edgar said.

Edgar and Gray said that the politics of running a large Baptist church, where the minister is expected to be a strong leader yet is hired by the congregation, are no simpler than those of Congress.

Family Traditions

Gray was born in 1941 into a family where politics provided a constant undercurrent to religion. His grandfather founded Bright Hope Church in 1925. He was succeeded as pastor after his death by Gray's father, who had a doctorate from the University of Pennsylvania and had been president of two black universities in Florida.

Gray's father was active in Democratic reform politics in Philadelphia and in the civil rights movement. Gray recalls that the Rev. Dr. Martin Luther King, Jr., was a frequent house guest, sometimes staying for weeks at a time.

Gray showed no particular interest in the ministry until late in college, when he decided he would go on to the seminary. His father, he says, "was quite pleased but quite shocked." Gray earned degrees from Drew and then from Princeton Theological Seminary. In 1972 he was recently married, teaching at a Catholic college, and running a Baptist church in Montclair, N.J., when his father died, and he returned to take over the family church.

Ministering to an urban area brought him into direct contact with secular politics, and in 1976 Gray challenged the incumbent Second District congressman, Robert N. C. Nix (1958-1979), in the Democratic primary. Nix was a member of the old-line black political hierarchy and one of the first blacks to chair a House committee (Post Office and Civil Service). Charging that Nix had lost touch with the district, Gray lost by only 339 votes. Two years later Gray ran again and won by almost 12,000 out of 63,000 votes cast.

That election left some resentment in Philadelphia among those in the local party organization who had been patiently waiting for Nix to retire to run for his seat.

But Gray has taken firm control of his district. His only significant challenge came in the 1982 primary from Milton Street, a tough-talking community activist and state senator. Gray won with 76 percent of the vote. In 1986 he faced opposition only in the May primary, and won 96.6 percent of the vote. He was unopposed in the November general election.

Off to a Fast Start

Even though he had never held a political office, Gray jumped quickly into House politics. He made friends with power brokers such as John P. Murtha, D-Pa., and won a coveted seat on the Democratic Steering and Policy Committee, which makes committee assignments.

Showing a precocious ability at behind-the-scenes dealing, Gray announced that he would not oppose any other freshman for a committee seat, and stood aside so someone else could take an opening he wanted on Banking, Finance, and Urban Affairs. When time came to select members for the Budget Committee, he spoke in favor of other freshmen—then sat back while other members of Steering and Policy put him on the panel.

In his other committee assignment, Foreign Affairs, Gray won establishment of a new African development program, a remarkable success for a freshman. He also became one of the leaders of the drive to impose sanctions on South Africa.

In 1981 Gray gave up his seats on Budget and Foreign Affairs to take a position on Appropriations, but two years later came back to Budget as a representative of the spending panel.

His campaign for the committee's chairmanship in 1984 was a model of quiet political acumen. Under House rules, members are allowed only six years on the committee, with an extra two possible for a chairman elected in his last term. At the end of 1984, Chairman Jones lost his eligibility, but announced that he would seek a rules change to permit him to keep the job. Jones was challenged by another committee member, Leon E. Panetta, D-Calif. But Panetta had himself served the full six years and needed a rules change to be able to serve as chairman.

While attention was focused on the Jones-Panetta race and the rules changes they sought, Gray used the Pennsylvania delegation and the Congressional Black Caucus to explore his chances for a dark-horse challenge. He went to members asking for their support in case the rules were not changed. The rules change was narrowly defeated in December, and when other Democrats—chiefly Martin Frost of Texas—attempted to mount a last-minute campaign for chairman, they found that Gray had sewn up the votes.

When Gray was sworn in as Budget

chairman, two thousand constituents flooded the Capitol for the brief ceremony in an unusual show of support. The trip was organized by his church. The congregation "is the root of my life," said Gray. "It is my family."

GOP Praise, Skepticism

House Republicans are left out of most budget maneuvers. They are kept to a committee ratio that understates their overall numbers in the House, and they are not invited to help write the House budget.

The Republicans complain bitterly about this system, but they do not, by and large, blame Gray for it. "On my side, I haven't heard a word spoken in anger about Bill Gray, and I've heard a lot of good things," said Bill Gradison, R-Ohio, a member of the Budget Committee.

Although their economic ideas could hardly be more different, Gray has joined forces with Jack F. Kemp, R-N.Y., on several issues such as tax-free "enterprise zones" for urban areas. "I think he's very open to ideas," said Kemp. "He's one of the fastest-rising stars of the party."

Independence Questioned

While they may like him personally, Republicans see the Budget chairman as something of a leadership puppet. "He is controlled by the Caucus," said Delbert L. Latta of Ohio, ranking Republican on Gray's committee. "I think he would prefer a little longer leash."

But Democrats on the committee said that in 1986, at least, Gray was more in the position of leading the leadership than vice versa. They point particularly to the tax issue. Speaker Thomas P. O'Neill, Jr., D-Mass., wanted no part of anything that could be labeled a tax increase so long as Reagan threatened to veto it. Senate conferees, meanwhile, had insisted that some sort of new tax initiative was essential.

Gray convinced O'Neill to go along with conditional "reserve funds" involving new taxes in both the House resolution and the conference report. And the final compromise, which would allow a revenue increase for defense and other "critical needs," raised the possibility of forcing Reagan to choose between defense spending and taxes.

The conditional nature of the deal was reminiscent of one of Gray's first major budget actions, in 1983. Negotiations on the fiscal 1984 budget had foundered until Gray, a junior member of the committee, came forward with a reserve fund to provide money for ten new initiatives, including farm relief and employment programs, if they were enacted by Congress. The idea broke a logjam and the budget was adopted. Few of the programs ever were enacted.

Rhetoric

One area of Gray's style that comes in for mild criticism is his rhetoric. While he is accessible and friendly, in dealings with reporters and colleagues he often relies on a few outworn metaphors: the deficit as a "sea of red ink" and Reagan's ".44-magnum veto gun" aimed at any bill increasing taxes. Sometimes solid information on where Gray stands is hard to come by. "I still don't know to this day whether Bill Gray supports [additional] revenues or not," Panetta said.

Some find Gray's rhetoric grating. "Gray places a high priority on being open and fair," said Vin Weber, R-Minn. "But because he feels he's open and fair, there is also an air of moral superiority. I think that rankles [Republican] members."

A House leadership aide said that Gray's rhetorical style sometimes left members uncertain. But he said that no one had complained that Gray misled a member.

From the viewpoint of the Senate, however, sources close to the conference on the budget said that at several points in negotiations, Gray agreed to a compromise from which he later backed away, apparently because of objections from chairmen of House authorizing committees.

Senate Budget Committee ranking member Pete V. Domenici, R-N.M., said that Gray was hemmed in by the short tenure of the Budget chairmanship, which gives him little independence. "That's not anything new," he said. "It's the result of the way they do business over there."

Some members also criticize Gray for playing virtually no role in the 1985 conference that established the final form of Gramm-Rudman. It is incongruous, they said, that the Budget chairman played no part in the most important budgetary law of the decade.

Gray says he stayed out of the conference because, "I don't want to have responsibility for carrying the ball on something I don't support."

An Eye on the Future

The Budget chairmanship is considered a House leadership position, and as the first black member to have such a post, Gray is often referred to as "the most powerful black member of Congress." Said Edgar, "Here's a black, urban progressive doing good at the worst time in history for black, urban progressives."

It is not clear how much real power Gray exercises, or whether his popularity among his colleagues will last. "It's still pretty early in his career," observed a leadership aide. But, the aide went on, "the bottom line is completing the budgets and not alienating people in the process." On that score, he said, Gray is two-for-two.

At the time Gray was elected Budget chairman, some Democrats feared that putting a black northeastern liberal in a key post was the wrong signal for a party that, in the wake of its 1984 electoral rout, needed to appeal more to white voters in the South and West.

But today, members agree that Gray has been able to overcome both stereotypes and limitations imposed by his race in a way that will help his future career—in the House or beyond it.

"It's important for people in the South to understand that he's making it on his own merit," said MacKay. "He's not part of 1970s tokenism."

Gray resents being characterized as a "black committee chairman," but he acknowledges that his race affects others' perceptions of his performance. "Every black person carries a burden of limitations, no matter how high they go," Gray says. "I have had more opportunities than the overwhelming majority, but that doesn't mean that I have broken through the limitations."

His challenge, Gray says, is to push the limits farther so race will be less of a factor when other black members seek powerful positions in Congress.

3

Leaders Without Portfolio

Congress can be miserly in the opportunities it offers members to have an impact on its workings.

There are few formal positions of power—a handful of leadership posts in both houses, plus committee chairmanships and positions as ranking minority member. The institution gives control over the flow of legislation and policy initiatives to the people who hold those spots; those who don't often feel impotent.

But Congress is made up of men and women who have learned, sometimes after much effort, how to influence a majority of voters in their districts or states. So it is natural that some of those outside the leadership loop develop the political skills necessary to influence their colleagues as well.

Robert L. Peabody of Johns Hopkins University, in a 1976 book on congressional leadership, described them as "informal leaders, people whose intelligence, integrity, demonstrated experience, or active pursuit of higher office have earned them an added measure of esteem or respect from their peers."

The following are profiles of seven members of the 100th Congress who personify ways of wielding power or influence outside of official leadership channels.

Included are three senators—Democrats Bill Bradley of New Jersey and Howard M. Metzenbaum of Ohio, and Republican Phil Gramm of Texas—and four House members—Democrats John P. Murtha of Pennsylvania and Henry A. Waxman of California, and Republicans Henry J. Hyde and Edward R. Madigan, both of Illinois.

Why They Were Chosen

The seven are lawmakers who, through some combination of personal qualities and legislative skills, have managed to put their imprint on Congress. The group is not meant to be all-inclusive or definitive. Its members were chosen based on interviews with senators, House members, and congressional aides conducted over several months at the end of the 99th Congress. No one was a unanimous choice of those interviewed.

Several hold institutional positions that help them exercise power. Madigan, for example, is ranking minority member of the Agriculture Committee and of the Energy and Commerce Subcommittee on Health and the Environment—positions that would make him chairman if Republicans ever took control of the House. Moreover, Madigan entered the House Republicans' leadership circle in December 1986 when he was chosen chief deputy whip.

Waxman is chairman of the Energy and Commerce Subcommittee on Health and the Environment, which puts him in the broad second tier of committee leadership below committee chairmen.

Nevertheless, both stand out in the House as tacticians whose influence rests more on the qualities they have brought to their roles than on strengths inherent in the positions themselves.

Metzenbaum was an early choice, one made long before Democrats in the November 1986 elections regained control of the Senate. Now he, too, is a subcommittee chairman, on not one, but three, panels.

But like Waxman and Madigan, Metzenbaum is a force to be reckoned with in his chamber because of traits distinct from any institutional power that might accrue to him by virtue of his positions.

Others With Influence

The ranks of untitled but influential members include any number of others who are likely to leave their mark on the 100th Congress.

Texas Democrat Marvin Leath, for example, is carving out a role as a bridge between the House Democratic leadership and conservative southern Democrats who have at times felt shut out of its deliberations. It is a role that for years was quietly performed by Charles Whitley of North Carolina, whose retirement in 1986 left a void that Leath may fill.

There are others, such as House Democrats Lee H. Hamilton of Indiana and Morris K. Udall of Arizona, whose integrity and respectful treatment of colleagues on both sides of the aisle have brought each a measure of personal influence.

Many House Republicans look for guidance to Bill Gradison of Ohio and Bill Frenzel of Minnesota. Both are widely recognized as intellectual guardians of GOP economic orthodoxy who can nevertheless reach compromises with the Democratic majority.

Both houses and parties abound with energetic younger members who seem certain to grow in influence as they gain seniority. These include Republican senator William S. Cohen of Maine, a tenacious and artful moderate who has had a major impact on nuclear arms issues; California Republican representative Dan Lungren, who used his post on the House Judiciary Committee to carve out a central role in rewriting the nation's immigration laws; and Democratic representative Charles E. Schumer of New York, who has dealt himself roles in issues such as the budget, immigration, and housing.

Bill Bradley: Compelling Ideas

Bill Bradley has an idea, although he is having trouble getting people who count to go along with it.

The Democratic senator from New Jersey is worried about Third World debt, and in particular about the $350 billion that Latin American countries owe the developed world.

In the summer of 1986, at a conference in Zurich, Switzerland, of financial officials from industrialized nations, Bradley proposed that the interest rate on all outstanding commercial and bilateral Third World loans be cut, that there be an annual 3 percent forgiveness of the loan principal, and that $3 billion worth of new loans be made to eligible countries. In exchange, debtor countries would lower trade barriers and work for economic growth.

The plan has won praise from some international economists, but drew immedi-

Sen. Bill Bradley, D-N.J.

ate fire from the Reagan administration, which has its own debt-relief plan developed by Treasury Secretary James A. Baker III. One Treasury official called Bradley's proposal "an extremely short-term and rather naive view of the debt situation."

Not surprisingly, the commercial banking community also has taken a dim view of Bradley's notions, as have World Bank President Barber B. Conable, Jr., and Federal Reserve Chairman Paul A. Volcker.

But Bradley is nothing if not patient. The idea is out there and drawing attention, and Bradley has been doing everything he can to make sure that people know about it.

He has delivered testimony to congressional colleagues, written articles for newspapers, addressed conferences and met with finance ministers, bankers, and politicians from around the globe. What counts is that he is being taken seriously.

There is a reason for that. After eight years in the Senate, Bradley is reaping the rewards of his dedication to thoughtful legislating. His focus has always been on the intellectual side of policy making—a concentration not known for guaranteeing success in politics and an early surprise for those who expected Bradley to trade on his celebrity as a professional basketball player when he arrived in Washington.

But Bradley's hard-working and thorough—some would say driven—approach to understanding an issue and developing his position on it has won him enormous respect from his colleagues and Congress-watchers of all political stripes. It is a style that has led some to consider Bradley aloof and distant; it is also the major reason Bradley's name has been surfacing in presidential speculation since a few years after he took office.

"The only Democratic think tank in this town is in Bill Bradley's head," former Reagan budget-office aide Michael J. Horowitz told the *Wall Street Journal* in 1986. And Kirk O'Donnell, a one-time aide to former House Speaker Thomas P. O'Neill, Jr., D-Mass., said of Bradley, "Members of Congress who are attracted by ideas and who know how to sell them will be the powers of the future."

O'Donnell's sales imagery is apt for Bradley. He is neither an arm-twister nor a legislative tactician. People have to buy his ideas. But he can be tireless at promoting them, and at helping his colleagues make up their minds to invest in them.

In Congress that can mean the difference between political influence and irrelevance. "The fact that an idea is floating in a vacuum," said Oregon Republican Bob Packwood, who chaired the Senate Finance Committee on which Bradley sits, "doesn't make any difference unless someone grabs it, hones it, and pushes it."

That is precisely what Bradley did for four years with his plan to overhaul and simplify the tax code. Starting in 1982, he began pushing the notion of a tax overhaul that would lower individual rates, simplify the tax rate structure, and close loopholes for both individuals and corporations.

He wrote a book, *The Fair Tax,* to try to build public support for the idea, and spent a good bit of his time touting the proposal in articles and speeches. In 1984 he urged Democratic presidential nominee Walter F. Mondale to make it a key part of his platform. But Mondale was enmeshed in his conviction that he would have to raise taxes, and Bradley's colleagues were having a hard time taking the idea seriously.

"Bradley and Gephardt . . . are putting everyone to sleep," commented Minnesota Republican senator Dave Durenberger at one point, referring to Missouri Democrat Richard A. Gephardt, who had sponsored the tax-overhaul proposal in the House.

By 1985, however, President Reagan had made tax reform the top domestic priority of his second term, and Congress began to pay heed. An overhaul bill reached the House floor at the end of the year, and Bradley worked with Ways and Means Chairman Dan Rostenkowski, D-Ill., to win its passage. In an unusual step for a senator, he spent a good bit of time lobbying House Democrats on the issue.

Spurred by the House, the Senate Finance Committee took up tax overhaul in 1986. Bradley was reform's beacon on the committee. But his colleagues loaded their plan with one special-interest benefit after another—oil and gas breaks, advantages for the timber industry, help for farmers and miners, favors for businesses investing in new equipment. With each committee session, the list grew longer.

Though Bradley made a few stabs at stemming the tide, he spent most of his time reminding other senators that there was an alternative, and that their measure would topple under its own weight if they kept on. At the end of each day of markup, he would stick around to talk to reporters, ensuring that his side of the argument got prominent mention the next day.

As it turned out, the chairman came around. Packwood suspended markups after the committee had cobbled together a tax bill that, at a time of soaring deficits, would have cost the government $29 billion in lost revenue. Then he started over. He huddled with Bradley and five other committee activists, and a week later returned with the skeleton of what eventually became the Tax Reform Act of 1986, a proposal that, in many of its basics, was the plan Bradley had been pushing.

In the weeks that followed, Bradley played a key role in bringing along liberal Democrats, arguing the intellectual merits of major sections of the measure and dealing with the press. When the bill eventually passed, Packwood and Rostenkowski gave Bradley considerable credit for its success.

It is that experience that makes it hard to write off Bradley's international debt plan, despite the arguments against it. Bradley's track record suggests that however many officials oppose his proposal now, its time may yet come.

Phil Gramm: Seizing Opportunities

Phil Gramm's southern political roots are years and miles way from New York's Tammany Hall, but the epitaph that Tammany's George W. Plunkitt once suggested for himself could just as well be said of Gramm: "He seen his opportunities and he took 'em."

Twice in his eight-year congressional career, the Texas Republican has seen an opportunity and seized it. And twice he's come away with top billing on landmark legislation—the 1981 Gramm-Latta law embodying President Reagan's budget priorities and the 1985 Gramm-Rudman-Hollings law for cutting the deficit.

In each case Gramm dramatically showed that even a junior member with an idea and good timing can overcome Congress's hierarchical and institutional roadblocks. In 1981 he was beginning only his second House term, and his first on the Budget Committee. In 1985 he was a first-year senator who had been kept off that chamber's Budget Committee.

Never mind that many colleagues, and outside experts, grouse that Gramm's first law set in motion the $200 billion-plus annual deficits that his second law is designed to conquer. Or that the second law promised budgetary salvation that it could not deliver as long as Congress and Reagan remained deadlocked over spending and taxing priorities. The fact is, Congress passed both.

In 1981 the time was Reagan's honeymoon with Congress. The idea was the new Republican president's proposed budget that would boost defense while cutting domestic programs enough to balance the budget. Gramm, though a Democrat at the time, capitalized on both.

After persuading House Democratic leaders to give him a Budget seat, he privately connived with Reagan budget director and former House ally David A. Stockman, R-Mich. (1977-1981), to draft the president's budget. Then he helped steer it through the House, bringing disgruntled southern Democrats into a winning coalition with Republicans.

Four years later, 1985 was a time of palpable frustration in Congress with spiraling deficits. As the year advanced without major cuts, it was widely expected there would be a showdown in the fall, when members had to vote on an annual resolution raising the government's debt limit. Approval of the essential measure was unlikely without simultaneous action against deficits.

Gramm, who by now had jumped to the Republican Party and the Senate, worked over the summer on the idea that would become Gramm-Rudman-Hollings, reviving a proposal he had cosponsored with House Majority Leader—now Speaker—Jim Wright, D-Texas, in 1981. The two men did not push their bill at the time. "I felt then the time had not come—but it was going to come," Gramm said in 1986. Fall 1985 was his time. As Democratic opponent J. Bennett Johnston, La., said afterward, "It was the idea of the moment."

In pursuit of his goals, Gramm's energy and ego seem boundless, even Messianic. A few Republicans recall his private exclamation, just moments after Senate passage of Gramm-Rudman-Hollings, that it was "the Lord's work." He has announced to Washington audiences, "I came here to change America."

Gramm's style and success have not been without potential cost to his effectiveness in the future. Many Democrats loathe him for his 1981 betrayal, and some Republicans distrust him. Members of both parties envy his headline-making triumphs, and gripe that his self-deprecating, hayseed humor masks an opportunistic, even dangerous, ideologue.

Gramm now confronts the added obstacle of life in the Senate minority. But he dismisses talk that it will impede him. No longer, he says, will he be "forced to support compromises that you do not believe in" by a Republican leadership anxious to move legislation. "In the minority," he said, "you have an opportunity to present alternatives. I'll be carrying the ball more."

He told the *Houston Post*, in the kind of remark that shows why fellow Republicans are wary, that he would no longer be constrained by "a prima donna Republican chairman." (Gramm denied the reference was to Budget Chairman Pete V. Domenici, R-N.M., saying that "there were others.")

At home meanwhile, his antipathy to Washington—"the devil's city," he calls it—

Sen. Phil Gramm, R-Texas

is not so popular now that a depressed oil industry wants help. And his free-market ideological consistency is not so appealing now that he opposes an oil-import fee, which oilmen seek to boost domestic prices. A Houston oilman, a former contributor to Gramm's campaign, publicly condemned him as "the third senator from Massachusetts"—the ultimate epithet for a Texas politician.

Whatever problems Gramm may face on the Hill and at home, few members underestimate his ability to step forward again with the idea of the moment—least of all his enemies. One Texas politician, former House Speaker Sam Rayburn, gave junior members this advice: "If you want to get along, go along." Gramm, by his example, has quite a different message: To get ahead, just go ahead.

Or, as Gramm said, "If you're willing to tackle tough issues, you don't have to worry about stepping on people's toes. They're going to step out of your way and shove you to the front."

Henry J. Hyde: Rhetorical Sword Play

In 1980, while still a relatively unknown House member, Henry J. Hyde became a hero to the anti-abortion movement when the Supreme Court upheld his legislation preventing federal payments for abortion. Caught in the flare of publicity brought on by the decision, Hyde was modest about his place in the drama.

"Somebody once said that we can't be great, but we can attach ourselves to something that is great," he told a reporter at the time. "I'm a spear-carrier in the opera. And way in the back, I might add."

His metaphor needs some updating these days. No opponent who has been skewered by one of Hyde's rhetorical thrusts would deny that the Illinois Republican comes on stage well-armed. But Hyde, now starting his seventh term, is no longer the anonymous member of the House chorus that "spear-carrier" implies.

Rather, on issues ranging from nuclear strategy to U.S. policy in Central America to the Equal Rights Amendment, he is often one of the principals, his tenor prominent among the few voices at the center of the debate.

Hyde is one of the premier orators in the House. Watching him in action, it is easy to see flashes of the Chicago trial lawyer he once was. He speaks with wit, passion, and deep conviction about the conservative causes he holds dear, and displays a delight in rhetorical engagement that is matched by only a few other members. He is quick on his feet, shrewdly finding flaws in his liberal opponents' arguments and pouncing on them with ready sarcasm.

Hyde admits that playing a downstage-center role in debates carries risks. "The more you speak on a variety of subjects, the less credence you're given," he said. "You have to husband your pearls before you cast them profligately about the chamber."

But that has not kept him from becoming something of a cleanup batter for Republicans on foreign policy issues. Whoever is nominally responsible for initiatives backing President Reagan's policies on Nicaragua or arms control, it is Hyde who tends to offer the most compelling arguments in their favor.

In a chamber where legislative dirt under the fingernails tends to be more highly prized than soulful oratory, there are people who question whether Hyde's verbal skills make a difference. "He's able to pull the strands together and find the slogans," said one Democratic Hill aide, "but I'm not sure what impact all that has."

One clear effect is that it gives Hyde considerable influence on his side of the aisle. In 1982 Hyde's decision to support extension of the Voting Rights Act of 1965—after initially opposing it—proved crucial in the legislation's movement toward passage.

"It made what we were doing respectable," said California Democrat Don Edwards, chairman of the subcommittee that oversaw the measure. "After all, Reagan didn't want to do it. . . . It moved the bill into a new level of acceptance and softened the problem we had with the White House and the Justice Department."

Hyde's rhetorical skills also give the GOP one of the few weapons allowed the minority party. Hampered in their ability to pull the House's institutional levers of power, Republicans often have to depend for legislative success on winning Democrats over to their side.

"One of the ways you establish coalitions in this House is you show that coalitions are worth belonging to," said Lungren of California. "You have to attract people not only because of the politics of the matter, but because of the force of the idea. . . . If you don't have a Henry Hyde articulating those views very forcefully, very well, and with intelligence behind them, it's hard to attract people to come over."

Rep. Henry J. Hyde, R-Ill.

One of Hyde's most effective moments came in the 1983 fight over proposals for a nuclear freeze. He had led the opposition in 1982—"government by bumper sticker," he called the idea—helping defeat the freeze narrowly. But grass-roots pressure in its favor had grown, and freeze supporters felt they would have little trouble getting it through on their next try.

They were wrong. The first day of debate took thirteen hours, with conservative Republicans quarterbacked by Hyde pressing freeze backers onto the defensive. They pointed out inconsistencies, peppered the proposal with weakening amendments, and forced proponents to limit their claims for the resolution's effect.

When the freeze eventually emerged from the floor after six days of debate spread out over two months, it was in a marrowless version, far from the potent rallying point that grass-roots organizers had hoped to have available.

Though Hyde is a warm and genuinely funny man, his occasionally acerbic humor can raise the ire of a Democratic opponent, costing Hyde the chance for compromise. "His wit seems like a Molotov cocktail thrown into the debate sometimes, even when he doesn't mean it to be," said one Democratic aide who has watched him at work.

In the next Congress, with Democrats in charge on both sides of Capitol Hill, it may be even more risky to inflame the opposition. But Hyde is unlikely to give the other side any breaks because of that.

"Conflict and disputation," he said, "are the heart and soul of drama, the heart and soul of literature, and the heart and soul of the legislative process—if we're not all to die of boredom."

Edward R. Madigan: The Art of Negotiation

A few years back, Edward R. Madigan was negotiating with a House Democratic subcommittee chairman over funding for a new program. The Democrats wanted it to run for four years; the Reagan administration, Madigan knew, hoped to limit it to three. So Madigan pressed for two.

That was just astute bargaining. But he transformed the affair into art when his Democratic counterpart decided to compromise and proposed three years' funding. Rather than agreeing immediately, Madigan hesitated. He had another matter he wanted to bring up. One of his aides needed a parking place in the crowded House lot; if that was taken care of, he allowed, then he might agree to three years' funding.

The ploy worked. The Democrat went

Rep. Edward R. Madigan, R-Ill.

along with the deal, the staffer got a coveted House parking spot, and Madigan won the level of funding he had been playing for all along.

It was a vintage performance, a small lesson in negotiating prowess. It was also a vivid illustration of why, after seven terms in the House, this Republican from a central Illinois farm district has been able to rival all but a handful of senior Democrats in his impact on public policy.

Madigan is a master of tactical subtlety, an inside player for whom legislative politics has more in common with a carefully considered game of chess than with brute tests of strength. He is a walking rejoinder to Republican colleagues who argue that their minority status compels confrontation with a Democratic majority that has robbed them of their legislative potency.

"I wouldn't be opposed to confrontation if I thought it would be successful," Madigan said. "But you force people in the majority party to stick with their ranks. . . . I can't pass up the opportunity to defeat something or pass something in order to be confrontational."

That approach, though it has come under fire from conservatives who worry that he has been too ready to compromise, is generally appreciated by his GOP colleagues—enough so that in December 1986 Madigan was appointed by party leaders to be chief deputy whip for the 100th Congress.

"There is probably no better agricultural strategist in the House, and no one who better uses timing," said Wisconsin Republican representative Steve Gunderson. "He's low-key and sometimes suggests he's not even focusing on an issue, then at the proper time will be in his seat and moving."

Madigan's first rule of operating appears to be to get along with subcommittee chairmen. When he was ranking minority member on their panels, he worked closely with James J. Florio of New Jersey, head of the Energy and Commerce subcommittee on transportation, and with Ed Jones of Tennessee, chairman of the Agriculture subcommittee on credit. His relations with Energy and Commerce Health Subcommittee Chairman Henry A. Waxman, D-Calif., are somewhat less warm, but the two men retain a cordial respect for each other.

He also draws on a solid understanding of his colleagues. He knows, for example, which members of each state delegation are looked to by others for direction on votes, and is careful to touch base with them before one of his bills comes to the floor. On agricultural issues in particular, he knows other members' districts and the pressures they face—so that, for example, he will not waste time pushing an idea to cut growers' dependence on federal crop payments with a member who represents poor farmers.

And if he is adept at subtly misdirecting his bargaining opponents, as his parking-spot deal suggests, he is also not above blunter forms of negotiating. After he flared up against a proposal to cut soybean programs more deeply than other commodities in the 1985 farm bill—and won soothing assurances from the chairman of the subcommittee involved—Madigan explained to the *Wall Street Journal*, "That's just under the heading of making them know they have to deal with me."

The 1986 elections took away one of Madigan's chief leverage points. As long as the Senate was in GOP hands, he could use a conference committee as his arena of last resort. That option has been important to him, for example, in his dealings on Waxman's subcommittee, which is firmly under the Democrat's control.

In trying to block an initiative in the full committee or on the House floor, he could rely on the threat posed by Republican Senate conferees to help win concessions. But with the Democrats in control of both chambers, Madigan has lost a major bargaining tool.

Still, Madigan's track record suggests he will adjust. "Sure we're in the minority," said Lungren of California. "But Ed knows there are pressure points all around this place. All you have to do is find what those pressure points are."

Howard Metzenbaum: Democratic Gatekeeper

In late 1973 a *Washington Post* profile introduced the Senate's newest member. Ohio Democrat Howard M. Metzenbaum vowed to "speak softly," in deference to senior senators. "I won't come in riding a white horse and being gung ho," he added. "I hope to be effective, but in a quiet voice."

Truth-in-labeling that was not. Metzenbaum has been effective; even critics agree he is one of Congress's premier leaders-without-portfolio. But he didn't earn that rank by being soft-spoken or deferential.

Instead, Metzenbaum from the start has been outspoken in his self-appointed role as watchdog for the consumer and the Treasury against big business. He defies Senate traditions of quiet, mutual back-scratching, publicly exposing the tax breaks and special-interest provisions that members bury deep within big bills and opposing federal spending for local projects that otherwise would get a rubber stamp of approval.

Consequently, Metzenbaum perhaps more than anyone has burst the myth of the Senate as a club, and epitomized its modern-day evolution as a place where mavericks and individualists can thrive, regardless of party or length of service. The trick is simply to play by the rules.

Metzenbaum does so best at the end of a session, when time is short. A filibuster, or just his threat of one, kills dozens of proposals a year. Near the end of the 99th Congress, a two-hour interview was interrupted four times by phone calls on behalf of colleagues seeking his go-ahead on a variety of proposals.

He was Democrats' gatekeeper to the floor when Republicans were in control, routinely vetoing GOP leaders' bids for the unanimous consent they needed to bring measures to the floor. If he was not at his seat, an aide was—alert and armed with a black book summarizing every pending bill, and Metzenbaum's position on each. At any time, he has up to twenty "holds" on bills, barring them from the floor.

Critics chortle that Metzenbaum has no major legislation to his credit, and that his amendments often fail by wide margins. But if bills do not bear his name, many bear his mark through the changes he wins. Many of his amendments are not meant to pass, but to eat time until a weary Senate either modifies a bill to his liking—he is usually a willing compromiser—or kills it.

Metzenbaum's role in the Senate legislative process has become all but institutionalized. "When you prepare an amendment or a bill, subconsciously you're thinking about Howard Metzenbaum. Will it pass the Metzenbaum test?" said Sen. David Pryor, D-Ark., in 1986 when members' special-interest additions threatened to drag down the landmark tax bill.

Sen. Howard Metzenbaum, D-Ohio

Republican leaders and committee chairmen not only consulted him before bringing bills to the floor, but also conspired to block fellow Republicans' proposals. Reporters go to his office to research end-of-the-year stories on the "cats and dogs" bills that members try to sneak through. The Senate Democrats' form that clears bills for action late in the session has checkoff boxes for their leader, appropriate committee head—and Metzenbaum. "Now that may seem officious," he said, "but I want to know what I'm passing. I would relish if every senator took this position. I don't enjoy being Peck's bad boy."

It helps that he has a skin grown thick over a long, successful life. A self-made millionaire and nearly 70, he is "past the point in his life where he needs constant peer approval," a former aide said.

"His beliefs override his concerns about being a thorn in anybody's side," said Orrin G. Hatch, R-Utah, Metzenbaum's frequent political sparring partner. "I respect him for that."

Metzenbaum traces his combativeness to years of fighting discrimination, especially against fellow Jews. He says his mission as public defender reflects *tsedaka*, which he defined as "the obligation of the Jews to give, and to pay their dues in society." And his independence, he says, is a luxury he can afford because "I have no other aspirations."

He is not the most popular member of the Senate. Even some colleagues in his party will vote against anything with his name on it. He is vulnerable to suggestions of hypocrisy; stories in recent years of an attempt to help a relative in a federal job, or to profit by using his influence in a business deal, drew more negative attention than usual.

The thick skin is not impervious: "I've walked out of the Senate sometimes after being trounced, and I've worried, 'You've lost your effectiveness. You only got twelve votes. The members don't respect you.' . . . There isn't any of us who goes out there and gets twelve votes and doesn't feel bad about it. And then you come back the next day and win overwhelmingly."

Being Peck's bad boy was one thing when Republicans held the Senate. But now Metzenbaum's party has the majority, and the responsibility to govern. Moreover, he is chairman of three subcommittees—one each on the Labor and Human Resources, Judiciary, and Energy and Natural Resources committees. He will have to be a coalition-builder, and less a maverick; a bill-passer more than a bill-killer. The test is whether Metzenbaum can succeed as well in his new role, or whether he will find himself the one Democrat who prefers life in the minority.

Rep. John P. Murtha, D-Pa.

John P. Murtha: Hidden Influence

In bold black and yellow, billboards along the southwestern Pennsylvania highway immodestly proclaimed, "John P. Murtha—The 'P' is for Power."

As campaign boasts go, that slogan in Murtha's tough 1982 primary race carried more truth than many. But it sent the wrong message about how Murtha built that power in the House: Public braggadocio and self-promotion are just what he assiduously avoids in his role as Congress's ultimate insider.

His influence after a dozen years has several origins—membership on the Appropriations Committee; leadership of a three-state bloc of votes in his coal-mining region; the gratitude of senior members for his repeated efforts at winning pay raises, higher limits on outside earnings, and pension benefits for members; and especially his renowned talent for "whipping," counting votes for Democratic leaders in advance of floor action.

Enhancing his effectiveness is his almost unique aversion to the media. Murtha declines interviews routinely. "He does the opposite of what everyone else up here does, and that's to discourage the press," said one House Democrat. This colleague compared Murtha to professional baseball pitcher Steve Carlton, whose avoidance of reporters contributed to an aura of mystery and an image of a player obsessed with his game.

If Murtha is not shuttling between back rooms, he typically can be found huddled with his coal-state cronies in the dark left-front corner of the House, nicknamed "the Pennsylvania corner." Members say it is inaccurate to claim Murtha controls the votes of these friends from Pennsylvania, West Virginia, and Ohio, because they generally would vote like him whether he asked them to or not. On a close vote, however, Murtha can deliver.

But it is his whipping among members outside his geographic base that better accounts for his influence, and his value to House leaders. For the only thing members like less than saying how they plan to vote is asking someone else for a commitment.

"It's a myth that anybody can whip," a leadership aide said. "There are very, very few people who can work the House and fewer who like it. But Murtha has energy and nerve, a second skin. He has absolutely no fear of rejection, of going back to members again and again for their votes."

"He is working 100 percent of the time on this stuff. He loves it," said Mike Lowry, D-Wash. Added Marvin Leath, D-Texas, "He moseys up to you and starts talking and the next thing you know, he's 'whipped' you."

On the Democratic Steering and Policy Committee, an insider's heaven given its responsibility for making committee assignments, he is a master. In the 99th Congress he cut deals that put one ally on Ways and Means and another on Appropriations, defeating the candidates of the Speaker and majority leader. In 1984 he engineered Pennsylvania Democrat William H. Gray III's rise to Budget Committee chairman, persuading then-Speaker Thomas P. O'Neill, Jr., Mass., and conservative southerners to back Gray.

Murtha's ties to southerners are based on their frequent alliances on defense and foreign policy issues. A decorated Marine veteran of the Korean and Vietnam wars, Murtha has backed the Reagan administration's efforts to deploy the MX missile and to aid the Nicaraguan contras, making rare floor speeches and even helping House Republicans to count votes. A 1986 speech that seemed to impugn the patriotism of contra-aid foes reportedly enraged O'Neill, the chief opponent, yet Murtha's value to the leadership was such that his party transgressions were tolerated.

He also gets away with it, colleagues say, because he is no threat. Murtha was knocked off the leadership ladder in 1980, when he was entangled in the FBI's Abscam bribery sting. Though he never was charged, the scandal cost Murtha a likely appointment to the number three post of majority whip.

The 100th Congress poses challenges to Murtha's power. He had to leave Steering and Policy because the seat he held alternates between Pennsylvania and Ohio, and it is Ohio's turn. More important, his good friend O'Neill is gone and Murtha's relations with the new leadership team generally are not good.

Though an early supporter of Jim Wright for Speaker, Murtha is not close to the Texan; he is much closer to Rostenkowski, whom Wright views as his chief rival. Murtha has little in common with Majority Leader Thomas S. Foley of Washington.

And he is an open foe of Majority Whip Tony Coelho of California, having backed first Bill Alexander of Arkansas and then Charles B. Rangel of New York for whip against Coelho.

Nevertheless, colleagues predict that Murtha will adapt. As Gray said, "The leadership always likes a good insider-man."

Henry A. Waxman: Persistent Pursuit

To understand Henry A. Waxman, it helps to understand his House district. It is a jumble of "Westside" Los Angeles communities: verdant enclaves of entertainment-industry wealth; quiet Jewish, Asian-American, and Hispanic neighborhoods; gaudy stretches of urban bohemia. What ties them together are a liberal temperament and a strong inclination to support politicians who share it.

That is ideal for Waxman. As one of the strongest House backers of government funding for social welfare programs, he is absolutely secure at home.

And that, in turn, is crucial to the way Waxman operates. He is the Democrats' legislative equivalent of water forging a new path to the sea: It may take him time to reach his goal, to find a way around obstacles if he cannot wear them down, but he gets there in the end.

Persistence is a rare—and valuable—quality in the House. Said a former Democratic leadership aide, "Members' attention spans don't allow for plugging away day after day; a member who does has an enormous asset on his side." But patience and persistence are effective only over time. Waxman's safe district buys him time.

For a legislator who does not jump from cause to cause with each new session, the benefits are obvious.

Rep. Henry A. Waxman, D-Calif.

In 1979 Waxman introduced legislation expanding health care for poor women during pregnancy and steered it through the House. The idea was to help states that broadened their Medicaid coverage of low-income women during pregnancy. But the bill died when the Senate, threatened by a string of anti-abortion amendments and concerns that it would cost too much, failed to take it up.

In 1984, in the restrictive climate of the Reagan administration, Waxman pushed the program through. He formed a coalition of liberals concerned with health care for the poor and conservative abortion foes who felt a moral obligation to ensure prenatal and infant care. With their help, he attached the measure to the fiscal 1985 budget reconciliation bill, then kept it there despite attempts to derail it.

The new program, though more limited than the one Waxman had wanted in the freer days of the Carter administration, was among the few social spending initiatives of the year.

Waxman's tenacity in trying to enact his values into law is a reflection of his belief that results are what count; he is interested in winning, not in scoring debating points.

An example: Chosen to sit on the House Democrats' task force on the Gramm-Rudman-Hollings budget-balancing legislation in 1985, he used the opportunity to try to dilute its effects—not simply to waste his energy arguing against a measure that was inevitably going to pass. With his colleagues' help, he ensured that the House alternative to the Senate's version protected a number of poverty programs against the measure's automatic cuts.

"Henry is responsible for most of the exemptions we put in there," said Texas Democrat Marvin Leath, who sat on the task force with Waxman and who, despite his conservative budgetary beliefs, went along with his more liberal colleague's arguments.

Waxman's goal-oriented style sometimes rubs colleagues the wrong way—he can be hard-nosed when going after something he wants—but he has also gained respect for playing power politics as a means toward his ends, not as an end in itself.

Some liberals note, for example, that if he had been concerned solely with consolidating his position, Waxman might never have taken on the powerful chairman of the Energy and Commerce Committee, Democrat John D. Dingell of Michigan, on the Clean Air Act and acid rain legislation. While other environmentalists on the committee have been wary of crossing Dingell, Waxman has been fighting a longstanding battle against the chairman to strengthen the Clean Air Act and to pass a strong acid rain bill; the balance of power tends to shift with changes in the committee's makeup.

In addition to his legislative wiliness, a chief source of Waxman's influence is his willingness to use the enormous pool of campaign cash available in Hollywood to help other members in reelection bids. Waxman donates to incumbents and promising challengers through his campaign organization and through his Twenty-fourth District of California PAC (political action committee).

There is no question that Waxman is a leading beneficiary of that strategy. He won his 1979 bid for the chairmanship of what is now the Energy and Commerce Subcommittee on Health and the Environment after contributing to the reelection campaigns of committee members. Should he ever try for the leadership, he will have a long list of Democrats who have benefited from his help.

But Waxman argues that his largess represents just another way to achieve his goals of protecting the environment and aiding the needy.

"One of the fundamental rules of my politics," Waxman said, "is there is no clear distinction between the political process and the legislative process. . . . It is important to get people into office to get the things done I believe in. It's not enough to just make the most of those natural allies already there."

4

The Influential Committees

When Sen. Thomas A. Daschle got his committee assignments for the 100th Congress, it was a freshman's dream come true. The South Dakota Democrat won places on three of the four committees he applied for, including a prize rarely awarded to newcomers: a seat on the Finance Committee, one of the most prestigious panels in Congress.

That's a far cry from the experience of an ambitious freshman senator at the turn of the century. When Robert M. La Follette, R (1906-1925), sought a seat on the Interstate Commerce Committee, the Wisconsin progressive wound up on seven minor committees, including one investigating the condition of the Potomac River front.

La Follette was elected at a time when the Senate had some fifty-five standing committees, but even in that plethora of panels he could see where the real power lay. "Of first importance is the great Finance Committee, which has charge of all bills affecting the tariff, currency and banking," he wrote.

Three-quarters of a century later Finance remains one of a handful of committees at the center of power. Some panels wax and wane, but Finance, Appropriations, and Ways and Means are never wholly eclipsed because they control the flow of money into and out of federal coffers.

Their institutional clout may pale in comparison to what they once had: Until 1975, Ways and Means made all committee assignments for Democratic members. And the Appropriations Committee before 1974 had fewer institutional constraints in determining federal spending.

But legislatively, other forces are at work in the 100th Congress that enhance the power of that charmed circle of committees. Their members are the dominant voices in debate on the leading issues of the day: deficit reduction and trade.

And these taxing and spending committees have been thrust to the center of action more than ever before by Congress's increasing tendency to pile most of its legislative work onto a handful of essential fiscal measures.

Those on panels that draft omnibus bills—such as continuing appropriations resolutions and debt limit legislation—enjoy privileged access to the bulk of Congress's work.

"Life outside those committees can be pretty dreary," said Rep. Thomas J. Downey, D-N.Y., a Ways and Means member who also served on Budget in the 99th Congress. "It's like a coal mine—only the people in the car have access to the coal."

Issues of the Moment

While the importance of money committees is as enduring as death and taxes, the influence of other committees rises and falls as the national agenda shifts one way and another.

For example, the now-quiescent House Education and Labor Committee had its days in the sun in the 1960s, when Congress was enacting landmark school aid laws; the Senate Energy Committee shone in the 1970s when energy policy was a major economic issue.

In the 100th Congress, trade has shaped up as an ascendant issue. Democratic leaders in both the House and Senate have identified it as a top priority.

A sign of its political sex appeal is the scramble among committee leaders for jurisdiction over trade legislation.

House Energy and Commerce Committee Chairman John D. Dingell, D-Mich., an aggressive chairman known for his skill at grabbing new jurisdictional territory, may move to expand his panel's authority over trade. And while the Finance Committee has primary jurisdiction over trade in the Senate, Commerce Committee Chairman Ernest F. Hollings, D-S.C., also wants to get into the act.

The attraction of the panels involved in trade and fiscal matters is reflected in the committee preferences filed with the Democratic Steering Committee by 1987's freshman class of Senate Democrats: They overwhelmingly requested assignments to the Finance, Appropriations, and Commerce committees.

"There might as well be only three committees around this place, as far as these new members are concerned," an aide to a Steering Committee member said. "You might as well take Labor, Judiciary, and the others and put them off in another building."

Democrats in Charge

The balance of power among committees in the 100th Congress may also be affected by the Democrats' return to majority status in the Senate, under the leadership of Robert C. Byrd of West Virginia, and the reshuffling of the House Democratic leadership in the wake of the retirement of Speaker Thomas P. O'Neill, Jr., D-Mass.

In the Senate the change of party control has brought in a new team of committee chairmen. Although the personnel change may do little to enhance or detract from the dominance of such committees as Finance or Appropriations, it may make a substantial difference on others.

For example, some observers question whether mild-mannered, patrician Claiborne Pell, D-R.I., will as Foreign Relations chairman be able to maintain the influence and prestige the panel regained under the 1985-1986 chairmanship of Richard G. Lugar, R-Ind., after a decade of decline.

Another key question is whether the Democratic-dominated Senate committees are going to "run in all directions or whether there will be some sense of coordinated effort," said Richard F. Fenno, Jr., a political scientist at the University of Rochester who has studied congressional committees.

Challenges in 1984 and 1986 to Byrd's reelection as Democratic leader may increase pressure on him to assert stronger leadership and coordinate the legislative agenda. But if his past performance as majority leader from 1977-1980 is a guide, he will be giving his committee chairmen wide latitude to set their own agendas and build the party consensus from them.

"The key question about these guys is always, do they want a real leader or someone to make the trains run?" said a former top Democratic staffer. "Byrd has been an adjudicator of powerful chairmen."

A different tack may be taken in the House by the new Speaker, Jim Wright of Texas, who has indicated that he intends to exercise the leadership's agenda-setting authority more aggressively than O'Neill. Some Democrats fear that approach will result in a clash with committee chairmen, but others point to Wright's 1986 success in engineering passage of omnibus antidrug, trade, and antiterrorism bills that spanned several committee jurisdictions.

Wright's ascension is also likely to affect the committee most closely associated with Democratic leaders—Rules, which is considered essentially an arm of the Speaker's office. The changing of the guard may mean a tighter rein on the committee, which had a relatively free hand toward the end of O'Neill's tenure, according to Rules member David E. Bonior, D-Mich.

"Especially in the last two years, we've developed more of a sense of independence because Tip left us on our own to do whatever we wanted," said Bonior, who is chief deputy whip. "I expect Jim will want to put his imprimatur on us to an extent."

Sources of Power

Although Democrats' control of Congress may bring some new life to authorizing committees that have been inhibited in recent years by Republican control of the Senate, the yawning federal deficit will still keep domestic initiatives in check.

"What the budget process has done to the whole situation is devalue all the committees," said Rep. David E. Price, a freshman Democrat from North Carolina who, as a political science professor at Duke University, studied the congressional committee system."

"Even Ways and Means and Appropriations are less autonomous, but they have a piece of the action in a way that authorizing committees don't."

House Energy and Commerce Committee chairman John D. Dingell of Michigan is an aggressive chairman known for his skill at grabbing new jurisdictional territory.

An exception, Price said, is the House Energy and Commerce Committee, which has grown in influence and is a testament to enduring sources of committee power: an expansive jurisdictional reach and an aggressive chairman.

As the scope of congressional activity has been sharply reduced by budget constraints, a committee's ability to claim a piece of whatever action there is has grown in importance.

"Increasingly the John Dingells of this world are going to build power bases by taking a piece of everybody's jurisdiction and making sure that every bill goes through the Energy and Commerce Committee," former representative Bob Edgar, D-Pa., said.

Dingell has been known as the most assertive chairman in the House since he took over his post from Harley O. Staggers, D-W.Va. (1949-1981), in 1981. Energy and

Commerce now has the largest staff and budget of any House committee.

Energy and Commerce lays claim to legislation touching major regulatory agencies, nuclear energy, toxic wastes, health research, Medicaid and Medicare, railroad retirement, telecommunications, tourism, and commerce. The committee also has one of the most active oversight subcommittees in the House. "Everything that moves comes under the jurisdiction of Energy and Commerce," said panel member Jim Slattery, D-Kan.

The payoff for members is not just in the currency of legislative influence: The committee also seems to be a veritable magnet for campaign contributions. According to Common Cause, the self-styled citizens' lobby, Energy and Commerce members in the 98th Congress received, on average, more political action committee contributions than members of any other House committee.

A broad jurisdictional reach also is part of the appeal of Appropriations and Budget, which oversee the full range of federal activity.

"Appropriations is involved in everything the government does," said House committee member Mickey Edwards, R-Okla. "Its [members have] a mandate or license to get involved in virtually anything the government spends money for."

The tax-writing committees handle not just the flow of all revenues into the federal Treasury, but also billions in federal spending for major entitlement programs, including Medicare, unemployment compensation, Social Security, and welfare.

Programs under Ways and Means's jurisdiction accounted for 37.8 percent of the total federal outlays in fiscal 1985—up from 25.3 percent in fiscal 1970. Finance's reach spreads even farther because, unlike Ways and Means, the Senate panel also has control over Medicaid.

"Finance has a huge jurisdiction," said Senate Budget Committee ranking member Pete V. Domenici, R-N.M., "and jurisdiction is power."

Tax Panels: Where the Action Is

Even if the Ways and Means and Finance committees keep their implicit promise not to make major tax changes in the wake of 1986's landmark overhaul of the tax code, their broad jurisdiction ensures they will continue in a leading role in the 100th Congress.

Former senator Thomas F. Eagleton, D-Mo., who was a member of the Appropriations Committee for much of his Senate career, said, "The power committee now is Finance. That's where the action is now and in the future."

Recalling that Finance and Appropriations were more on a par when he first came to the Senate in 1968, Eagleton said he would choose to sit on the tax-writing panel if he had his congressional career to do over.

"The real policy decisions of the next decade are going to be centered at Ways and Means—Medicare financing, Social Security, entitlements," said Rep. Buddy MacKay, D-Fla., a Budget Committee member who lobbied unsuccessfully for more than a year for a Ways and Means seat in the 100th Congress. "Long-term health care for the elderly is the next regularly scheduled crisis."

Ways and Means' and Finance's jurisdiction over major entitlement programs means they will continue to be central forces in deficit-reduction initiatives. These panels have been the major contributors to budget "reconciliation" packages—omnibus legislation that makes spending cuts mandated by the annual budget resolution.

In addition, these two will be the lead committees handling welfare reform and catastrophic health insurance, the only major domestic initiatives that both Congress and Reagan administration officials have tackled.

They also have jurisdiction over legislation to raise the federal debt ceiling—one of the few "must-pass" bills that in recent years have become vehicles for scores of legislative initiatives that might not pass on their own.

But for all its influence, even Ways and Means has seen its role fluctuate with stronger and weaker chairmen. Under the chairmanship of Wilbur D. Mills, D-Ark. (1939-1977), from 1958 through 1974, Ways and Means enjoyed almost unchallenged authority over legislation under its jurisdiction—a tribute in part to Mills's long tenure and command of tax law.

His successor, Al Ullman, D-Ore. (1957-1981), who was chairman from 1975 to 1981, was a weaker leader, and the committee became more fractious. This contributed to defeats on the floor during debate on Ways and Means bills.

In the early years of President Reagan's tenure, with Ways and Means chaired by Dan Rostenkowski, D-Ill., the initiative on tax matters came mostly from the Senate and the Reagan administration. But Rostenkowski went a long way toward restoring the committee's status with his firm handling of the 1986 tax-overhaul legislation, whose final shape he negotiated practically one-on-one with Senate Finance Chairman Bob Packwood, R-Ore.

"Rostenkowski has brought Ways and Means back to a position of prominence," Downey said. "He has the committee going along with him. We pretty much can deliver whatever we are asked to deliver."

Appropriations: Pork Power

Unlike other congressional panels, Appropriations is propelled by necessity. Tax-writing committees may or may not report major legislation in a given year, but

Chairman of the House Ways and Means Committee Dan Rostenkowski of Illinois strengthened the committee's influence with his firm handling of the 1986 tax-overhaul bill.

Appropriations must draft the bills—or one big continuing resolution as it did in 1986—to keep the government running each year.

Increasingly, Appropriations panels are doing more than that, including in their massive bills authorizations for such pivotal policies as aid to Nicaraguan guerrillas and such controversial programs as family planning that may not or cannot pass on their own.

"[Appropriations is] the only committee in the Senate that is required to perform or the government collapses," said Senate Appropriations ranking member Mark O. Hatfield, R-Ore. "These other committees can endure paralysis, but [Appropriations has] to perform."

However, the share of the government outlays that Appropriations controls has dwindled, as the growth of entitlement programs and interest on the national debt has put more of the federal budget out of the committee's reach.

According to the Congressional Budget Office, expenditures under the jurisdiction of the Appropriations committees have dropped from about two-thirds of gross federal outlays in fiscal 1970 to less than half in 1987. And while the panels' subcommittee chairmen once ran their baronies without external constraint, appropriators now must abide by limits set by the annual budget resolution and the newer strictures of the Gramm-Rudman-Hollings antideficit law.

But while the Budget Committee may breathe down their necks about obeying spending limits, the appropriators still are the ones dealing in hard currency. The budget may say spend $10 billion less, but the Appropriations Committee says how.

As a result, Appropriations remains the choice sty for pork-barrel politics, with members retaining the ability to do favors for their constituents and colleagues. Witness the first money bill to pass under the Gramm-Rudman system: The fiscal 1986 supplemental appropriations measure included, among other things, provisions earmarking $55.6 million in defense funding for projects at universities in the home states of Appropriations members and other key lawmakers.

"Appropriations used to be able to spend whatever it wanted," a House Democratic leadership aide said. "Now it cannot spend as much as it wants but can still spend where it wants."

Especially as more and more legislation—such as the omnibus crime bill in 1984—is built into the annual continuing resolution, members who sit on Appropriations will continue to have an important source of leverage over their colleagues.

"Appropriations is the key spot," said Edwards. "Members need you and come to you for help. If you're not on Appropriations, you are really at the mercy of other people."

Budget: Powerless Influence

Deficit reduction remains a major item of unfinished business in the 100th Congress, assuring that the House and Senate Budget committees remain at center stage. Despite the politically thankless job facing the panels, more than a dozen Democrats applied for a seat on House Budget for the 100th Congress.

Although the Budget committees are generally counted among the inner circle of sought-after panels, the nature of their power is elusive and of a different sort from that of other panels.

The Budget committees report no substantive legislation. The budget resolution that is their principal product sets targets that can be breached whenever the political will to meet them evaporates—such as when Congress in 1986 voted to add $1.7 billion for a politically popular antidrug program in violation of the budget. Budget Committee members have no goodies to give out either to colleagues or their own constituents.

But the power to set broad spending priorities is a constraint on Appropriations and other committees unheard of before the budget process was set up in 1974. Until then, the Appropriations committees would write much of each year's federal budget, one bill at a time, without an overall blueprint.

Appropriations also has lost a subtler form of influence because the Budget committees now kick off the annual budget process. "In the old days, Appropriations had original jurisdiction and took the first look at the president's budget," said political scientist Fenno. "The committee that gets the first crack has enormous power to set boundaries of what's going to be discussed."

Budgeteers also are armed with "reconciliation" instructions included in the annual budget resolution, which mandate that other committees make cuts to hit the budget targets. They do not tell other committees how to comply with savings instructions, but sometimes the options for meeting the targets are few. Still, getting other committees to comply is often more a matter of persuasion and negotiation than of institutional clout.

"The Budget Committee has no power, They are not a necessary hoop through which any substantive legislation must go," said Carol G. Cox, president of the Committee for a Responsible Federal Budget, a nonpartisan research group headed by former members of Congress. "Finance and Ways and Means have power; the Budget Committee has influence, and its influence derives from moral suasion."

Important differences between the chambers have led many Budget Committee members to feel that the House committee is much weaker within the institution than its Senate counterpart. While there are no limits on the number of terms a senator can be a member or chairman of the Budget Committee, House rules bar members from sitting on the panel for more than three consecutive terms, or four in the case of chairmen.

"The House has a rotating committee, in my opinion, deliberately intended to keep it weak by its great adversaries in the House, the Appropriations Committee and . . . the Ways and Means Committee," said Robert N. Giaimo, D-Conn. (1959-1981), a former House Budget chairman.

Rules: Penniless Power

One of the most influential panels in either chamber handles not a dime of federal funding: The Rules Committee is the desk at which every major bill has to stop before going to the House floor. With authority to draft ground rules for floor debate, the committee can block legislation, set the parameters of debate, and limit or bar amendments.

But like Appropriations and Ways and Means, Rules's influence is in many respects a pale shadow of its former self. Because its chairman and Democratic members are appointed by the Speaker, Rules generally does the Speaker's bidding.

But before 1974, when the Democratic Caucus gave the Speaker authority to appoint Rules members, the committee operated more as an autonomous power base than as an arm of the leadership. It often thwarted the leadership by bottling up legislation and, before 1965, legislation could not go to conference with the Senate without Rules's consent.

The Rules Committee also saw its influence diminish for a time when it got too far out of step with the House as a whole. When it was stacked with liberals in the early 1970s, it suffered a series of defeats on the floor. In 1973 alone the House rejected thirteen rules; from 1929-1972 rules reported by the committee had been rejected on only fifty occasions.

But in a recent display of Rules's clout, the committee in 1986 thwarted the formidable chairman of the Appropriations Committee, Jamie L. Whitten, when the Mississippi Democrat tried to resuscitate the general revenue sharing program by slipping $3.4 billion into the massive continuing resolution for fiscal 1987.

Rules forced Whitten to write a new measure excluding revenue sharing, thus saving Democrats from having to make a public choice between letting the politically popular program die, busting budget limits, or cutting other programs.

While Democratic leaders now call the shots on Rules for many major bills, they are not involved in every piece of legislation that goes to the floor, leaving Rules members wide areas in which they exercise their own discretion.

"I never want to get off Rules," Bonior

said. "You get to dabble . . . . You're always doing favors for people."

Armed Services and Foreign Policy

Beyond those committees that handle must-pass bills, have broad jurisdiction, and have a handle on important institutional controls is not simply a vast wasteland of committee impotence.

The House and Senate Armed Services committees are the central arena of debate on arms control and the defense budget, which accounts for more than sixty cents of every dollar of discretionary federal spending. The macro-decisions about the amount of money spent on the Pentagon likely will continue to be made in the broader budget context, but Armed Services' role in deciding how that money will be spent is far more significant now than it once was.

"In the 1950s, we used to think of it as a real estate committee, a pork-barrel committee where members got together and got military bases for their states," Fenno said. "Now it's a weapons and policy committee."

Turf battles between the defense authorizers and appropriators had intensified after the GOP takeover of the Senate in 1981, when Sen. Ted Stevens of Alaska, eager to carve out a larger role for the Defense Appropriations Subcommittee, was installed as chairman of that panel. Some are hopeful that those jurisdictional squabbles will subside in the 100th Congress, with Appropriations Committee Chairman John C. Stennis, D-Miss., also sitting on the Armed Services Committee, and his protégé, Sam Nunn of Georgia, chairing Armed Services.

The troubles that afflicted the Reagan administration's foreign policy in the wake of the Iranian arms scandal were expected to turn the spotlight of public attention on the work of the Senate Foreign Relations Committee, adding to the already high level of media attention paid to Foreign Relations members. In the 99th Congress they were influential players in the development of U.S foreign policy toward the Philippines and South Africa. Another important source of the committee's influence is its jurisdiction over treaties and the nominations of ambassadors.

But the committee sometimes has had to struggle to maintain its legislative clout. The foreign aid authorization bill that is the panel's chief product is always in danger of falling victim to political problems. In 1985 Congress cleared a foreign aid bill for the first time in four years.

"Foreign aid is the least popular bill you can name," said House Foreign Affairs member Henry J. Hyde, R-Ill. "Any one who serves on Foreign Affairs does so out of sheer self-indulgence, not out of political profit back home."

The House Foreign Affairs panel is at a particular disadvantage because it operates on turf traditionally dominated by the executive branch and the Senate. But House members can parlay membership on the panel into high visibility. For example, in 1986 Stephen J. Solarz, D-N.Y., chairman of the House Foreign Affairs Subcommittee on Asian and Pacific Affairs, became a leading congressional critic of now-deposed Philippine President Ferdinand E. Marcos's corrupt rule.

The Outer Circle

Other committees, hard hit in the Gramm-Rudman era, are finding it all but futile to create new programs.

"The authorizing committees, which should comprise the heart of [the policy-making process], are rapidly approaching irrelevance—squeezed out by the budget and appropriations processes, and caught up in jurisdictional infighting and subcommittee strangulation," House Republicans said in a proposal for procedural reforms considered at their party caucus meetings in December 1986.

Some of the authorizing committees that were the cockpit for steering Great Society social programs through Congress in the 1960s are now inactive. The House Education and Labor Committee has been largely reduced to a bunker for defending existing programs through the Reagan years.

The House Education panel may be more active in the 100th Congress, because it has a more receptive counterpart in a Democratic-controlled Senate Labor and Human Resources Committee. That, however, will not compensate for budgetary forces sharply limiting the turf of these panels.

But even if some of the authorizing committees see a modest resurgence of activity, frustration in Congress about the imbalance of power among panels is likely to remain. The 100th Congress may see increasing debate—although probably not action—on proposals to overhaul the system.

Domenici, a veteran of past panels to study the committee system, is somewhat skeptical of the prospects for structural changes in a turf-conscious institution. But he does hold out hope that some procedural reforms might be wrought, such as instituting a two-year cycle for budget and appropriations that would allow more time every other year for authorizing activities and oversight.

The frustration level rose last year, when all thirteen appropriations bills were folded into one, but it remains to be seen where that frustration leads in the 100th Congress.

"We're headed at some type of revamping of the whole process," said Bonior. "We've left too many people out of the process."

In Conference: New Hurdles, Hard Bargaining

Only a few hundred feet separate the House and Senate chambers, but most members rarely venture to the opposite side of the Capitol.

The traffic between chambers becomes thicker, however, after Congress reconvenes at the end of summer, because members increasingly are drawn into the House-Senate conference committees that always proliferate around that time of year.

While the spotlight tends to focus on floor action, crucial decisions are made in conferences—the least visible stage of the legislative process.

"Conference committees are the ultimate high for legislators," said Rep. Dennis E. Eckart, D-Ohio. "They are the Supreme Court of legislation. If you don't get it here, there's no other place to go."

That's heady stuff, but institutional and political factors in recent years have complicated the job of conference committees that requires reconciling differences between House and Senate versions of major legislation.

In an era of budget austerity, negotiators rarely can afford to hammer out agreements with a tool once freely wielded: spending more money to buy off competing interests.

"In the old days, it was not a zero-sum game," said John E. Dean, who until 1985 was an aide to the House Education and Labor Committee. "You could come up with a package that gave the House and Senate everything they wanted."

Lawmakers also have had to adapt to growing complexity in the negotiating process itself. The proliferation of wide-ranging omnibus bills has spawned some conferences of almost unmanageable size, span-

Traditional full-scale conferences, like the one on the 1986 higher education reauthorization bill, sometimes give way to private, chairman-to-chairman negotiations.

ning the jurisdictions of several committees. In other cases, however, sweeping bills of great impact are negotiated by just a handful of people.

A testament to such variety is the contrast between budget-related conferences of the Reagan era that involved hundreds of members and the extraordinary chairman-to-chairman private negotiations between Rep. Dan Rostenkowski, D-Ill., and Sen. Bob Packwood, R-Ore., that produced the 1986 tax overhaul bill.

"Here in a short span we've seen the political process stretch its way from one extreme to the other, from a concentration of decision-making power to the other extreme of almost chaos," said Jeff Drumtra, director of the Tax Reform Research Group, an affiliate of Ralph Nader's Public Citizen group.

Few but Important

Conference committees are so critical to the legislative process that they are sometimes referred to as the "third house" of Congress. Although conferences are convened on a relatively small number of measures, these generally include the most important bills before Congress.

According to a study by Ilona B. Nickels of the Congressional Research Service, only 8 percent of the public laws enacted in the 98th Congress were the product of conference committees. But these included such major legislation as an overhaul of the Social Security system and all appropriations bills. Most other laws cleared when one chamber accepted the other's amendments, or when an identical bill was passed by both chambers.

In the fall of 1986 conference committees worked on such issues as appropriations, financing the "superfund" toxic-waste cleanup program, the defense budget, hydroelectric power, higher education programs, reorganizing the Pentagon, and correcting the constitutional flaws of the Gramm-Rudman-Hollings antideficit law.

A Modicum of Openness

House and Senate rules changes since the mid-1970s have broken down the barriers of secrecy and seniority that previously denied the public and junior members access to conference committee proceedings.

More than two decades ago, when the House and Senate Armed Services committees were headed by Rep. Carl Vinson and Sen. Richard B. Russell, both Georgia Democrats, a junior member gave a succinct description of the conference that produced the annual military authorization bill. The process, said then-Rep. Otis G. Pike, D-N.Y., in 1964, involved "two gentlemen from Georgia talking, arguing, laughing, and whispering in each other's ears."

Almost all conference committees then met in private. But in 1975 both chambers adopted rules changes requiring open conferences unless a majority of either side's conferees voted publicly to close the session. The House went a step further in 1977, voting to require open meetings unless the House itself voted to close them.

Even with those reforms, the conference remains the least accessible part of the legislative process. Transcripts are not always kept of proceedings, and meetings frequently are held in tiny rooms that cannot accommodate all who want to attend.

Typically, conferees are senior members of the committees with jurisdiction over the legislation at issue. But increasingly in recent years, more junior lawmakers have been named if they are members of the relevant subcommittee, sponsors of important amendments, or have special expertise.

The composition of conference committees is so critical that for legislation as monumental as the 1986 tax overhaul bill, the selection of conferees was itself a moment of high drama.

Usually the Speaker of the House and presiding officer of the Senate appoint conferees selected by the relevant committee chairmen. But occasionally, congressional leaders play a more active role.

For example, then-Speaker Thomas P. O'Neill, Jr., D-Mass., made critical decisions about whom to appoint as negotiators on the Gramm-Rudman-Hollings measure, because that proposal had never been considered by any House committee. Instead, it was attached by the Senate as an amendment to a bill raising the debt ceiling.

And before Rostenkowski chose conferees on the tax overhaul bill, sources said, O'Neill made it clear he wanted one of them to be Rep. Richard A. Gephardt, D-Mo., an early Democratic proponent of tax reform.

House-Senate Differences

As one of the few congressional institutions that is a creature of both chambers, a conference is a prime arena for institutional rivalries.

A legendary House-Senate stare-down came in 1962, when appropriations action was stalled by a feud between House and Senate committee chairmen over, among other things, whether the conferences would meet on the House or Senate side of the Capitol. That particular issue was later defused with the construction of a meeting room exactly halfway between the chambers.

House members sometimes have an advantage in conferences, because they serve on fewer committees than senators and thus tend to specialize more. House members may know the details of a bill, while senators rely on staffers for such information. "You find yourself arguing with Senate staff," said Rep. Tom Tauke, R-Iowa. "For a House member, that's a frustrating experience."

With more committee assignments and other demands on their time, busy senators also often leave negotiations to one or two senators who know conference issues best. In a conference this summer on a major higher education bill, Robert T. Stafford, R-Vt., at one point found himself the sole Senate conferee. After receiving a House proposal, he quipped, "I'm caucusing with myself. Can you give me a couple minutes to complete the arguments?"

Sometimes intramural rivalry between House and Senate is overshadowed by divisions within a chamber's own delegation. For example, during a grueling six-month conference on key elements of the superfund bill in 1986, there were frequently more bitter splits among House Democrats than between the two chambers. Senate conferees, too, were divided on many issues.

"There was not much traditional us-vs.-them," said Eckart, a House conferee. "There were lots of us-es and lots of thems."

Toeing the Line

The power of conference committees derives in large part from the great deference given to conference reports, which are rarely rejected and cannot be amended on the floor under ordinary procedures.

Although few rules bind negotiators, the conference report generally has to remain within the scope of what the House and Senate passed.

Conferees are expected to defend their own chamber's provisions even if they disagree with them. Those who wander too far from their chamber's position do so at their peril.

Last year, for example, House Armed Services Chairman Les Aspin, D-Wis., was bitterly castigated by some colleagues after a conference on the annual defense authorization bill in which critics, predominantly liberals, said that House conferees yielded too much to the pro-Pentagon Senate.

That was one of the complaints aired by some House Democrats who sought unsuccessfully to oust Aspin from his committee chairmanship after the 99th Congress.

The Few Bargain for the Many

The private chairman-to-chairman talks that wrapped up the tax conference flew in the face of the last decade's drive to reduce secrecy and reliance on seniority in conferences.

Although they are unlikely to herald a wholesale reversion to closed sessions, the private negotiations did continue a pattern of recent years in which tax writers increasingly have conducted business behind closed doors.

Conferees can circumvent "sunshine" requirements for open proceedings by meeting separately in House and Senate caucuses with staff shuttling between them, then ratifying decisions in the full conference.

"It's something of a reversion to the old way of doing things," said Drumtra. "Yet we have to admit the only way to pass good tax reform now is behind closed doors out of the glare of tax lobbyists. We [who supported sunshine rules] were hoisted on our own petard on that."

There have been other important occasions on major legislation when conferees have been willing to leave deal-making to their two chairmen or a small group of senior members.

More than once, for instance, a budget

House Budget Committee chairman Bill Gray of Pennsylvania, left, and Senate Budget Committee ranking member Pete Domenici of New Mexico discuss issues during Joint Budget Conference.

deadlock has been broken by marathon private negotiations among the chairmen and ranking minority members of the House and Senate Budget committees.

"Attitudes have changed in the last few years," said Rep. Leon E. Panetta, D-Calif., a member of the House Agriculture Committee. "There's a willingness to accept whatever it takes to resolve" tough issues.

During the second of two conferences on the Gramm-Rudman law, a sixty-six-member affair, many of the key compromises were made by a group of six House and Senate leaders. "When a conference is huge, it's not where the bill is written," said Lynn Martin, R-Ill., a senior Budget Committee member.

But back-room dealers today are more likely than their predecessors to be solicitous of their rank and file. "It's like a good marriage," said Martin. "If there are good communications, they say go ahead."

The Problem with Packages

Congress's increasing tendency to legislate in omnibus packages has introduced new complications in the final stages of the legislative process.

Some conferences are so large, or their subjects so complex, that they have to break into subconferences, task forces, and the like. The superfund conference, for example, drew negotiators from six House committees and three Senate committees. Much of the work was done by small subgroups that were more manageable and focused than the full conference.

A conference with such a broad jurisdictional spread was once rare. Former representative John N. Erlenborn, R-Ill. (1965-1985), said it was considered extraordinary in 1974 when a conference on pension legislation drew negotiators from four committees.

That pales in comparison with the scope of conferences now convened almost routinely to handle annual budget "reconciliation" bills. These bills tie together measures drafted by virtually all committees to bring programs under their jurisidiction into compliance with savings targets mandated by the budget resolution.

In 1981 the reconciliation law that was a critical part of President Reagan's first-year legislative program was handled by the largest conference on record: 280 members meeting in more than 50 subgroups. The second largest conference, which brought together 242 conferees in 31 subgroups, met on the fiscal 1986 reconciliation bill. But on other omnibus bills, a relatively small group of members may handle a wide range of issues.

It is now common for supplemental appropriations bills and continuing appropriations resolutions to become unwieldy packages, laden with measures that may fall outside the jurisdiction of the Appropriations committees that traditionally provide conferees for those measures.

One of the most extreme examples was in 1984, when a huge omnibus crime bill was attached to the annual continuing resolution. Members of the Judiciary committees were not named as conferees on the measure, although they were called in for consultation.

Conferences on continuing resolutions make decisions about financing large chunks of the government's operations in a single measure. They have tended to be dominated by senior members of the Appropriations committees, while junior members generally are more involved in conferences on regular appropriations bills.

But in 1985 junior members of the House Appropriations Committee secured several seats on the conference on the fiscal 1986 continuing resolution, following a drive led by Norman D. Dicks, D-Wash.

Dicks, a member of the Defense Subcommittee and a conferee on that portion of the resolution, said the presence of junior members was crucial to retaining a House provision to ban testing of antisatellite (ASAT) weapons.

"The conference would have never gotten that if we hadn't been there fighting for it," said Dicks. "In the old days, the chairman and ranking members, maybe four people, were deciding the entire defense budget. Let's face it, the conference committee is where it all happens."

5

State Delegations

"We have become . . . like luncheon clubs," one northeastern Democrat grumbled in 1986, expressing his frustration over state delegations' decline in influence. Even in large states such as California, New York, and Texas, this member fretted, no longer are "the delegations . . . particularly effective in getting things done for their states."

That view would cause a man like former House Speaker Sam Rayburn of Texas to roll over in his grave. During Rayburn's reign in the 1940s and 1950s, state delegations were one of the primary building blocks of power in Congress. The deans of the larger House delegations were crucial to Rayburn's leadership, because they could deliver their entire membership on home-state as well as some national issues—often bringing along the state's senators, too.

Fortunately for Rayburn's specter, the northeastern Democrat overstated his case somewhat. A number of states—Texas, California, and New York prominent among them—maintain a considerable amount of influence in the 100th Congress, as members of their delegations capitalize on seniority, committee assignments, and coalition-building skills to deliver for their local constituencies.

In doing so, those members have overcome an increasingly imposing set of obstacles. Ideological diversity and geographical schisms have always been barriers to delegation unity; today, in the changed congressional politics of the 1980s, those problems are compounded by intensified partisan rhetoric and a decentralized power structure in which members of the leadership sometimes cannot count on the support of a delegation until they have lobbied virtually every member.

Texas: Number One

Texas stands tall at the top of the list of power delegations—as even some of the state's rivals to influence are forced to agree.

"California, New York, and Illinois are three states that will have some significant impact and voice in the 100th Congress," said Republican representative Jerry Lewis, a key member of the California delegation. "But we are not on the same playing field as Texas."

Strategic Players

Having the Speaker of the House as a member of the delegation doesn't hurt. Jim Wright has taken pains to pay attention to regional diversity during the latter stages of his ten-year career as House majority leader, but—as a student of Rayburn, another Texas-bred Speaker—he has always kept a watchful eye out for the interests of the Lone Star State. There is little reason to believe he will abandon that practice.

Texas also draws power from its sheer size—its twenty-seven-member House delegation is the chamber's third-largest—as well as its membership's political placement and seniority. Although defeats, retirements, and deaths have robbed Texas of some powerful political veterans in recent years, the state's congressional ranks are still rife with key players strategically positioned on some of the most influential committees in Congress. And Texas's representatives in the committee assignment process work to keep it that way.

"When [Democratic representative] Jim Chapman came here [after winning a 1985 special election], he immediately went on Public Works, because we needed someone on Public Works," said Democratic representative Martin Frost. "We always try to make sure we have the major committees covered and covered adequately."

Adequately, indeed. In the 100th Congress, Texas Democrats chair the Senate Finance Committee (Lloyd Bentsen) and the House Agriculture and Government Operations committees (E. "Kika" de la Garza and Jack Brooks, respectively). On the influential House Ways and Means Committee, Texas interests are represented by Democrat J. J. Pickle, chairman of the Oversight Subcommittee, and Republican Bill Archer, who ranks second on the committee on the Republican side.

Other influential Texans include: Democratic representatives Frost on the Rules and Budget committees and Charles Wilson, a force on the Appropriations Committee and probably the most persistent defender of independent oil interests in the House. The state's junior senator, Republican Phil Gramm, was a prime proponent of the two most significant budget measures of the 1980s. *(See pp. 46-48.)*

Lone Star Togetherness

But perhaps even more important than the placement and political prowess of its individual members is the Texas delegation's tradition of cohesion and unity. Over the years, the state's representatives have developed an almost legendary reputation for their ability to draw their wagons in a circle on issues of interest to their home-state constituency.

One in a long line of examples of Texas's ability to pull together came during debate over fiscal 1987 appropriations for the National Aeronautics and Space Administration (NASA).

When NASA administrators announced plans to consider moving a major space station project from Houston's Johnson City Space Center to a facility near Huntsville, Ala., the Texas delegation closed ranks. Lobbying by Wright, Brooks, Gramm, and several other Texans paid off: The NASA appropriations bill ultimately included a ban on any unauthorized transfer of work from the Johnson Space Center for one year.

The delegation's ability to coalesce may be attributable in part to the state's political history. Texans declared their territory a nation unto itself between 1836 and 1845, equipping their independent republic with its own armed forces and currency. Some feel that the strong sense of self-determination that led the locals to erect their own country is still evident in Texas politics today.

"The Texas delegation has always seen itself . . . almost as a separate entity in the Congress," said Norman Ornstein, resident scholar at the American Enterprise Institute (AEI). "It has a kind of self-identification. . . . Most other states don't see things that way."

Texas also owes its knack for unity to the state's widespread dependence on the oil and gas industry. Through boom and bust, oil's fortunes affect the economy in districts as diverse as freshman Republican representative Larry Combest's West Texas plains country and black Democratic representative Mickey Leland's ethnically mixed, urban Houston constituency—and gives those seemingly disparate House members a common cause.

A third crucial factor is the fact that, throughout most of its history, Texas has been a one-party state. The Democrats' dominance of the delegation made the task of arranging bloc voting relatively easy; the tiny cadre of Republican members faced the choice of either going along with the Democratic majority or embracing political irrelevancy.

"It didn't do any good to be partisan in that delegation," said an aide to a former House GOP member from Texas, "because there wasn't a damn thing you could do."

One Republican who tried to do something was Bruce Alger, who represented a Dallas-area district in the House during Rayburn's tenure as Speaker. After being invited to sit in on the Texas Democratic delegation's regular luncheons, Alger enraged Rayburn by publicly suggesting that the Speaker had communist tendencies. Rayburn retaliated by banning anyone affiliated with the Texas GOP from attending. That was in 1956. Republicans were not invited to a Texas Democratic delegation luncheon again until 1986.

But the Democratic dominance in Texas is ending, as signaled by the GOP's impressive successes in 1984: Republicans elected Gramm to the Senate and brought to ten the number of seats they hold in the U.S. House. The state's delegation has been grappling with the problems of partisan competition—and the threat it poses to unity—ever since.

Gramm has organized weekly breakfast meetings for the Texas Republicans to discuss legislative and political strategy. He acknowledges significant differences with his Democratic colleagues, but feels the gap can be bridged. "We can be in the middle of a philosophical battle with strong feelings on both sides, but in the midst of that battle, we can come together on Texas issues," he said.

Many Texas Democrats are not so sure. Gramm alienated a number of them during his days as a House Democrat. (Stripped of his place on the House Budget Committee by Democratic leaders for his role in passing President Reagan's 1981-1982 budget, Gramm resigned his House seat and won reelection as a Republican in 1983. He was elected to the Senate in 1984.) They are not likely to look favorably upon him in his new role as de facto Texas GOP leader.

California: Political Fault Lines

The problems of coordinating a two-party delegation may be new to Texas, but to members of the California contingent, they are old hat.

"The Democratic delegation works pretty well together, and the Republican delegation works pretty well together," said GOP representative Lewis, whose position as California's representative in his party's committee assignment process makes him the voice of the biggest single bloc of Republicans in the House. "But we're usually working against each other. On the question of how well the two parties come together . . . we have stumbled at evolving, and we have evolved, at best, very poorly."

California's problems stem largely from the delegation's ideological diversity. Anyone doubting that should imagine the difficulties involved in bringing together

Republican representative Bob Dornan, one of the most outspoken and militant conservatives in Congress, and Democratic representative Ronald V. Dellums, a member of the Democratic Socialists of America.

Those natural political differences have only been exacerbated by the delegation's seemingly interminable wrangling over redistricting. The late Democratic representative Phillip Burton earned his party's lasting love by crafting a district map that created four new Democratic seats—and dismembered three GOP-held districts—in 1981. But he also invited the California GOP's lasting enmity. Leaders in the two parties have been battling over the map virtually since it was implemented, and likely will continue to clash on the subject for months, if not years, to come.

The delegation has made some progress in burying the partisan hatchet. "You're beginning to get people in the Bay area to at least talk about export-import issues that affect southern California agriculture," Lewis said. Others cite examples of bipartisan cooperation on attempts to fund a mass transit system for Los Angeles, and on some offshore oil drilling issues.

But what is most significant about California's partisanship is that the state's delegation manages to succeed anyway. The forty-five-member contingent—the largest in the House, constituting just over ten percent of the chamber—exercises substantial influence, even when the parties operate independently.

For example, the twenty-seven-member Democratic unit frequently pulls together whenever legislation allocating federal education assistance or agricultural aid to the states hits the House floor.

Dictatorship to Democracy

Leadership of the Democratic contingent has in recent years undergone a dramatic shift, one of proportions normally seen only in Third World countries. Rep. Burton led the Democrats as a dictator would; under Rep. Don Edwards, the current dean of the Democrats, the delegation more closely approximates a democracy.

Rep. Jerry Lewis's position as California's representative in his party's committee assignment process makes him the voice of the biggest bloc of Republicans in the House.

Burton never achieved the position of delegation dean; that title belonged to Rep. Harold "Bizz" Johnson during Burton's most powerful days. But there was little question in the minds of most California Democrats about who ran the show.

"Phil was a very strong paternalistic figure," said one California Democrat. "He . . . felt very much as if he had to stand at the top and bring the boys together behind him. There's no way he could share his ultimate powerful role.

"As a result," the Democrat continued, "members of the delegation dealt with him in two ways. One, they became soldiers in his army. . . . Or two, they'd opt out, essentially stop participating in the delegation."

The contrast under Edwards, a devout

liberal, could not be more stark. "Don understands the need to be a collegial leader," said Democratic representative Vic Fazio. "He can be fairly laid back about issues of personal ego. . . . Now the delegation has more lead players in more places. That's the basis of our power. We don't have a person who plays Burton's role, we have a lot of key people who deal with each other more openly."

There is no shortage of key people. Among the most prominent are Democratic representative Tony Coelho, majority whip for the 100th Congress and former chairman of the Democratic Congressional Campaign Committee, and Democratic representative Henry A. Waxman, who has combined personal political prowess with access to copious campaign contributions (among the communities he represents are Hollywood and Beverly Hills) to forge a potent organization. *(See pp. 55-56.)*

Orchestrating harmony among all the egos in the delegation can be difficult at times. But Edwards has coped fairly well, in Fazio's words, by "looking to the people who have their own power centers, looking to them for leadership on their issues . . . and making us all more aware of our mutual interests."

To improve cooperation and coordinate the flow of information on issues of interest to California, Edwards has organized regular Wednesday morning meetings of Democrats and periodic press conferences. He also has established a full-time, two-person delegation office responsible for researching legislation and assessing the impact bills have on California. "I want to run it like a business," Edwards said.

California Republicans

Things are structured more loosely on the Republican side.

The dean of the GOP delegation is veteran representative Carlos J. Moorhead, an amiable conservative not known for his leadership abilities.

The current dean of California Democrats, Rep. Don Edwards has allowed the state's delegation more lead players in more places.

Perhaps more influential in rounding up California Republicans are Lewis, who serves as chairman of the House GOP Research Committee in addition to watching out for his delegation in the GOP committee assignment process; Robert E. Badham, who has served as secretary of the California Republican delegation; and Robert J. Lagomarsino, who serves as secretary of the House Republican Conference.

Other influential California Republicans include Reps. Dan Lungren, ranking Republican on the Judiciary Subcommittee on Immigration, Refugees, and International Law; and William M. Thomas, an active player on Ways and Means.

New York: Upstate vs. the City

While California has often managed to steer around the problems of delegation disunity, New York has sometimes seemed to wallow in them.

"When we get together for meetings," said Republican representative Sherwood Boehlert, "the question of whether to have chocolate or butterscotch as topping for our ice cream will divide our delegation. If the question of nuts comes up, woe be it."

Partisanship has played a part, as has the presence of some senior members over the years who placed their personal goals—and personal vendettas—over the interests of the delegation as a whole.

But New York's problems historically have been rooted more in its geographic and demographic diversity than in partisanship. There long has been a political schism between the upstate conservative Democrats and Republicans and the liberal Democrats of New York City.

"When I first arrived," said Democratic representative Matthew F. McHugh, who represents part of upstate's southern tier, "I had a sense that the New York City people were generally focused on city issues, and were not sensitive enough about issues affecting upstate New York."

McHugh recalls a debate during his first House term over farm legislation affecting the dairy industry, which is important to his constituency. "We made a particular effort to communicate to others in the delegation about the importance of the issue.... We found that it wasn't fully appreciated among city members how important agriculture and dairy is to the state's economy."

The upstate-downstate split has not gone away in the years since McHugh first came to Congress, but the situation has improved. A key catalyst for the improvement, both Democrats and Republicans say, was New York City's brush with fiscal insolvency in the mid- to late-1970s.

"The financial crisis was a sharp awakening," said Democratic representative Charles E. Schumer, New York City whip for the New York delegation. "It showed that we needed one another."

Boehlert, whose district is anchored in central New York's traditionally Republican territory, agrees. "It became apparent that our fates are intertwined." As evidence of increased cooperation among members of the delegation, Boehlert points to New Yorkers' successful efforts to win authorization for some construction of Army facilities to be used as part of a new light division at Fort Drum, located upstate in Watertown.

Members of the Illinois delegation, too, have wrestled with a tradition of upstate-downstate tensions; members from more rural and small-town sections of downstate have sometimes expressed resentment over the influence exercised by members from Chicago. But those tensions also have eased somewhat in recent years, as the once monolithic Chicago-area organization has lost some of its muscle and economic problems have helped bind together members from various parts of the state.

Pennsylvania's Problems

Partisanship and geography are not the only enemies of delegation unity.

Pennsylvania maintains a twenty-three-member House delegation, whose stars include Democrat William H. Gray III, chairman of the Budget Committee; Republican Bud Shuster, an influential force on Public Works; and Democrat John P. Murtha, whose influence on the Appropriations Committee is only part of his broader impact on House affairs. *(See pp. 53-55.)*

But some Pennsylvania members admit that stark differences in political style within the delegation have hampered its ability to coalesce.

The trademark style of Murtha and fellow Democrat Joseph M. Gaydos "is highly focused on trading votes and ... the pork-barrel process," said one Pennsylvania

Democrat. The politics practiced by other members of the delegation—Democrats Peter H. Kostmayer and Budget Chairman Gray—is, according to this same Democrat, "the issues model. Where the Murthas of the world build their power base by trading ... votes and chits, the Kostmayers ... and Grays gained influence by trying to make sure they had more knowledge than anybody else on their issues; by articulating their issues, they'd be able to get things done.

"Occasionally the first group respects the second because of their knowledge, and occasionally the second respects the first because they're able to accomplish some maneuver," the Democrat continued. "But ... much of the time, it's mutual tolerance ... hoping one doesn't do anything negative to the other."

Led by House Majority Leader Thomas S. Foley, Washington state is an example of a smaller state's delegation possessing power disproportionate to its size.

Florida's Growing Pains

In Florida the goal of delegation unity has been made somewhat more difficult to attain by the state's helter-skelter growth.

"The problems of diversity are growing more pointed in Florida," said Ornstein of the American Enterprise Institute. "You can see West Coast vs. East Coast sentiment, Tampa vs. Miami, coastal-central differences, generational differences. ... There are a lot of fault lines."

Members of the Florida delegation are quick to defend themselves, arguing that they have done a good job of coping with the problems presented by growth and suggesting that some of those problems arise simply because other state delegations do not understand their boom-related needs.

"Many states don't recognize what tremendous growth we have," said Republican representative C. W. Bill Young, who represents a swath of Florida anchored in St. Petersburg. "We try to make this point to them fairly often: 'Most of our constituents were at one time your constituents.'"

Young said that the failure of some other state delegations to understand that hurts Florida in a variety of federal formula fights, such as those pertaining to government funding of veterans' programs and housing.

But some Florida members acknowledged that the state's growth has also caused problems internally for the delegation.

"We've got a major generation gap problem," said one Democrat. "Florida went through tremendous stresses ... in the late 1960s and early 1970s. Those who came into politics after that look at politics one way; those who came in before look at it another way." The Democrat characterized it as a split between "those interested in legislative reform" and those possessed of "an Old South mentality.

"It's not like we have a range war," continued the member. "But the problem is

[that] none of us can say in advance, 'I speak for my delegation.' . . . You can't be sure how they're going to vote until you go ask them."

Smaller States' Tactics

There is one problem that all the large state delegations have in common. The sheer numbers that serve as a source of power for those states also make them a convenient target for the frustrations of small- and medium-sized delegations tired of playing second fiddle to the bigger states. When those frustrations grow too great, the small- and medium-sized delegations sometimes band together to gain revenge.

"There's no question that almost every significant question where you deal with formulae, whether it involves housing grant programs, or some form of distribution of transportation . . . any mix and variety, we constantly have to be on guard for that ganging-up process," said GOP representative Lewis of California.

"Your sheer size and power is always making you a giant to be brought to earth," echoed Democrat Fazio.

According to House Republican Boehlert, New York felt the sting of small- and mid-sized state revenge during debate over Westway, an urban highway system for New York City that was refused funding by Congress. Although the project failed to receive unanimous support from the state delegation, Boehlert feels that its defeat owed more to states looking for a chance to stick it to New York.

"Outside of New York, there was a feeling that the state was so powerful for so long, if we have a chance to beat the big guys, let's do it," Boehlert said. "Westway was viewed essentially as a New York issue and . . . we took a royal bath. . . . If an issue becomes viewed in the Congress as a New York issue, we lose every time."

"It's bound to occur," said Democratic representative Steny H. Hoyer of Maryland, speaking for the smaller states.

"Small countries get up and say, 'We're not going to take it anymore' from the United States. . . . At some point, you've got to get up and tell the big boys where to get off."

Little Can Be Powerful

Of course, "the big boys" are not the only ones who exercise influence in the 100th Congress. A number of smaller states' delegations possess power disproportionate to their numbers.

Washington state is a good example. Led by House Majority Leader Thomas S. Foley, the delegation has won praise from members around the country for having a preponderance of thoughtful, diligent politicians in its ranks who have demonstrated a capacity to work well side by side. "Their size doesn't justify the influence they've got," said one southern Democrat.

Arkansas is another. "That state has been particularly influential over the years because it comes up with so many good lawmakers," said Ornstein of AEI. Ornstein cited Democratic senators Dale Bumpers and David Pryor and House Democrats Bill Alexander and Beryl Anthony, Jr., as being part of a tradition of congressional leaders active in national affairs as well as in delivering for their home state. Anthony chairs the Democratic Congressional Campaign Committee, the House Democrats' fund-raising organization.

Perhaps the best example of disproportionate small-state influence is Wyoming. Its congressional delegation includes only three members, but two occupy top leadership positions. That makes Wyoming, in the words of one political scientist, "perhaps the most important state in the 100th Congress, pound for pound."

6

Press Coverage

Emergence of Media Stakes: The O'Neill House

Former Speaker Thomas P. O'Neill, Jr., turned over to his successor a House of Representatives far different from the one whose gavel he had assumed nearly a decade before. It is an institution in which media and public opinion have become a common preoccupation both of the leadership and of much of the rank and file in both parties.

One small, symbolic way to measure the change might be to review one of O'Neill's press conferences, which he conducted just before the opening of each House session.

Ten years before, Speaker Carl Albert of Oklahoma would meet quietly with a handful of reporters prior to the session each day, answering a few perfunctory questions about the upcoming schedule. Few things that he said were printed or broadcast anywhere; none of them was calculated to influence the media.

An O'Neill press conference was a media event, not only because dozens of print and broadcast reporters crowded his office to hear him, but because much of what he said was designed for their benefit.

O'Neill often began with a prepared statement challenging one or another aspect of Reagan administration policy, drafted for him by press secretary Christopher J. Matthews, a glib wordsmith and specialist in one-liners. Often, O'Neill's comments were repeated on the evening news; even more often, they were printed in the *New York Times* and the *Washington Post* the next day.

A decade before, and for most of its history prior to that, the House had been a relatively insular place outside the circle of national publicity and attention. Its members had responded to each other, and to their constituents.

In the last six years of O'Neill's tenure, when Republicans were in control of the presidency and the Senate, the House was the one visible outpost of Democratic strength. The words of its leaders took on an importance far beyond the walls of the Capitol; they helped shape public opinion on all the important issues of the day. And they were uttered for that purpose.

"Ten years ago, nobody paid any attention to us," said Tony Coelho of California, House majority whip in the 100th Congress. "The Reagan years have forced the House into the spotlight. The question is whether we can go back anymore. I don't think the press is going to let the House go back to where it was. It's a goldfish bowl."

Media Symbol

In the center of the bowl swam the largest and unlikeliest goldfish. O'Neill, who spent a quarter-century in the House, not only failed to attract media attention but actively avoided it. "I'm a back-room operator, no question about it," O'Neill told a television interviewer, and his long career leaves little room for doubt about the issue.

Before he took over as Speaker, O'Neill had had few dealings with the national press and virtually none with network television. He was a rank-and-file Massachusetts Democrat who arrived in Washington on Tuesday mornings, returned home on Thursday afternoons, and conducted his congressional business over poker, golf, and dinner at Duke Zeibert's restaurant at Connecticut Avenue and L Street in downtown Washington.

Even as a national figure, O'Neill consistently avoided the Sunday TV interview programs, insisting that his Sabbath was reserved for church, golf, and family.

Nevertheless, in the glare of attention the House has commanded during the Reagan years, it was O'Neill who became the first media celebrity in the history of the speakership. None of his recent predecessors was the subject of endless cartoon caricature in newspapers across the country, and none provided material for monologues on late-night TV talk shows.

Some House Democrats, acknowledging this ironic development, take pains to point out that little of it was O'Neill's doing. The media needed a symbol for the Democratic Party, and the Republicans helped out by choosing O'Neill as the symbol of what they hoped to portray as an obsolete political generation.

For the future of the House, though, what is important is that the speakership has worked its way out of its historic low profile, and nearly all members seem to agree with Coelho that it will not return there.

"Sam Rayburn could have walked down the streets of Spokane, Wash., without anybody noticing him," said Majority Leader Thomas S. Foley of Washington. "Tip O'Neill couldn't do that," Foley said. "And it is very unlikely that any future Speaker will be anonymous to the country. The Speaker is going to join the vice president, the chief justice, and a few Cabinet members in the forefront of public recognition."

Winning the Nation at Large

The implications of this change have borne down heavily on O'Neill's successor, Jim Wright of Texas. An accomplished orator, but a less-than-commanding TV performer and a man who has tended to be wary of the press in general, Wright has had to make adjustments.

"I don't think you can turn the clock back," he said. "We live in an electronic age—the public gains its knowledge from the ever-present tube. I don't shrink from it. I think it's an opportunity." It is an opportunity he has had no choice but to confront.

Still, if the only impact of the past few years of media coverage were to give future Speakers a familiar face and more quotes in the *New York Times*, the significance for life in the House would be limited.

In reality, something more has been going on. The media are not only using House leaders as a political symbol and source of news—House leaders are coming to use the media to accomplish their legislative goals.

A decade ago, nearly all influential House members would have said that legislative arguments are won on the floor, by the tireless personal cultivation of colleagues.

Nowadays, many of them say that sort of work is only part of the story. Increasingly, they believe, floor fights are won by orchestrating a campaign aimed over the heads of the members, at the country at large.

"The idea is growing more and more," said a leadership aide, "that you have to have a media strategy to win an important vote."

The passage of President Reagan's 1981 economic program convinced leading House Democrats that an important legislative battle is a media engagement, not just a lobbying effort.

When Reagan used national television to promote his budget-reduction plan in May 1981, O'Neill found himself unable to hold the support of nervous Democrats whose constituents liked the president's speech.

"Am I lobbying?" O'Neill said at one point. "The answer is yes. Am I getting commitments? The answer is no." He said Reagan had done "the greatest selling job I've ever seen."

From that day on, House leaders have operated on the assumption that traditional inside tactics are no longer enough.

"Sometimes to pass a bill," Foley said, "you have to change the attitude of the country."

For the past few years, nearly any showdown on a major issue—a budget resolution, an arms control proposal, sanctions against the government of South Africa, or aid to the Nicaraguan antigovernment "contras"—has been preceded by a House leadership media effort orchestrated to match whatever campaign the administration is waging.

That means, among other things, floor speeches by Democratic members meant for inclusion on TV news programs, and op-ed articles in national newspapers by senior members of key committees.

Representative Dan Lungren, R-Calif., side stepped media attention while helping to shape an overhaul of the 1986 immigration bill.

Taking the Pulse

In the 99th Congress, developing a media and public opinion strategy moved beyond the ad hoc stage and become a year-round element of leadership thinking. It remains so in the 100th Congress.

At least twice a week, a core group of House Democrats led by Californian Don Edwards meets over breakfast to talk about using media to help them win on the floor. "When you don't put public pressure on your colleagues," said Edwards, "just enough of them succumb to the other side for you to lose."

Early in 1986 Edwards and the Democratic leadership fell narrowly short in their bid to block Reagan from sending $100 million in aid to the contra forces fighting Nicaragua's leftist regime.

Members of the media group regularly call producers of TV talk shows to suggest House Democrats as guests. On Sundays, if a national newspaper has not given space to the Democratic response to the president's Saturday radio address, they call one of its editors to complain.

Edwards himself has a far more ambitious plan for building a public relations apparatus in the post-O'Neill era. He wants to persuade Wright to abandon the current Tuesday-through-Thursday schedule of House action, arguing that it affords Reagan and the Republicans three days of uncontested media exposure. "We die on weekends in the media," Edwards complained. "Meanwhile, there's the president smiling and getting into his plane and waving at everybody."

What Edwards has in mind is a seven-days-a-week, 365-days-a-year plan of action that would include not only a full schedule of Monday-through-Friday committee hearings chaired by Democrats, but also a regular press conference each Saturday by the Speaker or one of his top allies.

Moreover, he wants Wright to become a more familiar media personality than his TV-shy predecessor. "We've got to polish Jim Wright up," he said. "We want an important, persuasive national figure."

The Edwards plan may or may not be adopted. It remains to be seen how many key Democrats will be willing to devote their weekends to promoting their party on television. What is clear, though, is the direction in which things are moving. In the O'Neill years, media strategy became indispensable to House leadership, and it is going to remain that way.

Competing for Prime Time

But House leaders are not the only ones who have turned the House into a media-minded institution. In fact, they are several steps behind some of their more enterprising rank-and-file colleagues.

The House today—as opposed to the one of 1976—is a place where literally any members who want to publicize their issues or themselves can do it with relatively little effort.

This does not mean that the average U.S. representative is a television star. It remains true that the average member has virtually no continuing name recognition outside his or her district. But it is also true that the opportunity for coverage exists on a day-to-day basis, and even the most junior members realize it and think about ways to take advantage of it.

In 1986 Democrats Thomas J. Downey of New York and Edward J. Markey of Massachusetts used up spare time on the House floor by ranking the value of television exposure that was readily available to them.

In first place, they decided, was coverage on all three network news programs on the same night. That constituted "hitting for the cycle."

An appearance on the Public Broadcasting System's "MacNeil-Lehrer NewsHour" was less of a coup, but still very valuable.

Further down the list were other PBS public-affairs programs, such as the now-defunct "Lawmakers" or its successor, "Capitol Journal." Below those was an appearance on network radio, which, they agreed, any member can obtain simply by calling up and asking for it.

"If you want to reach your colleagues," Downey explained later, "sometimes the best way is to let them see you on TV or read your name in the paper. If you say something pithy or clever, you can find yourself on the national news in a matter of hours. . . . News management by members through the electronic media is a more viable option than it ever was."

Few House members in either party are as media-minded as Downey or Markey. But nearly all recognize the opportunities that have surfaced for them in the past ten years.

To start with, there is C-SPAN. Since the cable network began televising House proceedings in 1979, the number of people able to receive the broadcasts has grown to 25 million.

Only a tiny fraction of those people are watching the House at a given moment, of course, but nearly every member returns home on weekend trips to find at least a few constituents who saw him or her perform recently on the House floor.

One day-to-day consequence of C-SPAN has been the thinning out of House floor attendance. Members who used to spend part of each afternoon on the floor to follow debate now do the same thing by watching TV in their offices.

In a broader way, though, C-SPAN has sensitized members to the importance of TV in their work. There is always the chance that something they say in debate might turn up on a news program—or even in the campaign commercials of their opponents many months down the road.

C-SPAN is only the beginning. Cable News Network went on the air in 1980; its nonstop broadcasting gives members of Congress who want to be interviewed a twenty-four-hour target to shoot at.

Three years later, MacNeil-Lehrer expanded its nightly public affairs program from thirty minutes to a full hour. Instead of dealing with one subject each evening, it now tackles as many as four, and its need for a credible spokesperson on major issues neatly matches the entrepreneurship of articulate members of the House.

"You have members talking on the floor all the time about how they are using the media," said Democrat Dan Glickman of Kansas. "And the media encourage us to do that—especially the electronic media. The media have found Congress to be a lot more interesting than they used to."

Great Television

There is no evidence that either newspapers or TV are focusing more on how the House works as an institution than they used to. The *Washington Post*, which maintained a full-time reporter for routine institutional House coverage until about 1980, has since then used a series of people to perform that job more selectively.

But at the same time, there is unprecedented opportunity for individual members to present themselves as analysts, commentators, polemicists, and specialists in quick reaction to events around the world.

Some of the more traditional members find this disturbing. "You've got a bunch of verbalizers who have a smattering of the jargon and who have natural media ability," said Illinois Republican Henry J. Hyde. "A lot of them have been touched by the aphrodisiac of seeing their name in the papers or going on the evening news. It's a heady experience for them."

Matthews, O'Neill's press secretary, is just as critical. "You ask these guys why they want to be on TV," he said, "and it's like asking a moth why he likes a light bulb. It's why they're there."

But not all of them seem to be in it simply for self-gratification. New York Democrat Charles E. Schumer, elected in 1980, has made himself a significant force on a variety of issues with a media offensive that has been relentless and brilliant in its understanding of media needs.

A typical year for Schumer almost always includes op-ed articles in the *Washington Post*, the *New York Times*, and the *Wall Street Journal*, and so many MacNeil-Lehrer appearances that it is sometimes hard to tell whether he is a guest or a host.

The Foreign Affairs Committee has become a media gold mine for newly elected members. Some have attracted national news coverage remarkably soon after their arrival.

The Foreign Affairs Committee is worth focusing on as a clue to the ways the House changed in the O'Neill years. It is not primarily a legislative committee. Its only regular legislative responsibility is an annual foreign aid authorization, which in most years does not clear both chambers and become law. The Foreign Affairs Committee is a debating society.

And yet, it has evolved in the past decade from a backwater committee with a lackluster membership to a prize assignment that draws some of the best legislative talent arriving in any given year.

What the Foreign Affairs Committee offers its members is the unparalleled chance to talk, and to be listened to. The freedom to talk is precious in the House, and it is growing more important all the time. That is because the freedom to legislate for many is disappearing.

Coverage Now: It's What You Do That Counts

Before the 1986 elections, Sen. Lloyd Bentsen of Texas, second-ranking Democrat on the Finance Committee, had difficulty getting press attention. "We would work so hard to get an item in the Friday column of the *Wall Street Journal,*" said an aide, referring to the paper's well-read "Washington Wire."

But after the Democrats took control of the Senate and Bentsen was designated the incoming Finance chairman, all that changed. Now reporters pester him for news tips, and he can barely find time for all the interview requests.

In the last year of his Senate career, Colorado Democrat Gary Hart, who was contemplating a second run for the presidency, was one of dozens of House and Senate members attending a March 1986 fund-raiser in Ohio. When he made his entrance, the television camera crew covering the event turned their attention to him, ignoring committee chairmen and other more senior members in favor of the presidential hopeful.

The press interest in Bentsen and Hart represents the flip sides of congressional media power. In one case, a member makes news because he or she is influential within Congress, a legislative mover and shaker. A scrapbook of press clips and a shelf full of TV tapes did not make Bentsen Finance chairman.

But for Hart and other White House contenders—Rep. Jack F. Kemp, R-N.Y., and Sen. Joseph R. Biden, Jr., D-Del., to name two—press attention comes because of national political aspirations and the subsequent perception that the candidate could be president.

While a media presence was not essential for Bentsen's rise, it is critical for presidential contenders. The press is a major, and free, avenue for getting publicity outside Washington and attracting potential supporters.

With 1,600 print reporters accredited to cover Congress, along with 2,400 broadcast personnel, it is rare for members not to find themselves the subject of an interview at least once. Whether they get a second round beyond the local paper or TV station may depend on how well they do the first time. But if they are a committee chairman or party leader, or at the center of a topical issue, their performance may make no difference at all.

Reporters will want to talk to them regardless of how articulate they are or how well they look before a camera. What they have to say is important because of who they are, not how they say it.

Live television broadcasts from the House and Senate have magnified the situation. Indeed, press attention to Congress has become a growth industry, spawning the C-SPAN television network and a bevy of private media consultants and congressional press secretaries to help members make the most of the new technologies.

How members use press coverage and whether it makes for a more productive or responsive Congress is subject to debate. And some members worry that reporters' constant presence can interfere with effective legislating.

In a 1986 speech at Delta State University in Cleveland, Miss., Sen. Nancy Landon Kassebaum, R-Kan., asserted that "government must now operate under the microscope of the news media. That can make the outlandish claim and the fervent war cry seem to be the most effective tools for a successful campaign for or against an issue. The frequent victim of such tactics is effective government, the ability and the willingness to accommodate and shape a consensus."

Sending a Message

Using the press well, members say, is a special skill that can bring a variety of rewards.

"One of the ways you reach colleagues is through the media because they read the papers and watch the news at night," said Schumer. "The media really help you establish your position on an issue."

But Schumer also suggests some caution. "If you get the reputation for doing media for media's sake, I think it hurts your effectiveness on the Hill," he said. Schumer believes that members tend to lose respect for those colleagues they consider to be grandstanders.

Moreover, press attention can take a member only so far. Schumer's numerous TV appearances and opinion pieces may put him in the spotlight, but they will not make him chairman of the Judiciary Committee or the Banking Committee on which he serves.

One veteran Senate press secretary summed up the dichotomy in the following way: "A member of Congress has to court two constituencies, the constituency that sends him here and the constituency he has to work with. As a general rule, the home-state press has got to be any smart member's priority."

But echoing Schumer's observation, he adds that "the national press can be very effective in getting your views across to people you work with."

Most members believe, though, that influence within Congress is less the result of media attention and more the result of sustained diligence and hard work. "I think you earn your spurs with your colleagues not so much because the press quotes you a lot but because you know what you're talking about," said Rep. Hyde of Illinois.

Rep. Dick Cheney, R-Wyo., agreed: "I don't see [media attention] having that much impact on the ability to round up votes."

The new Democratic congressional leaders illustrate that point as well as anyone. Neither Sen. Robert C. Byrd of West Virginia, majority leader for the 100th Congress, nor Rep. Jim Wright of Texas, Speaker of the House, drew very much press attention in recent years compared with many of their colleagues.

Their power derives instead from the work each did within his chamber, which required building relationships and mastering the intricacies of legislation so that he was virtually unstoppable in the quest for the leadership.

Now that each is at the pinnacle of his

career, Byrd and Wright have become regulars in the national media, print, and broadcast.

Conversely, former Senate majority leader Robert Dole, R-Kan., and former assistant majority leader Alan K. Simpson, R-Wyo., are less in demand. Though they remain articulate, witty Republican spokesmen, they receive less press attention because they no longer run the Senate.

"When I was minority leader, I didn't necessarily seek out opportunities to be out front," said Byrd. "I tried to put my [Democratic] colleagues in those positions. Now as majority leader I can speak with greater confidence about what I can do or cannot do" in the Senate.

Byrd faced leadership challenges in 1984 and 1986 in part because some Democrats thought he was not an effective public spokesman. Byrd countered that there was more to good leadership than "a pretty face."

However, television producers, who once worried about Byrd's somewhat wooden style, say his media presence is improving. "He has come out swinging," said Karen Sughrue, executive producer of CBS's "Face the Nation." "He has been much more effective than we imagined before."

Influence in the Shadows

Byrd and Wright are among a myriad of members who have influence out of the klieg lights. Sometimes their relative anonymity is by choice; other times anonymity results, members believe, from reporters' oversight.

Sen. Orrin G. Hatch, R-Utah, who gets considerable press for defending the administration's civil rights policies and its judicial nominees, includes on his Senate list of the overlooked Dennis DeConcini, a conservative Democrat from Arizona who was frequently a swing vote on crucial Judiciary Committee votes between 1981 and 1986, and Robert T. Stafford, R-Vt., who has played a significant role in education legislation, particularly in 1981 when he fought the administration's proposed cuts in education programs.

Hearings held by Rep. Stephen J. Solarz, D-N.Y., on the wealth of Philippine president Ferdinand E. Marcos helped undermine U.S. support for Marcos, who was ultimately forced to step down.

Another senator regularly on such lists is Hawaii Democrat Daniel K. Inouye, a crafty but fair-minded politician whose views and instincts are respected by colleagues. A longtime member of the leadership, Inouye has been a back-room player, and it is largely because of his colleagues' esteem for him and his lack of zest for the spotlight that he won appointment in December 1986 to head a select Senate committee investigating the Iranian arms deal and diversion of funds to the Nicaraguan contras. As a result, Inouye is sure to move out of the background and onto center stage.

Any similar list in the House would have near the top Dave McCurdy, a Democrat from Oklahoma, and California Republican Dan Lungren.

McCurdy is considered an important inside strategist on defense and foreign policy issues. He was one of a handful of members who, in January 1985, helped orchestrate the successful drive by Les Aspin, D-Wis., to take the chairmanship of the Armed Services Committee from the aging Melvin Price, D-Ill. And prior to the Iran arms deal scandal, McCurdy was a central figure in hammering out compromises on aid to the contras.

Lungren, an articulate conservative, rarely gets the publicity of some of his GOP colleagues, partly because of the issues he has worked on and partly because he is neither a party leader nor a ranking member of a committee.

Yet Lungren played a critical role in shaping an overhaul of the immigration bill, and helped devise a successful strategy to force the House to pass a controversial anticrime bill in 1984.

"In getting legislation through, it's really the reputation you have with members," said Lungren. "And that rarely, I think, is reflected in the media, and I don't think it is determined by the media."

The converse of an Inouye or a Lungren is the member who generates publicity but accomplishes very little within Congress. A Who's Who of show horses is hard to pin down, however, because members are reluctant to criticize their publicity-minded colleagues for the record. But in private, members are universally disdainful of what could be termed the TV lights caucus.

Shaping Public Opinion

While some in Congress may call it grandstanding, generating media exposure is a useful political tool: It can help shape public opinion, which in turn may yield legislation or alter government policy.

Rep. Stephen J. Solarz is a skilled practitioner of this approach. The New York Democrat believes that hearings he held in 1986 on the hidden wealth of Philippine President Ferdinand E. Marcos helped undermine U.S. support for Marcos, who ultimately was forced to step down.

"I think the media can be most helpful in situations where one is attempting to influence public opinion, and by influencing public opinion to influence government action," Solarz said. "I want to be able to have an opinion if I can, to shape public perception" of an issue.

Solarz and Lungren do not have much in common politically, but they agree on the importance of aggressive media strategies. Members who fail to take advantage of the press, said Lungren, "don't realize the electronic world in which we now live."

Lungren added that press coverage is especially important for Republicans in the House. "We many times are at the peril of the rules imposed on us by the majority," he said. As a result, Lungren said, the minority has to try to make its case to the TV-watching public through carefully planned floor speeches. Lungren calls it "enlarging the debate outside the walls of Congress."

Solarz understands that too much press can be harmful. "Obviously one of the down sides is the extent to which it can generate sentiments of resentment on the part of other people who don't particularly care to see somebody else in the limelight," he said.

And Sen. Byrd agrees that a member can "get too much exposure. People get tired of seeing the same face, so much of the same thing," he said.

Media attention also can be politically costly if a member becomes identified with an issue that is not popular in his or her district.

Solarz recalls that he received a num-

The O'Neill era saw unprecedented growth in media coverage of Hill activity.

ber of hostile calls after he told reporters he believed President Reagan knew in advance about the diversion of funds to Nicaraguan contras from the profits of U.S arms sales to Iran.

One caller, he said, suggested "I go back to Moscow. He said how dare I criticize the president."

Another problem, which Solarz believes he has avoided, is getting the reputation of a grandstander. "This can also lead to a diminution of influence. Your colleagues won't take you seriously even if the press does give you more coverage than others," he said.

After his comments on Reagan, which he says reporters sought, Solarz appeared on all three network news shows and was interviewed on MacNeil-Lehrer and Larry King's program on CNN.

"I very rarely call press conferences," Solarz said. "Ninety percent of the coverage I get is because of something I am doing. . . . I am not running naked down Pennsylvania Avenue to get the attention of the press."

A Media Springboard

For members seeking a different office—the representative who wants to be a senator or the member who wants to be president—the press becomes an important tool. When a Schumer or Solarz is interviewed on national television about his legislative work, the voters in Rochester, Albany, and Elmira see him, not just his constituents in Brooklyn.

This broad exposure would be a help if either decides to run for the Senate. Both have been mentioned as possible challengers to Republican senator Alfonse M. D'Amato in 1992, but both say that at present they intend to stay in the House.

For someone like Biden, who is weighing a presidential run, the spotlight has been virtually automatic. As chairman of the Senate Judiciary Committee, he makes news because of his position. The same is not true for former senator Hart, nor for Kemp, whose main congressional position is ranking minority member of an Appropriations subcommittee.

However, like Biden, Kemp and Hart are in a unique category. Having established themselves as credible presidential contenders, they are regularly approached for their views on issues as well as their timetable for announcing their campaign plans.

When Biden gave an address in December 1986 at West Chester University in Pennsylvania, for example, reporters came to cover the event but also to ask Biden about the Iran-contra scandal. The same happened when Biden spoke in San Antonio to the National League of Cities.

In his book, *The Ultimate Insiders—U.S. Senators in the National Media,* Stephen Hess of the Brookings Institution quantified this presidential phenomenon. After surveying senators' appearances in the media in 1983, Hess noted that one of the best ways to get press attention was to run for the presidency. Four senators—Alan Cranston, D-Calif., Hart, Ernest F. Hollings, D-S.C., and John Glenn, D-Ohio, were candidates, and they were at the top of the list of senators who commanded the most press, Hess found.

Getting Good Press

For whatever reason they want it, members of Congress have ample opportunities to receive the attention of the media: mention in the daily newspapers, television and radio broadcasts; appearances on MacNeil-Lehrer; and interviews in weekly print publications and on the weekend network TV news programs—ABC's "This Week with David Brinkley," CBS's "Face the Nation," and NBC's "Meet the Press."

(Because C-SPAN and CNN require cable hookups, they are not so widely available to viewers as are the network shows.)

Members consider TV appearances to be the most significant in making a media mark because of the wide and immediate audience. As Kassebaum said, "TV has such an impact today on how the public feels about issues. It's an emotional response, which is different from the response you get reading something."

Barbara Cohen, the executive producer of "Meet the Press," has some basic criteria for choosing guests. "The main goal of the show is to have the biggest newsmaker, or newsmakers, on whatever the biggest story of the week is," she said.

"We want to carry weight with newsmakers and other interested observers of the governmental process," she added. "Also we want, very crassly, to make the front page of the *Washington Post* and the *New York Times* on Monday.

"Position counts for a lot," Cohen continued. "A chairman of a committee ... that's going to count. But there also may be a ranking member or maybe the number two person who is more eager to do television, who may give a good television interview—that's important."

Programs involving Senate Judiciary Committee issues in recent years illustrate Cohen's point. Chairman Strom Thurmond, R-S.C., was very much in control of the committee process and conducted all the negotiating with Democrats on key matters. But Thurmond is not entirely comfortable with extended interviews, and, as a result, Hatch, who shares Thurmond's political views, frequently got the nod to represent the Republicans.

In lining up guests for their shows, producers are careful to distinguish between the member who can give a fast quip for the nightly news and the one who can engage in a five- or ten-minute discussion on a subject.

Some members of Congress can do both. Simpson and Rep. Barney Frank, D-Mass., are two who manage to weave quick repartee into longer debates or interviews.

In talking about an overhaul of the immigration laws, a task that took six years, Simpson said it was "like giving birth to a porcupine."

Frank, a master at the spur-of-the moment jibe, told colleagues during a 1981 abortion fight related to funding for social programs that "the Reagan administration believes life begins at conception and ends at birth."

Kassebaum is at the other extreme. She shies away from television because "I'm not that good with sort of the one-line quip." While she is respected by her peers and considered to be a thoughtful politician, Kassebaum said, "You can be so thoughtful sometimes that you bore people."

Senate vs. the House

Viewers are more likely to see senators on news shows than House members. Said Sughrue, "We tend to go for the senators because there are fewer of them. They are more well-known nationally and tend frankly to speak out more on national policy than members of the House."

That is an observation that rankles many representatives. Cheney believes it's a reflection of the "conventional wisdom that the Senate is a step up. I don't share that view."

Said Edwards, the California Democrat who has been working to get more visibility for House Democrats, "We want to compete better with the Senate."

In a pamphlet he prepared for the Democratic Caucus, Edwards noted that "the president has 36 speech writers and press people, the Speaker has one. Senators and White House personnel dominate the weekend network TV interview shows." In October and November 1986, he reported, 24 percent of the guests on the three network Sunday shows were senators, 10 percent were administration spokesmen, and 3 percent were from the House.

Edwards wants to have a bank of House Democratic experts available to comment on major events, and he wants more House members to start thinking in broad political terms.

Beauty's Only Skin Deep

While a member's appearance—whether he or she is "telegenic" in the current parlance—can help, it is of secondary importance.

"I've never considered how they look," Sughrue said. "It's more that they have something to say and how forthcoming they are."

"Is Claude Pepper telegenic?" asked MacNeil-Lehrer producer Peggy Robinson, referring to the eighty-six-year-old Florida Democratic House member. "He's a slow talker, but he is certainly the point man on some issues. You'd be doing a disservice if you ignored him."

Robinson is clear on which came first, the power or the publicity. "I don't think we make them," she said. "I think they have already established their credibility."

The counterpart to the committee and subcommittee chairmen are the representatives of the opposing view. Hyde, for example, has carved out a niche for himself as one of Reagan's chief foreign policy defenders and is regularly invited to debate the president's critics.

"There is an anti-Reagan establishment [in the media] in abundance," said Hyde. "If you get a reputation for being a Reaganaut defender who is somewhat articulate, there is always a market for you."

But even some of the lesser-known members get their chance on the air. As MacNeil-Lehrer's Robinson put it: "Sometimes when we have a cast assembled . . . we lose a member who can't come out to the studio, and we end up going down the line just trying to find a body."

The Folks Back Home

Whether or not members are regulars on the national news broadcasts or in the major print publications, they are likely to be something of a star back home. Simply because they are in Washington, they are in a position to make news, say, by announcing a grant for the district or asking a round of questions of a top official, like Secretary of State George P. Shultz, when he comes to testify.

The media stakeout: Hill reporters interviewing outside congressional offices.

With the development of satellite communications and portable camera equipment, every state can receive live television coverage from Washington.

During a daylong seminar in 1986 on Congress and the media, Cokie Roberts, a reporter for National Public Radio, noted that the "instant news out of Congress" puts a member of Congress in his constituents' living room "night after night." The effect, she said, "is seeing the congressman as a nice guy. . . . This does more to promote incumbency than newsletters" that are mailed by every congressional office.

Not everyone agrees. Rep. Lungren complains that his local paper in Long Beach hardly covers him. He says he often gets better press in the Northeast corridor between Washington, D.C., and Boston than he does in Southern California.

Rep. Edwards said he believes most members still "concentrate on their communication through newsletters and town meetings."

Does It Make a Difference?

With so many reporters and television cameras on Capitol Hill, the questions arise: Does the press make a difference? Do members do their jobs better because they know so many people are watching?

"What would this place be like without the press?" asked Hyde. "With all of its warts and flaws it would be a terrible place. We need to be watched, hissed, booed, and applauded on occasion like all human beings."

But Cheney sees what he calls the "herd mentality" with the majority of the press seizing on one particular story. "The story of the moment gets all the attention when there is an awful lot of stuff going on," Cheney said. "There is a real tendency for many in the press to sort of look around and say, 'What is running on CBS or NBC?' "

Schumer agrees, adding, "The thing that suffers is the detail, the non-glamorous work."

Schumer attracted a lot of press for his efforts on the immigration bill and on credit card interest rates, both highly visible issues. But, he said, "I have labored in the fields of housing for six years and I don't think anyone pays much attention to it."

Kassebaum worries that too much press can harm the process. She recalled in an interview that when the Senate was mired in a debate over farm credit in 1985, Majority Leader Dole convened private sessions in his office in an effort to break the impasse.

Agriculture reporters, eager to keep abreast of talks, set up a "stakeout" in the hallway nearby. Senators who walked to and from the meetings had microphones routinely thrust in their faces.

"I didn't feel it was that productive to the issue," Kassebaum said. "You run the risk of saturation coverage, everyone believing they should have some point of view." And that, the senator asserted, makes consensus more difficult.

For all of the press pursuit, the stories on Congress that result, members agree, are for the most part positive. They tend to be about issues and events, and if they are about members, they record their accomplishments, not their shortcomings. Said Cheney: "The fact of the matter is each of us got here the same way. Each of us claims to represent half a million Americans. You never pass judgment on another member's qualifications."

While that is the prevailing view in Congress, reporters, editors, and producers make their own judgments about members' abilities. They reward, with air time or print, those they think have something to say and ignore those they regard lightly.

In her speech at Delta State, Kassebaum observed that the "the age of mass media may have made life more difficult for politicians and private citizens," but she added that she and her colleagues must tread carefully through the media gantlet.

"Common sense, good judgment, and plain political courage still are the keystones of democracy, and the safeguards of our national consensus," she said. "We may place an increased emphasis on how our leaders look and sound on television, but we still expect them to govern wisely."

7

Sideline Positions: Two Views

House GOP: The Permanent Minority

What's a House Republican to do, when his party has been in the minority for more than thirty years, has little prospect of gaining control of the chamber, and faces an increasingly unified Democratic majority?

"Do your homework, know more about the issue than anyone else, arrive early, and stay late."

That is the prescription of Texan Steve Bartlett, who has been remarkably successful at leaving his imprint on important legislation even though he is one of the most conservative Republicans in an overwhelmingly Democratic House.

In June 1986 Bartlett won House approval of an amendment making a fundamental shift in federal housing policy, channeling hundreds of millions of dollars into renovation rather than construction of new dwellings for the poor.

At a time when Republicans in the House have suffered party-line defeats and complained about being "shut out" of the legislative process on such high-visibility issues as the federal budget, taxes, and trade, Bartlett's coup was a striking reminder that there is legislative life in the minority party.

For members in the minority party, it is not always a comfortable life, and victories often go unnoticed. But, said Henry J. Hyde of Illinois, "if you come to understand your role is to be a gadfly, a conscience factor, and try to work some influence in committee . . . if that's enough and you don't need to be chairman of a committee or subcommittee or see your name on a bill, this can be very rewarding."

Bartlett believes that Republicans trap themselves when they "think like a minority and then give up before the legislative battle begins."

Yet the battlefield is unquestionably sloped against them, and House Republicans sometimes find the only way they can assert themselves is through dramatic floor tactics—such as those deployed in April 1986 to derail a vote on aid to antigovernment rebels in Nicaragua or in the 1985 walkout to protest a contested election in Indiana's Eighth District.

Republicans in the House face a basic fact of political life: As members of the minority party, they can neither establish the legislative agenda nor prevail in a partisan showdown.

Minority Status Quo

In March 1987 Republicans were at an eighty-one-seat disadvantage in the House, which the Democrats controlled 258-177. On powerful committees such as Ways and Means and Rules, GOP representation was even less than in the House as a whole. "If we have a united Democratic position, Republicans are irrelevant," said Henry A. Waxman, D-Calif.

More discouraging to many Republicans is the seeming permanence of their status as the minority. The last time the GOP held a majority in the House was 1954, before any Republican now serving was elected. "I haven't chaired a subcommittee or full committee in my thirty years in Congress," said Minority Leader Robert H. Michel of Illinois. "It's a pretty doggone discouraging and debilitating thing."

Michel believes the lack of any immediate prospect for GOP control has contributed to some Republicans' decisions to leave the House. "The only difference between a freshman Republican and a ranking Republican is that the ranking Republican gets to ask questions first" at hearings, said John McCain, R-Ariz., who quit the House to run successfully for the Senate in 1986.

To add insult to injury, Republicans complain of mistreatment by House Democrats on such matters as committee ratios and staffing. They argue that the Democrats have been in the majority for so long that they have become arrogant in the use of power, riding roughshod over the minority.

"Democrats have run the House for so long, they have lost the capacity to be embarrassed by any partisan act," said Bill Frenzel, R-Minn.

Without more frequent changes in party control, said former representative Barber B. Conable, Jr., R-N.Y. (1965-1985), "there is a tendency for the majority to become flabby, the minority to become irresponsible and demoralized."

Democrats insist that they treat Republicans fairly. They say the House GOP has a "minority mentality" that is uncompromising, obstructionist, and unwilling to share in the responsibilities of governing.

A Taste of Power

The first two years of President Reagan's tenure were heady times for House Republicans, who put together a working majority on key tax and spending issues by holding their own troops in line and picking off votes of "Boll Weevil" conservative Democrats.

That period came to an end after the 1982 elections gave Democrats a net gain of twenty-six seats. The Democratic leadership later took steps to keep the Boll Weevils from defecting, and Republicans themselves became less willing to march in lock step behind increasingly unpopular Reagan policies.

"We had more success and greater activity in the 97th Congress than we'd had in thirty years," noted an aide to Michel. "We just got a horrible stomach punch in 1982, which set everybody and everything back." Now, the aide added, GOP leaders are trying to "pull out of the doldrums" with aggressive floor tactics.

Among the more eye-catching maneuvers was a procedural sneak attack in April 1986 that scuttled Democratic plans to attach a compromise package of aid to the contras to a supplemental appropriations bill that was opposed by Reagan. In another surprise move, House Republicans late in 1985 initially blocked consideration of the tax overhaul bill. But Democrats charge that such tactics win Republicans nothing but attention. The contra aid maneuver, they say, only delayed action on the president's request for aid.

Making a Difference

Opportunities for Republicans to shape legislation vary by committee, subject, and personality. But Tom Tauke, R-Iowa, said, "On most issues around here, Republicans can play a role. There are only a few issues on which Democrats decide to stake out a party position and ram it through."

Edward R. Madigan, R-Ill., identified by Republicans and Democrats alike as a skilled legislative player on the Agriculture and Energy and Commerce committees, argues that some of his GOP colleagues underestimate how much Democrats need their cooperation and votes.

Madigan himself often works on health legislation with Waxman, who is chairman of the Energy Subcommittee on Health and the Environment. Madigan's endorsement tends to bring along moderate and conservative votes that the liberal Waxman might otherwise lose. Madigan's price for cooperation is often lower authorization levels.

Madigan believes that on an array of issues that divide Democrats on the Energy and Commerce Committee, such as toxic-waste cleanup and acid rain legislation, Republicans do not have to wait until they are in the majority to have influence.

"The terrible shock for them will be on the day they are in the majority and realize they need Democrats in order to get things done," said Madigan. "Perhaps if more realized that now, they would be more involved in the process than they are now."

GOP Sore Thumbs

Wielding Madigan's kind of influence requires a willingness to compromise that comes easiest for legislators who are not rigidly ideological. Other House Republicans are just as happy to play defense.

"I don't have time to sit around feeling frustrated. I'm too busy trying to stop

House Republican leader Robert H. Michel, Ill., heads a seemingly permanent minority. The last time the GOP held a House majority was 1954.

[Democrats'] bills," said Dick Armey, R-Texas, a staunch conservative who calls himself the "resident sore thumb" on the liberal Education and Labor Committee. "I'd rather be alone and be right than be part of a compromise on legislation I so totally disagree with."

The confrontational style of minority politics has been the hallmark of "Young Turk" Republicans in the Conservative Opportunity Society (COS), a dozen-member group that made its biggest splash in the 98th Congress. More interested in partisan combat than in making incremental changes in Democrats' legislation, COS members used parliamentary maneuvers and "special order" speeches to promote conservative causes.

The faction has quieted down somewhat since then, in part because its leaders are busy with "other agendas," said COS leader Vin Weber, R-Minn.

Weber believes that the group's guerrilla floor tactics may no longer be appropriate in what he called a more "complex political environment." "In 1984 Reagan was in a strong position, Democrats were on the defensive and could be made more on the defensive," Weber said. "That's not the environment of 1986."

Weber and others say there is less need for COS activism now, in part because they think the GOP leadership itself has been more willing to confront House Democrats.

COS founder Newt Gingrich, R-Ga., says the group nonetheless prepared a fresh cycle of special order speeches in summer 1986 to spotlight Reagan administration targets such as as cocaine trafficking and welfare reform.

White House: Boon or Burden?

House Republicans have some additional leverage in shaping legislation with the White House in GOP hands. Although they cannot block or pass legislation without Democratic help, they do have enough votes to sustain a presidential veto.

Although having a Republican in the White House is mostly a boon, some House members say it can also be a burden when they must support unpopular administration positions.

For example, House Republicans opposed to the Ways and Means Committee's tax overhaul bill were at odds with the White House, which wanted to pass the bill. And a number of Republicans distanced themselves from the White House on the 1986 omnibus trade bill, which garnered fifty-nine GOP votes despite a Reagan veto threat.

Forget the Credit

Many House Republicans say it takes a certain tolerance for anonymity to be able to enjoy life in the minority. Tauke cited a maxim he attributes to Gen. Douglas MacArthur: "It's amazing how much you can get done if you don't care who gets the credit."

But junior Democrats, too, have problems getting attention, which tends to flow to subcommittee chairmen and others in conspicuous leadership positions. Indeed, it could be argued that many of the frustrations House Republicans feel are not peculiar to being in the minority.

"There is a certain amount of frustration built into the collective decision-making process," said Conable before he left the House. "A lot of folks who come here who think they are going to change the world overnight wind up very quickly frustrated because there are 534 other people who think they're going to change the world overnight, too."

Liberal Democrats: Adapting to a Hostile Climate

As recently as 1983 Rep. Augustus F. Hawkins, D-Calif., could sponsor and win solid House approval of a $3.5 billion jobs bill, the type of legislation that was once the heart and soul of the liberal agenda.

In 1986 one of the few new programs Hawkins brought to the House floor was a no-added-cost school improvement bill that would siphon funds from established programs.

Coming from Hawkins, a twelve-term veteran schooled in Lyndon Johnson's Great Society tradition of liberalism, that modest bill was a sign of how hostile the congressional climate had become for creating new social programs.

Liberals have had to resort to such approaches as redirecting existing funds and thinking small in domestic programs, as they have tried to adapt their vision of a government actively involved in solving social problems to an austere, conservative environment.

Although the Reagan era has been difficult for liberals of both parties, it is an especially trying time for Democrats, who have been forced into a seemingly permanent defensive crouch. They have had to accommodate the widespread view that the government cannot afford major new domestic expenditures and that public support is flagging for the kind of government programs that were a key tool of Great Society liberalism.

Broad consensus in Congress about the importance of reducing the federal deficit has blurred somewhat the distinction between liberal and conservative Democrats on fiscal matters: Everyone, it seems, is a fiscal conservative.

But budget constraints remain especially painful for liberals who have known flusher times and see continuing social problems they would like the federal government to address.

"It's disappointing and frustrating. We're not doing what we ought to be doing," said Waxman of California. "The liberal agenda is fighting to keep what we have."

As liberals looked for ways to cope with the inclement political weather, some were lying low, waiting for the storm to pass. Others were trying to adapt their arguments to a conservative era and were looking for new ways to translate their ideals into policy.

Down but Not Out

Despite a White House occupied by a popular conservative Republican and a Senate that, until recently, was in the hands of a Republican majority, liberal Democrats still held an important beachhead in the House of Representatives.

The Americans for Democratic Action (ADA), a political group whose ratings of members' votes on key issues have been a standard if disputed measure of how "liberal" they are, gave 140 House Democrats a "passing" liberal grade in 1985. According to ADA, that means they voted "correctly" on 70 percent or more of the key votes identified by the organization in 1985. Twenty House Democrats got a 100 percent score.

The Senate lost several leading liberals when Republicans took control of the chamber in 1981, but Ann F. Lewis, ADA national director, said she was encouraged by the number of liberal Democrats who were elected to the Senate in 1984 and 1986.

The notion that liberals are a dying breed is "outdated," said Rep. Barney Frank, D-Mass. "People might have thought that in 1981, but I think people feel a little more aggressive now. Liberals are on the attack" on several fronts, including arms control and the military budget, Frank said.

Democrats pointed to opinion polls showing that despite President Reagan's personal popularity, public support for liberal positions had not waned on such issues as opposing aid to the antigovernment contras in Nicaragua and supporting antipoverty programs.

Nonetheless, some members were weathering the conservative climate under another label. "I don't know anyone who, like me, comes from a marginal district who calls himself a liberal," said Rep. Thomas J. Downey of New York. He describes himself as a "progressive Democrat."

"Liberals have been associated with unpopular causes, like busing, and mushy thinking. It's unfortunate, but conservatives have done a good job of making it have a pejorative connotation," Downey said.

Many Democrats dispute the notion that a liberal's identity is inherently tied to the "tax and spend" epithet routinely used by Reagan. They emphasize instead the priorities and values that guide their thinking, and argue that the "big spending" label applies just as well to Reagan's defense policies.

Indeed, deficit pressures have cut both ways: The same fiscal pressures forcing liberals to abandon hopes of creating new domestic programs are helping them to slow the president's defense buildup.

Damage Control

At a time when some in the Democratic Party have concluded that they should move to the right, the principal job for liberals on Capitol Hill has been damage control—sometimes against measures supported by their fellow Democrats.

That was the role played in 1985 by some House Democrats such as Waxman who were vehemently opposed to the Gramm-Rudman-Hollings antideficit law but nonethless participated in negotiating changes, included in the final version, to protect key health and antipoverty programs against budget cuts.

"They were able to reshape Gramm-Rudman-Hollings, not that it was a good bill, for a liberal end," said David Cohen, co-director of the Advocacy Institute, which counsels public interest groups on lobbying strategy. "But how you negotiate the terms of surrender, how you apply triage, makes a tremendous difference."

Liberals mostly have had their hands full with a supposedly "conservative" chore—guarding key elements of the status quo against a hostile Reagan administration.

They have measured their success in defensive terms: Although domestic spending has been curbed, Congress has blocked administration efforts to abolish dozens of programs and to weaken major regulatory statutes of an earlier era.

"I have to look at stopping the Reagan administration from gutting the Clean Air Act as one of the great successes, and salvaging many of the health programs as an accomplishment," said Waxman, chairman of the Energy and Commerce Subcommittee on Health and the Environment.

Strategically placed liberals, including Hawkins and Judiciary Chairman Peter W. Rodino, Jr., D-N.J., have kept bottled up in committee administration initiatives such as a constitutional amendment to allow prayer in the public schools and proposals to lower the minimum wage for youths.

On foreign policy and defense, where presidents traditionally dominate, liberals have had mixed success. House Democrats could not prevent production of the MX missile, but they came close several times.

In June 1986 they failed to defeat Reagan's request for $100 million for the contras in Nicaragua, but they had blocked aid to the rebels since mid-1984.

And in a slap at Reagan's policies toward South Africa, the House in June approved a total trade embargo on the country proposed by liberal Ronald V. Dellums, D-Calif., rather than milder sanctions backed by Democratic leaders.

Incremental Gains

Liberal Democrats' accomplishments have not been solely defensive. Occasionally, in sometimes-obscure legislative corners, they have been able to achieve incremental gains by choosing their targets carefully, building coalitions with moderates, and seizing opportune moments.

For example, in both 1984 and 1985 Waxman helped win modest expansions of Medicaid eligibility for poor children and pregnant women—an effort to reduce infant mortality through the federal-state health program for the poor.

The moves pale in comparison with predecessor $2 billion child health legislation that died after passing the House in 1979. But even a modest expansion was considered a coup at a time when Congress was looking for ways to cut, not increase, Medicaid and other social programs.

The Medicaid initiatives have been buried in annual budget "reconciliation" bills that are supposed to reduce spending. Using reconciliation as the vehicle for proposals to boost spending has been an increasingly popular legislative strategy, despite complaints from some Republicans.

Changed Packaging

In areas like the infant mortality initiative, some liberal Democrats are finding it easier to win moderate and conservative support for antipoverty programs than in the past. New packaging has helped.

Because the programs were described as liberal, said one lobbyist, moderates and conservatives paid little attention to them.

But during debate on the fiscal 1987 budget resolution, conservative Democrats such as Marvin Leath of Texas joined moderates like Buddy MacKay, D-Fla., and liberals on the House Budget Committee in support of spending increases for selected antipoverty programs targeted on children.

Carefully packaged as a "children's initiative," the plan called for increases of $1.8 billion over three years for a handful of existing health and education programs with well-established track records, including Head Start for poor preschool children; compensatory education for the poor; and nutrition programs for women, infants, and children (WIC).

Backers of these programs say conservatives are increasingly receptive to arguments that education and health spending on children is an investment that pays off in the future.

"For a while we couldn't be heard, and our arguments weren't cogent enough to turn the onslaught of the Reagan forces," said Rep. George Miller, D-Calif., a member of the Budget Committee and chairman of the Select Committee on Children, Youth, and Families. "That's now changed.

"I've gone from begging people to give me a few dollars for WIC to having it be part of the Republican budget," he said.

Pushing the Private Sector

Faced with little immediate prospect of growth in the domestic budget, members who see new horizons for social activism—like curbing high-school dropout rates or helping the elderly pay for nursing home care—are under pressure to find solutions not involving large federal expenditures.

Some see this as a healthy rethinking of liberal strategies for domestic problem solving. "Where liberalism was at fault in preceding decades is that we got into the habit of assuming that the federal solution worked for every issue," said Lewis. "The legislation of the 1930s and 1960s is not going to solve the problems of the '80s."

Rather than launch major new federal initiatives, liberals increasingly have looked to the states or pushed the private sector to do jobs that, in the past, they might have assigned to the federal government.

For example, the old liberal dream of national health insurance has been all but abandoned. But Rep. Fortney H. "Pete" Stark, D-Calif., has pushed incremental measures to fill in the gaps of private health insurance coverage.

The fiscal 1986 reconciliation bill included provisions, drawn largely from legislation introduced by Stark and Sen. Edward M. Kennedy, D-Mass., penalizing hospitals that failed to provide emergency treatment to the indigent. The bill also required employers to continue offering health insur-

Ann F. Lewis, national director of Americans for Democratic Action, believes problem solving today requires rethinking of liberal strategies.

ance coverage at group rates to laid-off workers and spouses of deceased employees.

In the reconciliation bill approved in July 1986 by the House Ways and Means Committee, Stark backed a provision designed to encourage states to set up insurance risk pools and make affordable group health coverage available to all.

In another health area, Rep. Ron Wyden, D-Ore., has pushed measures to encourage private insurance companies to offer policies to cover nursing home care for the elderly—expenditures not generally covered by Medicare. Such measures provide a pragmatic backstop to more ambitious proposals calling for increased federal spending for long-term health care.

Thinking Small

Wyden is an able practitioner of the "think small" approach to domestic policy. "I'm as frustrated about the imbalance of priorities as anybody, but I think this has forced Democrats to do some rethinking, and look at new approaches," Wyden said. "You have to be very focused. You have to be willing to scale back your efforts."

For example, at a time when demands for better schools far outstripped the federal government's resources and role in education, Wyden authored a modest program of scholarships to encourage bright students to go into teaching. "It's small, but it's going to prove a point," he said.

Sen. Paul Simon, D-Ill., agreed that lawmakers must be pragmatic about budget constraints but argued that it is also important to think on a grander scale. For example, Simon said he may introduce a jobs bill that will go nowhere.

"I know in this atmosphere it isn't going to pass this year, but unless we start talking about these things, they'll never happen," said Simon.

"The danger is we all start fighting for the status quo, when in fact there is no such thing as the status quo—you're either making progress or slipping back," he added.

One Democratic aide to the House Education and Labor Committee lamented: "The president has been successful not just in making Congress prudent, but in constraining people's vision and aspirations. We don't consider whether something is a good idea. The only question is what something costs."

Awaiting Pendulum's Swing

Hawkins, for one, has not lost heart. He expects to see the political pendulum eventually swing back in favor of liberalism.

"There's a season for conservatism, a season for liberalism," Hawkins said. "I've seen it so many times over my fifty years in politics. I recognize when you can move a jobs bill and when you can't."

His school improvement bill would earmark funds from existing programs to implement research about what makes schools effective. Hawkins sees it as a seed that could flower in a more liberal future. "At least you have the principle there," he said.

Some liberals see signs that the clouds of conservatism already are starting to lift: The November 1986 elections left Democrats in control of the Senate. Liberals eagerly await the post-Reagan era, anticipating that the conservative agenda will lose its steam without an extraordinarily popular president to push it.

Even then, few assume that an ebbing of the conservative tide will mean a robust recovery of Great Society liberalism. However, it is not quite clear what might take its place.

"We're too inchoate to be labeled, but something will emerge," said Rep. Charles E. Schumer, D-N.Y. "The idea that government should be helping people that need help, that government is a necessary force for good—that will be the core. The government-bashing that's taken place in the last ten to twelve years I think will recede."

8

Historical Perspective

It is ultimately a mix of rules and people that creates the chemistry of power in Congress.

People come and go: Members win seats and lose them, swept into office and out again by variable political winds; old members are succeeded by much younger ones, who, if they are lucky, may themselves grow old in office.

Rules, to be sure, also change from season to season. The parliamentary bookshelf grows more crowded, with the likes of *Jefferson's Manual, Cannon's Precedents, Deschler's Procedure*, and *Hind's Precedents.*

But rules and the precedents created by people in power accumulate like leaves on a forest floor, transformed into something more permanent, like the soil that sustains the forest. In the end, the evolution of power in Congress can be traced through the history of its rules, and the people who have made and used them.

The Power of Charm: Clay

There are few better examples of the power of personality in Congress than the career of Henry Clay. The magnetism of his personality allowed him not only to lead Congress, but also to lead the nation into the War of 1812 with Britain. He was elected Speaker November 4, 1811, the day he arrived in the House at age thirty-four.

That kind of thing is less likely to happen today. The 12th Congress was much smaller than the 100th, new members made up a much larger proportion of the total, the seniority system was scarcely imagined, and the tradition of Speakers working their way up the "leadership ladder" had not taken hold.

Although he grew up in the East, Clay moved to frontier Kentucky to build a law practice, land holdings, and a political base. While he could mingle confidently within the more refined social circles of Richmond, Va., Clay was also the kind of man who could flourish in untamed areas—hard-drinking, adept at gambling, and ready to settle insults in a duel.

Even Clay's enemies conceded his charm, and his skill at oratory was important in the pre-electronic age when debate in Congress mattered more than today. His political genius came most of all from human chemistry. It was the after-dinner talks beside the fire at Mrs. Dawson's boardinghouse on Capitol Hill, where Clay lodged with half a dozen other freshman members, that became the breeding ground for the "War-Hawk" movement he led.

The magnetism of Henry Clay allowed him to lead not only Congress, but also the nation, into the War of 1812.

Clay's magic came not only from charisma, but also from compromise. He was the architect of several agreements—including the Missouri Compromise of 1820—that bridged the gap between feuding sections of the country. His talents were much needed as a glue to keep the nation together in the decades of deepening regional conflict that led to the Civil War.

Clay strengthened the power of the speakership. The seven Speakers before him had presided over the House only ceremonially; Clay was the first to lead it.

Tactical Approaches to Power

Power in Congress tends to be decentralized—a natural result of its democratic character. Sen. Daniel Webster referred to his chamber as a "Senate of equals" who bowed to no master. The House has been even more egalitarian. So egalitarian, in fact, and so large, that we may wonder that anything gets done. Only the stricter rules and stronger leadership in the House, in contrast to the Senate, make orderly business possible today.

But it was not always so. Former House Rules Committee chairman Richard W. Bolling, D-Mo. (1949-1983), recounts in his history of the House that there was near gridlock in the chamber in the decades of bitter divisiveness before and after the Civil War. It resulted from the delaying tactics of the minority.

A classic obstructive tactic was the "disappearing quorum"—in which members of the minority party simply sat in their seats and refused to answer when the clerk called the roll. With perfect attendance by the majority party rare, this could block passage of a bill when margins were slim. (Under the Constitution, a majority of members must be present for either chamber to do business.)

To counteract this tendency to obstruct, a stronger "leadership" structure has evolved in the House than in the Senate.

The House adopted rules limiting debate as early as 1841. The Senate, by contrast, has nurtured a tradition of almost unlimited debate, and cloture there is still unusual.

The Push for Power: Reed

Near the end of the nineteenth century, Republican Thomas Brackett Reed of Maine (Speaker, 1889-1891, 1895-1899) realized that for his party—which had only a slim majority in the House—to do anything, some changes would have to be made. As Speaker, he set his mind to strengthening the powers of the office and was so successful that he was nicknamed "Czar Reed."

Because the Republicans had only a small majority, it was easy for Democrats to block action with the disappearing quorum. One of Reed's most famous exploits came

Speaker Tom Reed was so successful in strengthening the powers of the office that he was nicknamed "Czar Reed."

when he decided to counter such a move by directing the clerk to record as present some Democrats he saw in the chamber who were refusing to answer the roll call.

Pandemonium raged. "I deny your right, Mr. Speaker, to count me as present," roared one member. Another simply said: "I am not here." After days of fierce parliamentary combat, Reed not only carried the point but pushed adoption of a new set of rules strengthening leadership powers.

Too Much Power

One justification for the "Reed rules" was stated by his lieutenant, Joseph G. Cannon, R-Ill. "I say that a majority under the Constitution is allowed to legislate, and that if a contrary practice has grown up, such practice is unrepublican, undemocratic, against sound policy, and contrary to the Constitution." Later, as a Speaker himself (1903-1911), "Uncle Joe" Cannon further consolidated and extended the powers of the office.

For example, the Speaker had the power to appoint members of committees since the earliest years. During his tenure as Speaker, however, Cannon appointed and removed members and chairmen at will, regardless of seniority, simply to get the legislation he wanted.

Cannon was equally blunt in extending other powers, too. Speakers long had held the power to choose who would speak when several members sought the floor; but Cannon simply refused to recognize members he did not want to hear.

As chairman of the Rules Committee, as well as Speaker, Cannon had complete control of what bills came to the floor. In his last years, Bolling writes, "Cannon had crossed the line separating strong leadership and absolutism."

The result was revolt. Insurgents in his own Republican party joined Democrats in 1910 to strip the speakership of some key powers and shatter Cannon's psychological dominance.

The opening wedge in their attack was the device of "Calendar Wednesday," a single day every week when bills approved by committees could be called up directly on the floor—bypassing the gatekeeping function of Rules. When Cannon maneuvered to sidestep the insurgents, for example by adjourning from Tuesday to Thursday or interposing privileged business, they eventually confronted him in open revolt. The battle continued for days on and off the floor, sometimes around the clock, and when it was done, the House had taken from the Speaker the power to chair Rules, appoint its members, or even sit on it.

The defeated Cannon, still in the Speaker's chair, dramatically asked for a motion for his own removal. One was offered but failed, 155-192. However, it was clear that the Speaker would thenceforth be as much the servant of the House as its master.

O'Neill's Ups and Downs

Cannon's iron hand is in sharp contrast to the style of the 47th Speaker of the House, Thomas P. O'Neill, Jr., of Massachusetts.

Colleagues had a right to feel some apprehension when O'Neill took over in 1977. After twelve terms, he was a familiar and popular member, but one without any real reputation as a legislator. He had been a compromise choice for Democratic whip in 1971, acceptable to liberals because of his antiwar record, and he had simply moved up the ladder after that.

Even during the previous four years, as majority leader under Speaker Carl Albert of Oklahoma, O'Neill had worked a short week in Washington, continuing to focus on life and politics in Boston and playing little role in the day-to-day management of the House. Some of O'Neill's contemporaries knew that he had been Speaker of the Massachusetts House in the late 1940s, and that he had been considered a strong one. But there was nothing in his easygoing congressional career to suggest much of an appetite for leadership.

The first few months seemed to bear out contentions that O'Neill as Speaker would be like the man who had run the Massachusetts House, not the one who had coasted through twelve terms in Washington. "Power is when people assume you have power," he told a reporter in 1977. O'Neill began his speakership by convincing people that he had it.

Thomas P. "Tip" O'Neill's tenure as Speaker saw tremendous growth in media coverage and a subtle shift of real legislative power into a relatively small number of hands.

Confronted with the challenge of enacting President Carter's energy package, he came up with a novel and successful idea, appointing an ad hoc committee to take up the bills on an emergency basis and thus bypass the parochial jealousies of the existing committee structure. Carter unveiled his proposals in April; by August 5 O'Neill had moved them through the House.

By the fall of 1977 there were stories claiming that O'Neill was the strongest congressional leader since Sam Rayburn. That early reputation was crucial, because he had to live off its capital for a long time. It was five years before O'Neill was able to win as impressively as he did the summer he took office.

By 1978 the perceived failures of the Carter administration had taken their toll on the Democratic Party in Congress, and given O'Neill a Democratic majority that was increasingly reluctant to follow him. In November of that year the midterm election brought in a belligerent crop of youthful Republicans, sensitive to the public relations potential of the House floor, and skillful at linking the Democratic leadership to the Carter White House and to overall economic decline.

The last two years of Carter's presidency marked the low point in O'Neill's personal management of the House. The leadership was embarrassed on issue after issue—energy, budget, foreign policy—by a coalition of Republicans and nervous conservative Democrats who thought it prudent to keep their distance from O'Neill as well as Carter.

"I've got a lot of good friends out there," the Speaker said one frustrating night in 1980, "who won't even give me a vote to adjourn."

Those frustrations, however, proved to be only a mild foreshadowing of what took place a year later, with President Reagan in the White House. Given Reagan's popularity and the Republican gain of thirty-three House seats in the fall of 1980, there may never have been much chance for O'Neill's Democrats to derail the president's economic program. But O'Neill's handling of the 1981 economic debate did not particularly reinforce his image as a leader.

In April, while other Democrats were struggling to stave off a Reagan budget victory, the Speaker took his usual springtime foreign tour, this one to Australia. On his return, he announced that Reagan could not be beaten, an observation that struck some Democratic colleagues as an abdication of responsibility.

A few months later he seemed to switch to the other extreme, fighting aggressively to win passage of a Democratic tax bill that had been laced with special interest concessions in an effort to hold southern Democratic votes. Reagan won easily on the tax issue; the simple fact was that the Democratic leadership did not have control of the chamber.

Had O'Neill chosen to retire in 1982, his speakership would have had an aura of failure about it. But he opted to stay on, and the last five years of his tenure brought a gradual revival, not only in his public reputation but in his ability to lead.

By early 1982 recession had ended the southern Democratic infatuation with Reagan policies, and there were no more Republican victories on major economic policy issues. In the fall of 1982 GOP candidates throughout the country campaigned by attacking the Speaker as an obsolete hack, and they failed spectacularly. With national unemployment cresting above 10 percent on Election Day, Democrats regained twenty-six of the seats they had lost in 1980, reclaiming political control of the House in addition to the nominal control that they had never lost.

The following two Congresses saw no landmark legislative initiatives from the Democrats. But they nevertheless established O'Neill as a Speaker who nearly always had the necessary votes when he needed them.

The key committees were packed with enough leadership loyalists to make most key votes predictable. Budget resolutions drafted in large part by the leadership won wide approval on the House floor, with Republicans offering only halfhearted opposition. The Republican strategy of making O'Neill their national campaign villain was a failure for the second time in 1984, and polls showed the Speaker's popularity rising among the American people in the closing months of his career.

Tip O'Neill was not a great legislator—his casual attitude toward detail is too well documented for that. "I don't know the depth of every piece of legislation. . . . The important stuff, I understand it," he told an

Seniority System Thrives . . .

Congress's seniority system is rooted in tradition, not law or rules. It dates to 1846, when fledgling parties took charge of committee assignments, but seniority did not evolve as the sole criterion for picking chairmen until after World War II.

As congressional service became a career, members with safe seats stayed for decades and enjoyed long tenures as chairmen and ranking minority members.

By the 1970s junior members—especially in the House—were growing frustrated. Often they felt separated from those at the top not only by age but also by geography and ideology. Many chairmen were conservative southerners, at a time when most House Democrats were more liberal.

House Reforms

In 1971 House Republicans agreed that their ranking committee members would be chosen by a secret-ballot vote of the full conference, and that nominations need not be based strictly on seniority.

In 1973 House Democrats compelled all chairmen to stand for election by secret ballot, though none was deposed. House Republicans challenged several ranking members that year, but none was ousted.

By the start of the next Congress in 1975, Democrats had adopted the procedures they now use. Power over committee nominations was transferred from Ways and Means Committee Democrats to the Steering and Policy Committee. A secret-ballot vote of the caucus was made standard.

In implementing those reforms, House Democrats ousted the chairmen of Armed Services, Agriculture, and Banking. But for the next decade, until Melvin Price was ousted as chairman of the House Armed Services Committee in 1985, Democrats routinely elected committees' senior members as chairmen, with scattered dissents.

Senate Changes

Senate Democrats and Republicans made changes in 1971. In the Democratic majority, the leadership's Steering Committee continued to name chairmen, but a senator could demand a caucus vote on any nominee. Because that exposed the dissident senator to retribution, in 1975 Democrats mandated a secret-ballot vote whenever one-fifth of the caucus returned, unsigned, a notice requesting a vote on a chairman.

interviewer. But like the Republican president who was his antagonist in the last five years of his tenure, O'Neill persuaded skeptics that there are elements of leadership that go beyond the mastery of facts.

"Tip is not a man who is interested in substance," John D. Dingell, the veteran Michigan Democrat, said of him in 1986. "But he has the ability to reduce complicated issues down to a few simple, easily understood points. That's not a weakness. It's an unbelievable political strength."

. . . Despite Reforms

Republicans in 1971 limited their members to serving as ranking member, or chairman, on one standing committee.

The entire Senate in 1971 defeated a bipartisan resolution to allow criteria other than seniority to determine chairmen or ranking members. The GOP sponsor was Charles McC. Mathias, Jr., of Maryland, one of his party's most liberal members, who retired after the 99th Congress.

Mathias's career showed that the seniority system can be bent to deprive members of committee chairs, even when it is not violated. In 1977 he was in line to be ranking member of Judiciary. But Strom Thurmond of South Carolina, prodded by conservatives, forfeited his Armed Services ranking position to assert seniority over Mathias on Judiciary. In 1981, when Republicans took control of the Senate, Thurmond became Judiciary chairman and Mathias was left with the relatively minor Rules and Administration Committee.

Senate Republicans' most notable action against the seniority system was a 1973 proposal sponsored by Howard H. Baker, Jr., of Tennessee. It allowed committees to choose their own leaders, without regard to seniority, subject to approval in the full GOP conference.

Since the reform years, "there haven't been many challenges to chairmen, in large part just because the chairmen have gotten the message and essentially caved in and found they have to respond to the members," said Roger H. Davidson, a scholar of Congress at the Library of Congress.

In the House, he said, "the ones who were left [after the 1975 coups] learned a lesson, and that lesson has not had to be relearned." However, Davidson said, the House theoretically could be more fertile ground than the Senate for rebellions. "The mathematics are a little different," he said. Because the Senate has fewer members, almost all senators can chair a committee or subcommittee, if their party is in the majority, or sit as a ranking minority member if not.

Also, Senate rules give members far greater freedom than House rules. Any senator can amend legislation on the floor or use parliamentary tactics to stall or block a bill. The sense of influence this conveys helps defuse potential rebellions. "It's much easier to get involved, even informally, than in the House," Davidson said. "Particularly in the majority party, the fact you don't have the chairmanship doesn't freeze you out of policy making."

Power by Committee

Woodrow Wilson, before he became president, described the U.S. form of government as "government by the chairmen of the standing committees of Congress."

Today, the power of committees is as formidable as any other kind of power in Congress. But it was not always that way.

There were few standing committees in the earliest Congresses; the practice then was to appoint a new, ad hoc committee to consider each piece of legislation. By the mid-nineteenth century, however, the size and complexity of the legislative workload had given rise to an extensive structure of committees. It was the power accumulated by their chairmen that caused Wilson's lament in 1885.

The rise of the Speaker to dominance in the House somewhat overshadowed the power of committee chairmen. In fact, the Speaker's authority to appoint members and chairmen of committees was one of his chief tools of leadership. The revolt against Speaker Cannon in 1910 reversed that and gave senior members an iron grip on the levers of power that lasted until the 1970s.

The seniority system was a key to the power of southern conservatives in Congress during the first part of the twentieth century. One legacy of the Civil War was that the rural South (and most of the South was rural) became virtually a one-party polity—and that party was the Democratic party, which dominated both chambers after 1930. The one-party system of the South guaranteed safe seats, and safe seats meant growing seniority. The result of this was that a disproportionate number of key committees were chaired by conservative southern Democrats.

That changed in the 1970s, an era of many attempted reforms and some successful ones. A new generation of members, swept en masse into office by public reaction against the Vietnam War and Watergate, revolted against the power structure and ended the system whereby simple seniority had guaranteed a member the committee chair. *(See box, pp. 108-109.)*

In the House today, chairmen are elected in the Democratic Caucus by secret ballot. And although seniority is still respected in most instances, many younger members have come to power as chairmen of subcommittees, which have grown in importance as Congress has tried to limit the proliferation of full committees.

In recent years, however, a new, more subtle change has been occurring that is quietly concentrating legislative power in a relatively small number of hands.

Many members like to refer to the current legislative process in the House as the "four bill" system. What they mean is that in the average year, there may be only four important domestic legislative vehicles—the budget resolution, continuing appropriations, supplemental appropriations, and the reconciliation package of spending cuts that the budget dictates. Sometimes legislation to raise the federal debt limit is another. "The only way to get things done in recent years," said Leon E. Panetta, a California Democrat, "has been to attach them to bills the Senate and the president cannot refuse."

Return to Oligarchy

Those who are able to influence one of the "must pass" bills can count on being important players in the process. Those who are not can count on being spectators. As a result, one of the most common clichés about the modern House—its open, democratic character—is ceasing to be accurate. The current House is democratic in the sense that all members are part of the debate. But when it comes to making decisions, democracy is the wrong word to use.

"The natural tendency of this institution is toward oligarchy," said Democrat Philip R. Sharp of Indiana. "What we have now is a technique for returning to a closed system where a few people make all the decisions."

This frustrates members not only in Washington but at home. Two decades ago, most of them could return to their districts and explain that the restrictions of the seniority system made it difficult to accomplish what they wanted to do. These days that explanation will not do, at least among sophisticated constituents.

The return to oligarchy tends to escape notice because it bears so little resemblance to the form of oligarchy that prevailed before the reform wave of the early 1970s. The current system concentrates power not in the chairmen of many committees, as before, but in virtually all the members of a few elite committees.

Political Parties Wield Power

Historically, another major source of congressional power has been the political party organizations. They are not mentioned in the Constitution and are often informal, but they nonetheless have evolved through tradition as highly powerful centers of decision making.

James Madison, in the *Federalist Papers*, spoke of parties or factions as a "dangerous vice" but an inevitable one in a society protecting political liberty. The framers created a system of checks and balances designed to "control the violence of faction."

And although organized parties did not exist when the first Congress convened, they quickly grew from casual clubs of like-minded members to serious organizations devoted to accomplishment of legislative programs.

The caucus (now more often called a conference) of the members of the House or Senate from a particular party had by the time Clay was in the House become a major power center.

Daniel Webster, shortly after he arrived as a freshman in the House in 1813, observed: "Before anything is attempted to be done here, it must be arranged elsewhere." Party discipline in the era of Clay was stiff enough to inspire the phrase "King Caucus."

The power of the caucus reached one of its peaks in the early nineteenth century because it did the job presidential nominating conventions do today. Caucus power declined after 1825 but saw a resurgence under strong Speakers like Cannon.

The caucus grew weaker in ensuing years—partly because southern Democrats viewed it as a tool for imposing policies of the more liberal majority of the national party. They often voted with Republicans in the so-called "conservative coalition."

One way the 1970s reformers weakened the grip of conservative southern chairmen on the committee system was to subject their appointments to caucus approval and oust some of the chairmen there.

A Senate Power: LBJ

While history books go on at length about the interesting and sometimes notorious House Speakers, less has been written about Senate leaders. That is changing, however, as legislating becomes more complex and the relationships between the White House and the Congress more symbiotic.

No one did more than Lyndon B. Johnson, the rough-hewn, crafty Texas Democrat, to turn the position of majority leader of the Senate, which he held from 1955 to 1961, into a power center.

His influence was the accumulation of hundreds of intense one-to-one relationships. He got his way by turning on victims his legendary "treatment"—cajoling, wheedling, pleading, accusing, threatening, and promising—until they relented. The tools of Johnson's Senate power were an informal network of intelligence-gatherers and political operatives who were largely outside of the traditional organizational structures by which the Senate is run.

Not surprisingly, the power Johnson accumulated could not be passed on to his successors.

Appendix A

Characteristics of the 100th Congress

Following is a compilation of information about individual members of the 100th Congress—their birth dates, occupations, religion, and seniority.

Senate

(Seniority rank is within the member's party.)

ALABAMA

Heflin (D)—June 19, 1921. Occupation: lawyer, judge. Religion: Methodist. Seniority: 32.

Shelby (D)—May 6, 1934. Occupation: lawyer. Religion: Presbyterian. Seniority: 51.

ALASKA

Stevens (R)—November 18, 1923. Occupation: lawyer. Religion: Episcopalian. Seniority: 3.

Murkowski (R)—March 28, 1933. Occupation: banker. Religion: Roman Catholic. Seniority: 34.

ARIZONA

DeConcini (D)—May 8, 1937. Occupation: lawyer. Religion: Roman Catholic. Seniority: 25.

McCain (R)—August 29, 1936. Occupation: naval officer, beer distributor. Religion: Episcopalian. Seniority: 44.

ARKANSAS

Bumpers (D)—August 12, 1925. Occupation: farmer, hardware company executive, lawyer, governor. Religion: Methodist. Seniority: 17.

Pryor (D)—August 29, 1934. Occupation: newspaper publisher, lawyer, governor. Religion: Presbyterian. Seniority: 29.

CALIFORNIA

Cranston (D)—June 19, 1914. Occupation: author, journalist, real estate executive. Religion: Protestant. Seniority: 9.

Wilson (R)—August 23, 1933. Occupation: lawyer. Religion: Protestant. Seniority: 39.

COLORADO

Armstrong (R)—March 16, 1937. Occupation: broadcasting executive. Religion: Lutheran. Seniority: 25.

Wirth (D)—September 22, 1939. Occupation: education official. Religion: Episcopalian. Seniority: 47.

CONNECTICUT

Weicker (R)—May 16, 1931. Occupation:

lawyer. Religion: Episcopalian. Seniority: 7.

Dodd (D)—May 27, 1944. Occupation: lawyer. Religion: Roman Catholic. Seniority: 36.

DELAWARE

Roth (R)—July 22, 1921. Occupation: lawyer. Religion: Episcopalian. Seniority: 6.

Biden (D)—November 20, 1942. Occupation: lawyer. Religion: Roman Catholic. Seniority: 14.

FLORIDA

Chiles (D)—April 3, 1930. Occupation: lawyer. Religion: Presbyterian. Seniority: 11.

Graham (D)—November 9, 1936. Occupation: developer, governor. Religion: United Church of Christ. Seniority: 54.

GEORGIA

Nunn (D)—September 8, 1938. Occupation: farmer, lawyer. Religion: Methodist. Seniority: 12.

Fowler (D)—October 6, 1940. Occupation: lawyer. Religion: Presbyterian. Seniority: 49.

HAWAII

Inouye (D)—September 7, 1924. Occupation: lawyer. Religion: Methodist. Seniority: 7.

Matsunaga (D)—October 8, 1916. Occupation: lawyer. Religion: Episcopalian. Seniority: 22.

IDAHO

McClure (R)—December 27, 1924. Occupation: lawyer. Religion: Methodist. Seniority: 9.

Symms (R)—April 23, 1938. Occupation: fruit grower, fitness club owner. Religion: Methodist. Seniority: 30.

ILLINOIS

Dixon (D)—July 7, 1927. Occupation: lawyer. Religion: Presbyterian. Seniority: 37.

Simon (D)—November 29, 1928. Occupation: author, newspaper editor and publisher. Religion: Lutheran. Seniority: 41.

INDIANA

Lugar (R)—April 4, 1932. Occupation: agricultural industries executive. Religion: Methodist. Seniority: 16.

Quayle (R)—February 4, 1947. Occupation: lawyer, newspaper publisher. Religion: Presbyterian. Seniority: 32.

IOWA

Grassley (R)—September 17, 1933. Occupation: farmer. Religion: Baptist. Seniority: 31.

Harkin (D)—November 19, 1939. Occupation: lawyer. Religion: Roman Catholic. Seniority: 41.

KANSAS

Dole (R)—July 22, 1923. Occupation: lawyer. Religion: Methodist. Seniority: 4.

Kassebaum (R)—July 29, 1932. Occupation: broadcasting executive. Religion: Episcopalian. Seniority: 20.

KENTUCKY

Ford (D)—September 8, 1924. Occupation: insurance executive, governor. Religion: Baptist. Seniority: 16.

McConnell (R)—February 20, 1942. Occupation: county judge/executive. Religion: Baptist. Seniority: 43.

LOUISIANA

Johnston (D)—June 10, 1932. Occupation: lawyer. Religion: Baptist. Seniority: 13.

Breaux (D)—March 1, 1944. Occupation: lawyer. Religion: Roman Catholic. Seniority: 46.

MAINE

Cohen (R)—August 28, 1940. Occupation: author, lawyer. Religion: Unitarian. Seniority: 25.

Mitchell (D)—August 20, 1933. Occupation: lawyer, judge. Religion: Roman Catholic. Seniority: 35.

MARYLAND

Sarbanes (D)—February 3, 1933. Occupation: lawyer. Religion: Greek Orthodox. Seniority: 24.

Mikulski (D)—July 20, 1936. Occupation: social worker. Religion: Roman Catholic. Seniority: 49.

MASSACHUSETTS

Kennedy (D)—February 22, 1932. Occupation: author, lawyer. Religion: Roman Catholic. Seniority: 6.

Kerry (D)—December 22, 1943. Occupation: lawyer. Religion: Roman Catholic. Seniority: 40.

MICHIGAN

Riegle (D)—February 4, 1938. Occupation: business executive, professor. Religion: Methodist. Seniority: 21.

Levin (D)—June 28, 1934. Occupation: lawyer. Religion: Jewish. Seniority: 32.

MINNESOTA

Durenberger (R)—August 19, 1934. Occupation: adhesives manufacturing company executive, lawyer. Religion: Roman Catholic. Seniority: 19.

Boschwitz (R)—November 7, 1930. Occupation: plywood company owner, lawyer. Religion: Jewish. Seniority: 22.

MISSISSIPPI

Stennis (D)—August 3, 1901. Occupation: lawyer, judge. Religion: Presbyterian. Seniority: 1.

Cochran (R)—December 7, 1937. Occupation: lawyer. Religion: Baptist. Seniority: 21.

MISSOURI

Danforth (R)—September 5, 1936. Occupation: lawyer, clergyman. Religion: Episcopalian. Seniority: 13.

Bond (R)—March 6, 1939. Occupation: lawyer, governor. Religion: Presbyterian. Seniority: 45.

MONTANA

Melcher (D)—September 6, 1924. Occupation: veterinarian, cattle feedlot operator. Religion: Roman Catholic. Seniority: 23.

Baucus (D)—December 11, 1941. Occupation: lawyer. Religion: United Church of Christ. Seniority: 28.

NEBRASKA

Exon (D)—August 9, 1921. Occupation: office equipment retailer, governor. Religion: Episcopalian. Seniority: 30.

Karnes (R)—December 12, 1948. Occupation: lawyer, agribusiness official. Religion: Methodist. Seniority: 46.

NEVADA

Hecht (R)—November 30, 1928. Occupation: clothing store owner. Religion: Jewish. Seniority: 39.

Reid (D)—December 2, 1939. Occupation: lawyer. Religion: Mormon. Seniority: 53.

NEW HAMPSHIRE

Humphrey (R)—October 9, 1940. Occupation: airline copilot. Religion: Baptist. Seniority: 28.

Rudman (R)—May 18, 1930. Occupation: lawyer. Religion: Jewish. Seniority: 29.

NEW JERSEY

Bradley (D)—July 28, 1943. Occupation: professional basketball player. Religion: Protestant. Seniority: 32.

Lautenberg (D)—January 23, 1924. Occupation: computer firm executive. Religion: Jewish. Seniority: 38.

NEW MEXICO

Domenici (R)—May 7, 1932. Occupation:

lawyer. Religion: Roman Catholic. Seniority: 10.

Bingaman (D)—October 3, 1943. Occupation: lawyer. Religion: Methodist. Seniority: 39.

NEW YORK

Moynihan (D)—March 16, 1927. Occupation: author, government professor. Religion: Roman Catholic. Seniority: 25.

D'Amato (R)—August 1, 1937. Occupation: lawyer. Religion: Roman Catholic. Seniority: 34.

NORTH CAROLINA

Helms (R)—October 18, 1921. Occupation: journalist, broadcasting executive. Religion: Baptist. Seniority: 10.

Sanford (D)—August 20, 1917. Occupation: lawyer, college president, governor. Religion: Methodist. Seniority: 45.

NORTH DAKOTA

Burdick (D)—June 19, 1908. Occupation: lawyer. Religion: United Church of Christ. Seniority: 4.

Conrad (D)—March 12, 1948. Occupation: state tax commissioner. Religion: Unitarian. Seniority: 55.

OHIO

Glenn (D)—July 18, 1921. Occupation: astronaut, soft drink company executive. Religion: Presbyterian. Seniority: 15.

Metzenbaum (D)—June 4, 1917. Occupation: newspaper publisher, parking lot executive, lawyer. Religion: Jewish. Seniority: 20.

OKLAHOMA

Boren (D)—April 21, 1941. Occupation: lawyer, political science professor, governor. Religion: Methodist. Seniority: 30.

Nickles (R)—December 6, 1948. Occupation: machine company executive. Religion: Roman Catholic. Seniority: 34.

OREGON

Hatfield (R)—July 12, 1922. Occupation: political science professor, governor. Religion: Baptist. Seniority: 2.

Packwood (R)—September 11, 1932. Occupation: lawyer. Religion: Unitarian. Seniority: 5.

PENNSYLVANIA

Heinz (R)—October 23, 1938. Occupation: food industry executive. Religion: Episcopalian. Seniority: 15.

Specter (R)—February 12, 1930. Occupation: lawyer, law professor. Religion: Jewish. Seniority: 34.

RHODE ISLAND

Pell (D)—November 22, 1918. Occupation: investment executive. Religion: Episcopalian. Seniority: 5.

Chafee (R)—October 22, 1922. Occupation: lawyer, governor. Religion: Episcopalian. Seniority: 14.

SOUTH CAROLINA

Thurmond (R)—December 5, 1902. Occupation: lawyer, judge, governor. Religion: Baptist. Seniority: 1.

Hollings (D)—January 1, 1922. Occupation: lawyer, governor. Religion: Lutheran. Seniority: 8.

SOUTH DAKOTA

Pressler (R)—March 29, 1942. Occupation: lawyer. Religion: Roman Catholic. Seniority: 27.

Daschle (D)—December 9, 1947. Occupation: congressional aide. Religion: Roman Catholic. Seniority: 51.

TENNESSEE

Sasser (D)—September 30, 1936. Occupation: lawyer. Religion: Methodist. Seniority: 25.

Gore (D)—March 31, 1948. Occupation: journalist, home builder. Religion: Baptist. Seniority: 43.

TEXAS

Bentsen (D)—February 11, 1921. Occupation: finance holding company executive, lawyer. Religion: Presbyterian. Seniority: 10.

Gramm (R)—July 8, 1942. Occupation: economics professor. Religion: Episcopalian. Seniority: 42.

UTAH

Garn (R)—October 12, 1932. Occupation: insurance executive. Religion: Mormon. Seniority: 12.

Hatch (R)—March 22, 1934. Occupation: lawyer. Religion: Mormon. Seniority: 16.

VERMONT

Stafford (R)—August 8, 1913. Occupation: lawyer, governor. Religion: Congregationalist. Seniority: 8.

Leahy (D)—March 31, 1940. Occupation: lawyer. Religion: Roman Catholic. Seniority: 18.

VIRGINIA

Warner (R)—February 18, 1927. Occupation: lawyer. Religion: Episcopalian. Seniority: 24.

Trible (R)—December 29, 1946. Occupation: lawyer. Religion: Episcopalian. Seniority: 38.

WASHINGTON

Evans (R)—October 16, 1925. Occupation: engineer, college president, governor. Religion: Congregationalist. Seniority: 41.

Adams (D)—January 13, 1927. Occupation: lawyer. Religion: Episcopalian. Seniority: 47.

WEST VIRGINIA

Byrd (D)—November 20, 1917. Occupation: lawyer. Religion: Baptist. Seniority: 3.

Rockefeller (D)—June 18, 1937. Occupation: public official, governor. Religion: Presbyterian. Seniority: 44.

WISCONSIN

Proxmire (D)—November 11, 1915. Occupation: journalist, printing company executive. Religion: United Church of Christ. Seniority: 2.

Kasten (R)—June 19, 1942. Occupation: shoe company executive. Religion: Episcopalian. Seniority: 32.

WYOMING

Wallop (R)—February 27, 1933. Occupation: rancher, meatpacking plant executive. Religion: Episcopalian. Seniority: 16.

Simpson (R)—September 2, 1931. Occupation: lawyer. Religion: Episcopalian. Seniority: 23.

House

(Seniority rank is within the member's party.)

ALABAMA

1 **Callahan (R)**—September 11, 1932. Occupation: moving and storage company executive. Religion: Roman Catholic. Seniority: 132.

2 **Dickinson (R)**—June 5, 1925. Occupation: railroad executive, lawyer, judge. Religion: Methodist. Seniority: 8.

3 **Nichols (D)**—October 16, 1918. Occupation: cotton gin company president, fertilizer manufacturing company executive. Religion: Methodist. Seniority: 33.

4 **Bevill (D)**—March 27, 1921. Occupation: lawyer. Religion: Baptist. Seniority: 33.

5 **Flippo (D)**—August 15, 1937. Occupa-

tion: accountant. Religion: Church of Christ. Seniority: 91.

6 **Erdreich (D)**—December 9, 1938. Occupation: lawyer. Religion: Jewish. Seniority: 166.

7 **Harris (D)**—June 29, 1940. Occupation: lawyer. Religion: Baptist. Seniority: 234.

ALASKA

AL **Young (R)**—June 9, 1933. Occupation: elementary school teacher, riverboat captain. Religion: Episcopalian. Seniority: 34.

ARIZONA

1 **Rhodes (R)**—September 8, 1943. Occupation: lawyer. Religion: Protestant. Seniority: 157.

2 **Udall (D)**—June 15, 1922. Occupation: professional basketball player, lawyer. Religion: Mormon. Seniority: 16.

3 **Stump (R)**—April 4, 1927. Occupation: farmer. Religion: Seventh-day Adventist. Seniority: 43.

4 **Kyl (R)**—April 25, 1942. Occupation: lawyer. Religion: Presbyterian. Seniority: 157.

5 **Kolbe (R)**—June 28, 1942. Occupation: real estate consultant. Religion: Methodist. Seniority: 132.

ARKANSAS

1 **Alexander (D)**—January 16, 1934. Occupation: lawyer. Religion: Episcopalian. Seniority: 37.

2 **Robinson (D)**—March 7, 1942. Occupation: sheriff. Religion: Methodist. Seniority: 221.

3 **Hammerschmidt (R)**—May 4, 1922. Occupation: lumber company executive. Religion: Presbyterian. Seniority: 11.

4 **Anthony (D)**—February 21, 1938. Occupation: lawyer. Religion: Episcopalian. Seniority: 115.

CALIFORNIA

1 **Bosco (D)**—July 28, 1946. Occupation: lawyer. Religion: Roman Catholic. Seniority: 166.

2 **Herger (R)**—May 20, 1945. Occupation: rancher, gas company president. Religion: Mormon. Seniority: 157.

3 **Matsui (D)**—September 17, 1941. Occupation: lawyer. Religion: Methodist. Seniority: 115.

4 **Fazio (D)**—October 11, 1942. Occupation: journalist. Religion: Episcopalian. Seniority: 115.

5 *vacant*

6 **Boxer (D)**—November 11, 1940. Occupation: stockbroker, journalist. Religion: Jewish. Seniority: 166.

7 **Miller (D)**—May 17, 1945. Occupation: lawyer. Religion: Roman Catholic. Seniority: 66.

8 **Dellums (D)**—November 24, 1935. Occupation: psychiatric social worker. Religion: Protestant. Seniority: 48.

9 **Stark (D)**—November 11, 1931. Occupation: banker. Religion: Unitarian. Seniority: 53.

10 **Edwards (D)**—January 6, 1915. Occupation: title company executive, lawyer, FBI agent. Religion: Unitarian. Seniority: 18.

11 **Lantos (D)**—February 1, 1928. Occupation: economics professor. Religion: Jewish. Seniority: 142.

12 **Konnyu (R)**—May 17, 1937. Occupation: public official. Religion: Roman Catholic. Seniority: 157.

13 **Mineta (D)**—November 12, 1931. Occupation: insurance executive. Religion: Methodist. Seniority: 66.

14 **Shumway (R)**—July 28, 1934. Occupation: lawyer. Religion: Mormon. Seniority: 54.

15 **Coelho (D)**—June 15, 1942. Occupation: congressional aide. Religion: Roman Catholic. Seniority: 115.

16 Panetta (D)—June 28, 1938. Occupation: lawyer. Religion: Roman Catholic. Seniority: 91.

17 Pashayan (R)—March 27, 1941. Occupation: lawyer, tire retailer. Religion: Protestant. Seniority: 54.

18 Lehman (D)—July 20, 1948. Occupation: legislative aide. Religion: Lutheran. Seniority: 166.

19 Lagomarsino (R)—September 4, 1926. Occupation: lawyer. Religion: Roman Catholic. Seniority: 35.

20 Thomas (R)—December 6, 1941. Occupation: political science professor. Religion: Baptist. Seniority: 54.

21 Gallegly (R)—March 7, 1944. Occupation: businessman. Religion: Protestant. Seniority: 157.

22 Moorhead (R)—May 6, 1922. Occupation: lawyer. Religion: Presbyterian. Seniority: 26.

23 Beilenson (D)—October 26, 1932. Occupation: lawyer. Religion: Jewish. Seniority: 91.

24 Waxman (D)—September 12, 1939. Occupation: lawyer. Religion: Jewish. Seniority: 66.

25 Roybal (D)—February 10, 1916. Occupation: social worker, public health teacher. Religion: Roman Catholic. Seniority: 18.

26 Berman (D)—April 15, 1941. Occupation: lawyer. Religion: Jewish. Seniority: 166.

27 Levine (D)—June 7, 1943. Occupation: lawyer. Religion: Jewish. Seniority: 166.

28 Dixon (D)—August 8, 1934. Occupation: legislative aide, lawyer. Religion: Episcopalian. Seniority: 115.

29 Hawkins (D)—August 31, 1907. Occupation: real estate salesman. Religion: Methodist. Seniority: 18.

30 Martinez (D)—February 14, 1929. Occupation: upholstery company owner. Religion: Roman Catholic. Seniority: 163.

31 Dymally (D)—May 12, 1926. Occupation: special education teacher, data processing executive. Religion: Episcopalian. Seniority: 142.

32 Anderson (D)—February 21, 1913. Occupation: banker, home builder. Religion: Episcopalian. Seniority: 37.

33 Dreier (R)—July 5, 1952. Occupation: public relations executive. Religion: Christian Scientist. Seniority: 77.

34 Torres (D)—January 27, 1930. Occupation: auto worker, labor official, international trade executive. Religion: unspecified. Seniority: 166.

35 Lewis (R)—October 21, 1934. Occupation: insurance executive. Religion: Presbyterian. Seniority: 54.

36 Brown (D)—March 6, 1920. Occupation: physicist, management consultant. Religion: Methodist. Seniority: 52.

37 McCandless (R)—July 23, 1927. Occupation: automobile dealer. Religion: Protestant. Seniority: 110.

38 Dornan (R)—April 3, 1933. Occupation: broadcast journalist and producer. Religion: Roman Catholic. Seniority: 131.

39 Dannemeyer (R)—September 22, 1929. Occupation: lawyer. Religion: Lutheran. Seniority: 54.

40 Badham (R)—June 9, 1929. Occupation: hardware company executive. Religion: Lutheran. Seniority: 43.

41 Lowery (R)—May 2, 1947. Occupation: public relations executive. Religion: Roman Catholic. Seniority: 77.

42 Lungren (R)—September 22, 1946. Occupation: lawyer. Religion: Roman Catholic. Seniority: 54.

43 Packard (R)—January 19, 1931. Occupation: dentist. Religion: Mormon. Seniority: 110.

44 Bates (D)—July 21, 1941. Occupation: marketing analyst. Religion: Protestant. Seniority: 166.

45 Hunter (R)—May 31, 1948. Occupation: lawyer. Religion: Baptist. Seniority: 77.

COLORADO

1 Schroeder (D)—July 30, 1940. Occupation: lawyer, law instructor. Religion: United Church of Christ. Seniority: 53.

2 Skaggs (D)—February 22, 1943. Occupation: lawyer. Religion: Congregationalist. Seniority: 234.

3 Campbell (D)—April 13, 1933. Occupation: businessman, jewelry designer. Religion: unspecified. Seniority: 234.

4 Brown (R)—February 12, 1940. Occupation: meatpacking company executive, tax accountant, lawyer. Religion: United Church of Christ. Seniority: 77.

5 Hefley (R)—April 18, 1935. Occupation: public official. Religion: Presbyterian. Seniority: 157.

6 Schaefer (R)—January 25, 1936. Occupation: public relations consultant, history teacher. Religion: Roman Catholic. Seniority: 129.

CONNECTICUT

1 Kennelly (D)—July 10, 1936. Occupation: public official. Religion: Roman Catholic. Seniority: 162.

2 Gejdenson (D)—May 20, 1948. Occupation: dairy farmer. Religion: Jewish. Seniority: 142.

3 Morrison (D)—October 8, 1944. Occupation: lawyer. Religion: Lutheran. Seniority: 166.

4 McKinney (R)—January 30, 1931. Occupation: tire retailer. Religion: Episcopalian. Seniority: 19.

5 Rowland (R)—May 24, 1957. Occupation: insurance agent. Religion: Roman Catholic. Seniority: 132.

6 Johnson (R)—January 5, 1935. Occupation: civic leader. Religion: Unitarian. Seniority: 110.

DELAWARE

AL Carper (D)—January 23, 1947. Occupation: public official. Religion: Presbyterian. Seniority: 166.

FLORIDA

1 Hutto (D)—May 12, 1926. Occupation: high school English teacher, advertising and broadcast executive, sportscaster. Religion: Baptist. Seniority: 115.

2 Grant (D)—February 21, 1943. Occupation: public official. Religion: Baptist. Seniority: 234.

3 Bennett (D)—December 2, 1910. Occupation: lawyer. Religion: Disciples of Christ. Seniority: 3.

4 Chappell (D)—February 3, 1922. Occupation: lawyer. Religion: Methodist. Seniority: 37.

5 McCollum (R)—July 12, 1944. Occupation: lawyer. Religion: Episcopalian. Seniority: 77.

6 MacKay (D)—March 22, 1933. Occupation: lawyer, citrus grower. Religion: Presbyterian. Seniority: 166.

7 Gibbons (D)—January 20, 1920. Occupation: lawyer. Religion: Presbyterian. Seniority: 18.

8 Young (R)—December 16, 1930. Occupation: insurance executive. Religion: Methodist. Seniority: 19.

9 Bilirakis (R)—July 16, 1930. Occupation: lawyer, restaurant owner. Religion: Greek Orthodox. Seniority: 110.

10 Ireland (R)—August 23, 1930. Occupation: banker. Religion: Episcopalian. Seniority: 43.

11 Nelson (D)—September 29, 1942. Occupation: lawyer. Religion: Episcopalian. Seniority: 115.

12 Lewis (R)—October 26, 1924. Occupation: real estate broker, aircraft testing specialist. Religion: Methodist. Seniority: 110.

13 **Mack** (R)—October 29, 1940. Occupation: banker. Religion: Roman Catholic. Seniority: 110.

14 **Mica** (D)—February 4, 1944. Occupation: congressional aide. Religion: Roman Catholic. Seniority: 115.

15 **Shaw** (R)—April 19, 1939. Occupation: nurseryman, lawyer, judge. Religion: Roman Catholic. Seniority: 77.

16 **Smith** (D)—April 25, 1941. Occupation: lawyer. Religion: Jewish. Seniority: 166.

17 **Lehman** (D)—October 5, 1913. Occupation: high school English teacher, automobile dealer. Religion: Jewish. Seniority: 53.

18 **Pepper** (D)—September 8, 1900. Occupation: lawyer. Religion: Baptist. Seniority: 18.

19 **Fascell** (D)—March 9, 1917. Occupation: lawyer. Religion: Protestant. Seniority: 8.

GEORGIA

1 **Thomas** (D)—November 20, 1943. Occupation: farmer, investment banker. Religion: Methodist. Seniority: 166.

2 **Hatcher** (D)—July 1, 1939. Occupation: lawyer. Religion: Episcopalian. Seniority: 142.

3 **Ray** (D)—February 2, 1927. Occupation: exterminator, congressional aide. Religion: Methodist. Seniority: 166.

4 **Swindall** (R)—October 18, 1950. Occupation: lawyer, furniture store owner. Religion: Presbyterian. Seniority: 132.

5 **Lewis** (D)—February 19, 1940. Occupation: city councilman. Religion: Baptist. Seniority: 234.

6 **Gingrich** (R)—June 17, 1943. Occupation: history professor. Religion: Baptist. Seniority: 54.

7 **Darden** (D)—November 22, 1943. Occupation: lawyer. Religion: Methodist. Seniority: 217.

8 **Rowland** (D)—February 3, 1926. Occupation: physician. Religion: Methodist. Seniority: 166.

9 **Jenkins** (D)—January 4, 1933. Occupation: lawyer. Religion: Baptist. Seniority: 91.

10 **Barnard** (D)—March 20, 1922. Occupation: banker. Religion: Baptist. Seniority: 91.

HAWAII

1 **Saiki** (R)—May 28, 1930. Occupation: teacher. Religion: Episcopalian. Seniority: 157.

2 **Akaka** (D)—September 11, 1924. Occupation: elementary school teacher, public official. Religion: Congregationalist. Seniority: 91.

IDAHO

1 **Craig** (R)—July 20, 1945. Occupation: real estate salesman, cattle and grain farmer. Religion: Methodist. Seniority: 77.

2 **Stallings** (D)—October 7, 1940. Occupation: history professor. Religion: Mormon. Seniority: 221.

ILLINOIS

1 **Hayes** (D)—February 17, 1918. Occupation: labor official, packinghouse worker. Religion: Baptist. Seniority: 216.

2 **Savage** (D)—October 30, 1925. Occupation: newspaper publisher. Religion: Baptist. Seniority: 142.

3 **Russo** (D)—January 23, 1944. Occupation: lawyer. Religion: Roman Catholic. Seniority: 66.

4 **Davis** (R)—September 6, 1935. Occupation: public official. Religion: Protestant. Seniority: 157.

5 **Lipinski** (D)—December 22, 1937. Occupation: parks supervisor. Reli-

gion: Roman Catholic. Seniority: 166.

6 **Hyde** (**R**)—April 18, 1924. Occupation: lawyer. Religion: Roman Catholic. Seniority: 36.

7 **Collins** (**D**)—September 24, 1931. Occupation: auditor. Religion: Baptist. Seniority: 61.

8 **Rostenkowski** (**D**)—January 2, 1928. Occupation: insurance executive. Religion: Roman Catholic. Seniority: 12.

9 **Yates** (**D**)—August 27, 1909. Occupation: lawyer. Religion: Jewish. Seniority: 24.

10 **Porter** (**R**)—June 1, 1935. Occupation: lawyer. Religion: Presbyterian. Seniority: 75.

11 **Annunzio** (**D**)—January 12, 1915. Occupation: high school industrial arts teacher, labor official. Religion: Roman Catholic. Seniority: 25.

12 **Crane** (**R**)—November 3, 1930. Occupation: American history professor, author. Religion: Methodist. Seniority: 18.

13 **Fawell** (**R**)—March 25, 1929. Occupation: lawyer. Religion: Methodist. Seniority: 132.

14 **Hastert** (**R**)—January 2, 1942. Occupation: teacher. Religion: Protestant. Seniority: 157.

15 **Madigan** (**R**)—January 13, 1936. Occupation: automobile leasing company executive. Religion: Roman Catholic. Seniority: 26.

16 **Martin** (**R**)—December 26, 1939. Occupation: English teacher. Religion: Roman Catholic. Seniority: 77.

17 **Evans** (**D**)—August 4, 1951. Occupation: lawyer. Religion: Roman Catholic. Seniority: 166.

18 **Michel** (**R**)—March 2, 1923. Occupation: congressional aide. Religion: Apostolic Christian. Seniority: 1.

19 **Bruce** (**D**)—March 25, 1944. Occupation: farmer, lawyer. Religion: Methodist. Seniority: 221.

20 **Durbin** (**D**)—November 21, 1944. Occupation: lawyer. Religion: Roman Catholic. Seniority: 166.

21 **Price** (**D**)—January 1, 1905. Occupation: journalist. Religion: Roman Catholic. Seniority: 2.

22 **Gray** (**D**)—November 14, 1924. Occupation: car dealer, auctioneer, public official. Religion: Baptist. Seniority: 220.

INDIANA

1 **Visclosky** (**D**)—August 13, 1949. Occupation: lawyer. Religion: Roman Catholic. Seniority: 221.

2 **Sharp** (**D**)—July 15, 1942. Occupation: political science professor, congressional aide. Religion: Methodist. Seniority: 66.

3 **Hiler** (**R**)—April 24, 1953. Occupation: foundry executive. Religion: Roman Catholic. Seniority: 77.

4 **Coats** (**R**)—May 16, 1943. Occupation: lawyer. Religion: Baptist. Seniority: 77.

5 **Jontz** (**D**)—December 18, 1951. Occupation: public official. Religion: Methodist. Seniority: 234.

6 **Burton** (**R**)—June 21, 1938. Occupation: insurance and real estate agent. Religion: Protestant. Seniority: 110.

7 **Myers** (**R**)—February 8, 1927. Occupation: banker, farmer. Religion: Episcopalian. Seniority: 11.

8 **McCloskey** (**D**)—June 12, 1939. Occupation: lawyer, journalist. Religion: Roman Catholic. Seniority: 166.

9 **Hamilton** (**D**)—April 20, 1931. Occupation: lawyer. Religion: Methodist. Seniority: 25.

10 **Jacobs** (**D**)—February 24, 1932. Occupation: lawyer. Religion: Roman Catholic. Seniority: 64.

IOWA

1 **Leach** (**R**)—October 15, 1942. Occupa-

tion: foreign service officer, propane gas company executive. Religion: Episcopalian. Seniority: 43.

2 **Tauke** (**R**)—October 11, 1950. Occupation: lawyer. Religion: Roman Catholic. Seniority: 54.

3 **Nagle** (**D**)—April 15, 1943. Occupation: lawyer. Religion: Roman Catholic. Seniority: 234.

4 **Smith** (**D**)—March 23, 1920. Occupation: farmer, lawyer. Religion: Methodist. Seniority: 12.

5 **Lightfoot** (**R**)—September 27, 1939. Occupation: radio broadcaster, store owner. Religion: Roman Catholic. Seniority: 132.

6 **Grandy** (**R**)—June 29, 1948. Occupation: entertainer. Religion: Episcopalian. Seniority: 157.

KANSAS

1 **Roberts** (**R**)—April 20, 1936. Occupation: journalist, congressional aide. Religion: Methodist. Seniority: 77.

2 **Slattery** (**D**)—August 4, 1948. Occupation: lawyer, real estate agent. Religion: Roman Catholic. Seniority: 166.

3 **Meyers** (**R**)—July 20, 1928. Occupation: homemaker, public official. Religion: Methodist. Seniority: 132.

4 **Glickman** (**D**)—November 24, 1944. Occupation: lawyer. Religion: Jewish. Seniority: 91.

5 **Whittaker** (**R**)—September 18, 1939. Occupation: optometrist. Religion: Christian Church. Seniority: 54.

KENTUCKY

1 **Hubbard** (**D**)—July 7, 1937. Occupation: lawyer. Religion: Baptist. Seniority: 66.

2 **Natcher** (**D**)—September 11, 1909. Occupation: lawyer. Religion: Baptist. Seniority: 7.

3 **Mazzoli** (**D**)—November 2, 1932. Occupation: lawyer, law professor. Religion: Roman Catholic. Seniority: 48.

4 **Bunning** (**R**)—October 23, 1931. Occupation: investment broker, professional baseball player. Religion: Roman Catholic. Seniority: 157.

5 **Rogers** (**R**)—December 31, 1937. Occupation: lawyer. Religion: Baptist. Seniority: 77.

6 **Hopkins** (**R**)—October 25, 1933. Occupation: stockbroker. Religion: Methodist. Seniority: 54.

7 **Perkins** (**D**)—August 6, 1954. Occupation: lawyer. Religion: Baptist. Seniority: 219.

LOUISIANA

1 **Livingston** (**R**)—April 30, 1943. Occupation: lawyer. Religion: Episcopalian. Seniority: 52.

2 **Boggs** (**D**)—March 13, 1916. Occupation: high school teacher. Religion: Roman Catholic. Seniority: 60.

3 **Tauzin** (**D**)—June 14, 1943. Occupation: lawyer. Religion: Roman Catholic. Seniority: 140.

4 **Roemer** (**D**)—October 4, 1943. Occupation: banker, data processing executive. Religion: Methodist. Seniority: 142.

5 **Huckaby** (**D**)—July 19, 1941. Occupation: farmer, engineer. Religion: Methodist. Seniority: 91.

6 **Baker** (**R**)—May 22, 1948. Occupation: real estate broker. Religion: Methodist. Seniority: 157.

7 **Hayes** (**D**)—December 21, 1946. Occupation: lawyer, developer, businessman. Religion: Methodist. Seniority: 234.

8 **Holloway** (**R**)—November 28, 1943. Occupation: nursery owner. Religion: Baptist. Seniority: 157.

MAINE

1 **Brennan** (**D**)—November 2, 1934. Occu-

pation: governor, lawyer. Religion: Roman Catholic. Seniority: 258.

2 **Snowe** (**R**)—February 21, 1947. Occupation: concrete company executive, public official. Religion: Greek Orthodox. Seniority: 54.

MARYLAND

1 **Dyson** (**D**)—November 15, 1948. Occupation: lumber company executive. Religion: Roman Catholic. Seniority: 142.

2 **Bentley** (**R**)—November 28, 1923. Occupation: journalist, international trade consultant. Religion: Greek Orthodox. Seniority: 132.

3 **Cardin** (**D**)—October 5, 1943. Occupation: lawyer. Religion: Jewish. Seniority: 234.

4 **McMillen** (**D**)—May 26, 1952. Occupation: businessman, professional basketball player. Religion: Roman Catholic. Seniority: 234.

5 **Hoyer** (**D**)—June 14, 1939. Occupation: lawyer. Religion: Baptist. Seniority: 160.

6 **Byron** (**D**)—July 27, 1932. Occupation: civic leader. Religion: Episcopalian. Seniority: 115.

7 **Mfume** (**D**)—October 24, 1948. Occupation: city councilman. Religion: Baptist. Seniority: 234.

8 **Morella** (**R**)—February 12, 1931. Occupation: English literature professor. Religion: Roman Catholic. Seniority: 157.

MASSACHUSETTS

1 **Conte** (**R**)—November 9, 1921. Occupation: lawyer. Religion: Roman Catholic. Seniority: 3.

2 **Boland** (**D**)—October 1, 1911. Occupation: public official. Religion: Roman Catholic. Seniority: 5.

3 **Early** (**D**)—January 31, 1933. Occupation: teacher, basketball coach. Religion: Roman Catholic. Seniority: 66.

4 **Frank** (**D**)—March 31, 1940. Occupation: lawyer. Religion: Jewish. Seniority: 142.

5 **Atkins** (**D**)—April 14, 1948. Occupation: public official. Religion: Unitarian. Seniority: 221.

6 **Mavroules** (**D**)—November 1, 1929. Occupation: personnel supervisor. Religion: Greek Orthodox. Seniority: 115.

7 **Markey** (**D**)—July 11, 1946. Occupation: lawyer. Religion: Roman Catholic. Seniority: 89.

8 **Kennedy** (**D**)—September 24, 1952. Occupation: energy company executive. Religion: Roman Catholic. Seniority: 234.

9 **Moakley** (**D**)—April 27, 1927. Occupation: lawyer. Religion: Roman Catholic. Seniority: 53.

10 **Studds** (**D**)—May 12, 1937. Occupation: high school teacher. Religion: Episcopalian. Seniority: 53.

11 **Donnelly** (**D**)—March 2, 1946. Occupation: high school teacher. Religion: Roman Catholic. Seniority: 115.

MICHIGAN

1 **Conyers** (**D**)—May 16, 1929. Occupation: lawyer. Religion: Baptist. Seniority: 25.

2 **Pursell** (**R**)—December 19, 1932. Occupation: high school teacher, real estate salesman, office supply business owner. Religion: Baptist. Seniority: 43.

3 **Wolpe** (**D**)—November 2, 1939. Occupation: political science professor, congressional aide. Religion: Jewish. Seniority: 115.

4 **Upton** (**R**)—April 23, 1953. Occupation: legislative affairs specialist. Religion: Congregationalist. Seniority: 157.

5 **Henry** (**R**)—July 9, 1942. Occupation: political science professor. Religion:

Christian Reformed. Seniority: 132.

6 **Carr** (**D**)—March 27, 1943. Occupation: lawyer. Religion: Baptist. Seniority: 164.

7 **Kildee** (**D**)—September 16, 1929. Occupation: Latin teacher. Religion: Roman Catholic. Seniority: 91.

8 **Traxler** (**D**)—July 21, 1931. Occupation: lawyer. Religion: Episcopalian. Seniority: 63.

9 **Vander Jagt** (**R**)—August 26, 1931. Occupation: lawyer. Religion: Presbyterian. Seniority: 10.

10 **Schuette** (**R**)—October 13, 1953. Occupation: lawyer. Religion: Episcopalian. Seniority: 132.

11 **Davis** (**R**)—July 31, 1932. Occupation: funeral director. Religion: Episcopalian. Seniority: 54.

12 **Bonior** (**D**)—June 6, 1945. Occupation: probation officer. Religion: Roman Catholic. Seniority: 91.

13 **Crockett** (**D**)—August 10, 1909. Occupation: lawyer, judge. Religion: Baptist. Seniority: 141.

14 **Hertel** (**D**)—December 7, 1948. Occupation: lawyer. Religion: Roman Catholic. Seniority: 142.

15 **Ford** (**D**)—August 6, 1927. Occupation: lawyer. Religion: United Church of Christ. Seniority: 25.

16 **Dingell** (**D**)—July 8, 1926. Occupation: lawyer. Religion: Roman Catholic. Seniority: 10.

17 **Levin** (**D**)—September 6, 1931. Occupation: lawyer. Religion: Jewish. Seniority: 166.

18 **Broomfield** (**R**)—April 28, 1922. Occupation: insurance salesman. Religion: Presbyterian. Seniority: 1.

MINNESOTA

1 **Penny** (**D**)—November 19, 1951. Occupation: sales representative. Religion: Lutheran. Seniority: 166.

2 **Weber** (**R**)—July 24, 1952. Occupation: newspaper publisher. Religion: Roman Catholic. Seniority: 77.

3 **Frenzel** (**R**)—July 31, 1928. Occupation: warehouse company executive. Religion: unspecified. Seniority: 19.

4 **Vento** (**D**)—October 7, 1940. Occupation: science teacher. Religion: Roman Catholic. Seniority: 91.

5 **Sabo** (**D**)—February 28, 1938. Occupation: public official. Religion: Lutheran. Seniority: 115.

6 **Sikorski** (**D**)—April 26, 1948. Occupation: lawyer. Religion: Roman Catholic. Seniority: 166.

7 **Stangeland** (**R**)—February 8, 1930. Occupation: farmer. Religion: Lutheran. Seniority: 51.

8 **Oberstar** (**D**)—September 10, 1934. Occupation: language teacher, congressional aide. Religion: Roman Catholic. Seniority: 66.

MISSISSIPPI

1 **Whitten** (**D**)—April 18, 1910. Occupation: author, lawyer, grammar school teacher and principal. Religion: Presbyterian. Seniority: 1.

2 **Espy** (**D**)—November 28, 1953. Occupation: lawyer, businessman. Religion: Baptist. Seniority: 234.

3 **Montgomery** (**D**)—August 5, 1920. Occupation: insurance executive. Religion: Episcopalian. Seniority: 33.

4 **Dowdy** (**D**)—July 27, 1943. Occupation: broadcasting executive, lawyer. Religion: Methodist. Seniority: 161.

5 **Lott** (**R**)—October 9, 1941. Occupation: lawyer. Religion: Baptist. Seniority: 26.

MISSOURI

1 **Clay** (**D**)—April 30, 1931. Occupation: real estate salesman, insurance company executive. Religion: Roman Catholic. Seniority: 37.

2 **Buechner** (**R**)—June 6, 1940. Occupation: lawyer, real estate developer. Religion: Roman Catholic. Seniority: 157.

3 **Gephardt** (**D**)—January 31, 1941. Occupation: lawyer. Religion: Baptist. Seniority: 91.

4 **Skelton** (**D**)—December 20, 1931. Occupation: lawyer. Religion: Christian Church. Seniority: 91.

5 **Wheat** (**D**)—October 16, 1951. Occupation: public official. Religion: Church of Christ. Seniority: 166.

6 **Coleman** (**R**)—May 29, 1943. Occupation: lawyer. Religion: Protestant. Seniority: 42.

7 **Taylor** (**R**)—February 10, 1928. Occupation: automobile dealer. Religion: Methodist. Seniority: 26.

8 **Emerson** (**R**)—January 1, 1938. Occupation: government relations executive. Religion: Presbyterian. Seniority: 77.

9 **Volkmer** (**D**)—April 4, 1931. Occupation: lawyer. Religion: Roman Catholic. Seniority: 91.

MONTANA

1 **Williams** (**D**)—October 30, 1937. Occupation: elementary and secondary school teacher. Religion: Roman Catholic. Seniority: 115.

2 **Marlenee** (**R**)—August 8, 1935. Occupation: rancher. Religion: Lutheran. Seniority: 43.

NEBRASKA

1 **Bereuter** (**R**)—October 6, 1939. Occupation: city planner. Religion: Lutheran. Seniority: 54.

2 **Daub** (**R**)—April 23, 1941. Occupation: lawyer, feed company executive. Religion: Presbyterian. Seniority: 77.

3 **Smith** (**R**)—June 30, 1911. Occupation: farmer. Religion: Methodist. Seniority: 36.

NEVADA

1 **Bilbray** (**D**)—May 19, 1938. Occupation: lawyer. Religion: Roman Catholic. Seniority: 234.

2 **Vucanovich** (**R**)—June 22, 1921. Occupation: travel agent, congressional aide. Religion: Roman Catholic. Seniority: 110.

NEW HAMPSHIRE

1 **Smith** (**R**)—March 30, 1941. Occupation: real estate broker. Religion: Congregationalist. Seniority: 132.

2 **Gregg** (**R**)—February 14, 1947. Occupation: lawyer. Religion: Protestant. Seniority: 77.

NEW JERSEY

1 **Florio** (**D**)—August 29, 1937. Occupation: lawyer. Religion: Roman Catholic. Seniority: 66.

2 **Hughes** (**D**)—October 17, 1932. Occupation: lawyer. Religion: Episcopalian. Seniority: 66.

3 **Howard** (**D**)—July 24, 1927. Occupation: elementary school teacher, principal. Religion: Roman Catholic. Seniority: 25.

4 **Smith** (**R**)—March 4, 1953. Occupation: sporting goods wholesaler. Religion: Roman Catholic. Seniority: 77.

5 **Roukema** (**R**)—September 19, 1929. Occupation: high school history and government teacher. Religion: Protestant. Seniority: 77.

6 **Dwyer** (**D**)—January 24, 1921. Occupation: insurance salesman and executive. Religion: Roman Catholic. Seniority: 142.

7 **Rinaldo** (**R**)—September 1, 1931. Occupation: industrial relations consultant. Religion: Roman Catholic. Seniority: 26.

8 **Roe** (**D**)—February 28, 1924. Occupation: construction company owner, engineer. Religion: Roman Catholic. Se-

niority: 47.

9 Torricelli (D)—August 26, 1951. Occupation: lawyer. Religion: Methodist. Seniority: 166.

10 Rodino (D)—June 7, 1909. Occupation: lawyer. Religion: Roman Catholic. Seniority: 3.

11 Gallo (R)—November 23, 1935. Occupation: real estate broker. Religion: Methodist. Seniority: 132.

12 Courter (R)—October 14, 1941. Occupation: lawyer. Religion: Methodist. Seniority: 54.

13 Saxton (R)—January 22, 1943. Occupation: realty company owner. Religion: Methodist. Seniority: 130.

14 Guarini (D)—August 20, 1924. Occupation: lawyer. Religion: Roman Catholic. Seniority: 115.

NEW MEXICO

1 Lujan (R)—May 12, 1928. Occupation: insurance broker. Religion: Roman Catholic. Seniority: 15.

2 Skeen (R)—June 30, 1927. Occupation: rancher. Religion: Roman Catholic. Seniority: 77.

3 Richardson (D)—November 15, 1947. Occupation: business consultant. Religion: Roman Catholic. Seniority: 166.

NEW YORK

1 Hochbrueckner (D)—September 20, 1938. Occupation: electronics engineer. Religion: Roman Catholic. Seniority: 234.

2 Downey (D)—January 28, 1949. Occupation: personnel manager. Religion: Methodist. Seniority: 66.

3 Mrazek (D)—November 6, 1945. Occupation: congressional aide. Religion: Methodist. Seniority: 166.

4 Lent (R)—March 23, 1931. Occupation: lawyer. Religion: Methodist. Seniority: 19.

5 McGrath (R)—March 27, 1942. Occupation: physical education teacher, public official. Religion: Roman Catholic. Seniority: 77.

6 Flake (D)—January 30, 1945. Occupation: clergyman. Religion: African Methodist Episcopal Zion. Seniority: 234.

7 Ackerman (D)—November 19, 1942. Occupation: advertising executive, newspaper publisher and editor, social studies teacher. Religion: Jewish. Seniority: 214.

8 Scheuer (D)—February 6, 1920. Occupation: lawyer. Religion: Jewish. Seniority: 64.

9 Manton (D)—November 3, 1932. Occupation: lawyer. Religion: Roman Catholic. Seniority: 221.

10 Schumer (D)—November 23, 1950. Occupation: lawyer. Religion: Jewish. Seniority: 142.

11 Towns (D)—July 21, 1934. Occupation: social worker, teacher. Religion: Protestant. Seniority: 166.

12 Owens (D)—June 28, 1936. Occupation: librarian. Religion: Baptist. Seniority: 166.

13 Solarz (D)—September 12, 1940. Occupation: public official. Religion: Jewish. Seniority: 66.

14 Molinari (R)—November 23, 1928. Occupation: lawyer. Religion: Roman Catholic. Seniority: 77.

15 Green (R)—October 16, 1929. Occupation: lawyer. Religion: Jewish. Seniority: 53.

16 Rangel (D)—June 11, 1930. Occupation: lawyer. Religion: Roman Catholic. Seniority: 48.

17 Weiss (D)—September 17, 1927. Occupation: lawyer. Religion: Jewish. Seniority: 91.

18 Garcia (D)—January 9, 1933. Occupation: computer engineer. Religion: Pentecostal. Seniority: 114.

19 Biaggi (D)—October 26, 1917. Occupation: lawyer, police detective. Religion: Roman Catholic. Seniority: 37.

20 DioGuardi (R)—September 20, 1940. Occupation: accountant. Religion: Roman Catholic. Seniority: 132.

21 Fish (R)—June 3, 1926. Occupation: lawyer. Religion: Episcopalian. Seniority: 15.

22 Gilman (R)—December 6, 1922. Occupation: lawyer. Religion: Jewish. Seniority: 26.

23 Stratton (D)—September 27, 1916. Occupation: broadcast journalist, college instructor. Religion: Presbyterian. Seniority: 12.

24 Solomon (R)—August 14, 1930. Occupation: insurance salesman. Religion: Presbyterian. Seniority: 54.

25 Boehlert (R)—September 28, 1936. Occupation: congressional aide. Religion: Roman Catholic. Seniority: 110.

26 Martin (R)—April 26, 1944. Occupation: lawyer. Religion: Roman Catholic. Seniority: 77.

27 Wortley (R)—December 8, 1926. Occupation: newspaper publisher. Religion: Roman Catholic. Seniority: 77.

28 McHugh (D)—December 6, 1938. Occupation: lawyer. Religion: Roman Catholic. Seniority: 66.

29 Horton (R)—December 12, 1919. Occupation: lawyer. Religion: Presbyterian. Seniority: 5.

30 Slaughter (D)—August 14, 1929. Occupation: public official. Religion: Episcopalian. Seniority: 234.

31 Kemp (R)—July 13, 1935. Occupation: professional football player. Religion: Presbyterian. Seniority: 19.

32 LaFalce (D)—October 6, 1939. Occupation: lawyer. Religion: Roman Catholic. Seniority: 66.

33 Nowak (D)—February 21, 1935. Occupation: lawyer. Religion: Roman Catholic. Seniority: 66.

34 Houghton (R)—August 7, 1926. Occupation: glassworks company executive. Religion: Episcopalian. Seniority: 157.

NORTH CAROLINA

1 Jones (D)—August 19, 1913. Occupation: office supply company executive. Religion: Baptist. Seniority: 32.

2 Valentine (D)—March 15, 1926. Occupation: lawyer. Religion: Baptist. Seniority: 166.

3 Lancaster (D)—March 24, 1943. Occupation: lawyer. Religion: Presbyterian. Seniority: 234.

4 Price (D)—August 17, 1940. Occupation: educator. Religion: Baptist. Seniority: 234.

5 Neal (D)—November 7, 1934. Occupation: newspaper publisher, mortgage banker. Religion: Presbyterian. Seniority: 66.

6 Coble (R)—March 18, 1931. Occupation: lawyer. Religion: Presbyterian. Seniority: 132.

7 Rose (D)—August 10, 1939. Occupation: lawyer. Religion: Presbyterian. Seniority: 53.

8 Hefner (D)—April 11, 1930. Occupation: broadcasting executive. Religion: Baptist. Seniority: 66.

9 McMillan (R)—May 9, 1932. Occupation: food store executive. Religion: Presbyterian. Seniority: 132.

10 Ballenger (R)—December 6, 1926. Occupation: president of plastics packaging company. Religion: Episcopalian. Seniority: 155.

11 Clarke (D)—June 12, 1917. Occupation: farmer. Religion: Presbyterian. Seniority: 232.

NORTH DAKOTA

AL Dorgan (D)—May 14, 1942. Occupation: public official. Religion: Lutheran. Seniority: 142.

OHIO

1 Luken (D)—July 9, 1925. Occupation:

lawyer. Religion: Roman Catholic. Seniority: 90.

2 Gradison (R)—December 28, 1928. Occupation: investment broker. Religion: Jewish. Seniority: 36.

3 Hall (D)—January 16, 1942. Occupation: real estate salesman. Religion: Christian. Seniority: 115.

4 Oxley (R)—February 11, 1944. Occupation: FBI agent, lawyer. Religion: Lutheran. Seniority: 109.

5 Latta (R)—March 5, 1920. Occupation: lawyer. Religion: Church of Christ. Seniority: 3.

6 McEwen (R)—January 12, 1950. Occupation: real estate developer. Religion: Protestant. Seniority: 77.

7 DeWine (R)—January 5, 1947. Occupation: lawyer. Religion: Roman Catholic. Seniority: 110.

8 Lukens (R)—February 11, 1931. Occupation: business consultant. Religion: Lutheran. Seniority: 156.

9 Kaptur (D)—June 17, 1946. Occupation: urban planner. Religion: Roman Catholic. Seniority: 166.

10 Miller (R)—November 1, 1917. Occupation: electrical engineer. Religion: Methodist. Seniority: 11.

11 Eckart (D)—April 6, 1950. Occupation: lawyer. Religion: Roman Catholic. Seniority: 142.

12 Kasich (R)—May 13, 1952. Occupation: legislative aide. Religion: Roman Catholic. Seniority: 110.

13 Pease (D)—September 26, 1931. Occupation: newspaper editor. Religion: Methodist. Seniority: 91.

14 Sawyer (D)—August 15, 1945. Occupation: public official. Religion: Presbyterian. Seniority: 234.

15 Wylie (R)—November 23, 1920. Occupation: lawyer. Religion: Methodist. Seniority: 11.

16 Regula (R)—December 3, 1924. Occupation: lawyer. Religion: Episcopalian. Seniority: 26.

17 Traficant (D)—May 8, 1941. Occupation: county sheriff. Religion: Roman Catholic. Seniority: 221.

18 Applegate (D)—March 27, 1928. Occupation: real estate salesman. Religion: Presbyterian. Seniority: 91.

19 Feighan (D)—October 22, 1947. Occupation: lawyer. Religion: Roman Catholic. Seniority: 166.

20 Oakar (D)—March 5, 1940. Occupation: high school English and drama teacher. Religion: Roman Catholic. Seniority: 91.

21 Stokes (D)—February 23, 1925. Occupation: lawyer. Religion: African Methodist Episcopal Zion. Seniority: 37.

OKLAHOMA

1 Inhofe (R)—November 17, 1934. Occupation: real estate developer. Religion: Presbyterian. Seniority: 157.

2 Synar (D)—October 17, 1950. Occupation: lawyer, rancher, real estate broker. Religion: Episcopalian. Seniority: 115.

3 Watkins (D)—December 15, 1938. Occupation: real estate salesman, home builder. Religion: Presbyterian. Seniority: 91.

4 McCurdy (D)—March 30, 1950. Occupation: lawyer. Religion: Lutheran. Seniority: 142.

5 Edwards (R)—July 12, 1937. Occupation: journalist, lawyer. Religion: Episcopalian. Seniority: 43.

6 English (D)—November 30, 1940. Occupation: petroleum landman. Religion: Methodist. Seniority: 66.

OREGON

1 AuCoin (D)—October 21, 1942. Occupation: journalist, public relations executive. Religion: Protestant. Seniority: 66.

2 **Smith, Robert F.** (**R**)—June 16, 1931. Occupation: cattle rancher. Religion: Presbyterian. Seniority: 110.

3 **Wyden** (**D**)—May 3, 1949. Occupation: lawyer. Religion: Jewish. Seniority: 142.

4 **DeFazio** (**D**)—May 27, 1947. Occupation: county commissioner. Religion: Roman Catholic. Seniority: 234.

5 **Smith, Denny** (**R**)—January 19, 1938. Occupation: newspaper publisher, airline pilot. Religion: Protestant. Seniority: 77.

PENNSYLVANIA

1 **Foglietta** (**D**)—December 3, 1928. Occupation: lawyer. Religion: Roman Catholic. Seniority: 142.

2 **Gray** (**D**)—August 20, 1941. Occupation: clergyman. Religion: Baptist. Seniority: 115.

3 **Borski** (**D**)—October 20, 1948. Occupation: stockbroker. Religion: Roman Catholic. Seniority: 166.

4 **Kolter** (**D**)—September 3, 1926. Occupation: accountant. Religion: Roman Catholic. Seniority: 166.

5 **Schulze** (**R**)—August 7, 1929. Occupation: household appliance dealer. Religion: Presbyterian. Seniority: 36.

6 **Yatron** (**D**)—October 16, 1927. Occupation: professional boxer, ice cream manufacturer. Religion: Greek Orthodox. Seniority: 37.

7 **Weldon** (**R**)—July 22, 1947. Occupation: chairman, Delaware County Council. Religion: Protestant. Seniority: 157.

8 **Kostmayer** (**D**)—September 27, 1946. Occupation: public relations consultant. Religion: Episcopalian. Seniority: 165.

9 **Shuster** (**R**)—January 23, 1932. Occupation: corporate executive. Religion: United Church of Christ. Seniority: 26.

10 **McDade** (**R**)—September 29, 1931. Occupation: lawyer. Religion: Roman Catholic. Seniority: 5.

11 **Kanjorski** (**D**)—April 2, 1937. Occupation: lawyer. Religion: Roman Catholic. Seniority: 221.

12 **Murtha** (**D**)—June 17, 1932. Occupation: car wash operator. Religion: Roman Catholic. Seniority: 62.

13 **Coughlin** (**R**)—April 11, 1929. Occupation: lawyer. Religion: Episcopalian. Seniority: 15.

14 **Coyne** (**D**)—August 24, 1936. Occupation: accountant. Religion: Roman Catholic. Seniority: 142.

15 **Ritter** (**R**)—October 21, 1940. Occupation: engineering consultant, professor. Religion: Unitarian. Seniority: 54.

16 **Walker** (**R**)—December 23, 1942. Occupation: high school teacher, congressional aide. Religion: Presbyterian. Seniority: 43.

17 **Gekas** (**R**)—April 14, 1930. Occupation: lawyer. Religion: Greek Orthodox. Seniority: 110.

18 **Walgren** (**D**)—December 28, 1940. Occupation: lawyer. Religion: Roman Catholic. Seniority: 91.

19 **Goodling** (**R**)—December 5, 1927. Occupation: public school superintendent. Religion: Methodist. Seniority: 36.

20 **Gaydos** (**D**)—July 3, 1926. Occupation: lawyer. Religion: Roman Catholic. Seniority: 36.

21 **Ridge** (**R**)—August 26, 1945. Occupation: lawyer. Religion: Roman Catholic. Seniority: 110.

22 **Murphy** (**D**)—June 17, 1927. Occupation: lawyer. Religion: Roman Catholic. Seniority: 91.

23 **Clinger** (**R**)—April 4, 1929. Occupation: lawyer. Religion: Presbyterian. Seniority: 54.

RHODE ISLAND

1 **St Germain** (**D**)—January 9, 1928. Occupation: lawyer. Religion: Roman

Catholic. Seniority: 15.

2 **Schneider** (R)—March 25, 1947. Occupation: television producer and moderator. Religion: Roman Catholic. Seniority: 77.

SOUTH CAROLINA

1 **Ravenel** (R)—March 29, 1927. Occupation: businessman. Religion: Protestant. Seniority: 157.

2 **Spence** (R)—April 9, 1928. Occupation: lawyer. Religion: Lutheran. Seniority: 19.

3 **Derrick** (D)—September 30, 1936. Occupation: lawyer. Religion: Episcopalian. Seniority: 66.

4 **Patterson** (D)—November 18, 1939. Occupation: public official, homemaker. Religion: Methodist. Seniority: 234.

5 **Spratt** (D)—November 1, 1942. Occupation: lawyer, insurance executive. Religion: Presbyterian. Seniority: 166.

6 **Tallon** (D)—August 8, 1946. Occupation: clothing store owner. Religion: Methodist. Seniority: 166.

SOUTH DAKOTA

AL **Johnson** (D)—December 28, 1946. Occupation: lawyer. Religion: Lutheran. Seniority: 234.

TENNESSEE

1 **Quillen** (R)—January 11, 1916. Occupation: newspaper publisher, real estate and insurance salesman, banker. Religion: Methodist. Seniority: 5.

2 **Duncan** (R)—March 24, 1919. Occupation: lawyer. Religion: Presbyterian. Seniority: 8.

3 **Lloyd** (D)—January 3, 1929. Occupation: radio station owner and manager. Religion: Church of Christ. Seniority: 66.

4 **Cooper** (D)—June 19, 1954. Occupation: lawyer. Religion: Episcopalian. Seniority: 166.

5 **Boner** (D)—February 14, 1945. Occupation: high school and college teacher and coach, banker, lawyer. Religion: Methodist. Seniority: 115.

6 **Gordon** (D)—January 24, 1949. Occupation: lawyer. Religion: Methodist. Seniority: 221.

7 **Sundquist** (R)—March 15, 1936. Occupation: printing, advertising, and marketing firm owner. Religion: Lutheran. Seniority: 110.

8 **Jones** (D)—April 20, 1912. Occupation: dairy farmer, agricultural official. Religion: Presbyterian. Seniority: 45.

9 **Ford** (D)—May 20, 1945. Occupation: mortician. Religion: Baptist. Seniority: 66.

TEXAS

1 **Chapman** (D)—March 8, 1945. Occupation: lawyer. Religion: Methodist. Seniority: 231.

2 **Wilson** (D)—June 1, 1933. Occupation: lumberyard manager. Religion: Methodist. Seniority: 53.

3 **Bartlett** (R)—September 19, 1947. Occupation: tool and plastics company owner. Religion: Presbyterian. Seniority: 110.

4 **Hall** (D)—May 3, 1923. Occupation: businessman, banker, lawyer, judge. Religion: Methodist. Seniority: 142.

5 **Bryant** (D)—February 22, 1947. Occupation: lawyer. Religion: Methodist. Seniority: 166.

6 **Barton** (R)—September 15, 1949. Occupation: engineering consultant. Religion: Methodist. Seniority: 132.

7 **Archer** (R)—March 22, 1928. Occupation: lawyer, feed company executive. Religion: Roman Catholic. Seniority: 19.

8 **Fields** (R)—February 3, 1952. Occupation: lawyer, cemetery executive. Religion: Baptist. Seniority: 77.

9 **Brooks (D)**—December 18, 1922. Occupation: lawyer. Religion: Methodist. Seniority: 5.

10 **Pickle (D)**—October 11, 1913. Occupation: public relations and advertising executive. Religion: Methodist. Seniority: 23.

11 **Leath (D)**—May 6, 1931. Occupation: banker. Religion: Presbyterian. Seniority: 115.

12 **Wright (D)**—December 22, 1922. Occupation: advertising executive. Religion: Presbyterian. Seniority: 8.

13 **Boulter (R)**—February 23, 1942. Occupation: lawyer. Religion: Independent Bible Church. Seniority: 132.

14 **Sweeney (R)**—September 15, 1955. Occupation: congressional aide, White House personnel administrator. Religion: Methodist. Seniority: 132.

15 **de la Garza (D)**—September 22, 1927. Occupation: lawyer. Religion: Roman Catholic. Seniority: 25.

16 **Coleman (D)**—November 29, 1941. Occupation: lawyer. Religion: Presbyterian. Seniority: 166.

17 **Stenholm (D)**—October 26, 1938. Occupation: cotton grower. Religion: Lutheran. Seniority: 115.

18 **Leland (D)**—November 27, 1944. Occupation: pharmacist. Religion: Roman Catholic. Seniority: 115.

19 **Combest (R)**—March 20, 1945. Occupation: wholesale distributor. Religion: Methodist. Seniority: 132.

20 **Gonzalez (D)**—May 3, 1916. Occupation: lawyer, business consultant, translator. Religion: Roman Catholic. Seniority: 17.

21 **Smith (R)**—November 19, 1947. Occupation: rancher, lawyer. Religion: Christian Scientist. Seniority: 157.

22 **DeLay (R)**—April 8, 1947. Occupation: pest control company owner. Religion: Baptist. Seniority: 132.

23 **Bustamante (D)**—April 8, 1935. Occupation: teacher, judge. Religion: Roman Catholic. Seniority: 221.

24 **Frost (D)**—January 1, 1942. Occupation: lawyer. Religion: Jewish. Seniority: 115.

25 **Andrews (D)**—February 7, 1944. Occupation: lawyer. Religion: Methodist. Seniority: 166.

26 **Armey (R)**—July 7, 1940. Occupation: economics professor. Religion: Presbyterian. Seniority: 132.

27 **Ortiz (D)**—June 3, 1937. Occupation: law enforcement official. Religion: Methodist. Seniority: 166.

UTAH

1 **Hansen (R)**—August 14, 1932. Occupation: insurance executive, land developer. Religion: Mormon. Seniority: 77.

2 **Owens (D)**—May 2, 1937. Occupation: lawyer. Religion: Mormon. Seniority: 232.

3 **Nielson (R)**—September 12, 1924. Occupation: statistics professor. Religion: Mormon. Seniority: 110.

VERMONT

AL **Jeffords (R)**—May 11, 1934. Occupation: lawyer. Religion: Congregationalist. Seniority: 36.

VIRGINIA

1 **Bateman (R)**—August 7, 1928. Occupation: lawyer. Religion: Presbyterian. Seniority: 110.

2 **Pickett (D)**—August 31, 1930. Occupation: lawyer. Religion: Baptist. Seniority: 234.

3 **Bliley (R)**—January 28, 1932. Occupation: funeral director. Religion: Roman Catholic. Seniority: 77.

4 **Sisisky (D)**—June 9, 1927. Occupation: beer and soft drink distributor. Religion: Jewish. Seniority: 166.

5 **Daniel (D)**—May 12, 1914. Occupation:

textile company executive. Religion: Baptist. Seniority: 37.

6 **Olin** (**D**)—February 28, 1920. Occupation: electronics company executive. Religion: Unitarian. Seniority: 166.

7 **Slaughter** (**R**)—May 20, 1925. Occupation: lawyer. Religion: Episcopalian. Seniority: 132.

8 **Parris** (**R**)—September 9, 1929. Occupation: automobile dealer, commercial pilot, banker, lawyer. Religion: Episcopalian. Seniority: 76.

9 **Boucher** (**D**)—August 1, 1946. Occupation: lawyer. Religion: Methodist. Seniority: 166.

10 **Wolf** (**R**)—January 30, 1939. Occupation: lawyer. Religion: Presbyterian. Seniority: 77.

WASHINGTON

1 **Miller** (**R**)—May 23, 1938. Occupation: lawyer. Religion: Jewish. Seniority: 132.

2 **Swift** (**D**)—September 12, 1935. Occupation: broadcaster, television news and public affairs director. Religion: Unitarian. Seniority: 115.

3 **Bonker** (**D**)—March 7, 1937. Occupation: auditor. Religion: Presbyterian. Seniority: 66.

4 **Morrison** (**R**)—May 13, 1933. Occupation: fruit grower, nurseryman. Religion: Methodist. Seniority: 77.

5 **Foley** (**D**)—March 6, 1929. Occupation: lawyer. Religion: Roman Catholic. Seniority: 25.

6 **Dicks** (**D**)—December 16, 1940. Occupation: lawyer, congressional aide. Religion: Lutheran. Seniority: 91.

7 **Lowry** (**D**)—March 8, 1939. Occupation: public official. Religion: Baptist. Seniority: 115.

8 **Chandler** (**R**)—July 13, 1942. Occupation: public relations consultant, television newsman. Religion: Protestant. Seniority: 110.

WEST VIRGINIA

1 **Mollohan** (**D**)—May 14, 1943. Occupation: lawyer. Religion: Baptist. Seniority: 166.

2 **Staggers** (**D**)—February 22, 1951. Occupation: lawyer. Religion: Roman Catholic. Seniority: 166.

3 **Wise** (**D**)—January 6, 1948. Occupation: lawyer. Religion: Episcopalian. Seniority: 166.

4 **Rahall** (**D**)—May 20, 1949. Occupation: broadcasting executive, travel agent. Religion: Presbyterian. Seniority: 91.

WISCONSIN

1 **Aspin** (**D**)—July 21, 1938. Occupation: economics professor. Religion: Episcopalian. Seniority: 48.

2 **Kastenmeier** (**D**)—January 24, 1924. Occupation: lawyer. Religion: unspecified. Seniority: 11.

3 **Gunderson** (**R**)—May 10, 1951. Occupation: public official. Religion: Lutheran. Seniority: 77.

4 **Kleczka** (**D**)—November 26, 1943. Occupation: accountant. Religion: Roman Catholic. Seniority: 218.

5 **Moody** (**D**)—September 2, 1935. Occupation: economist. Religion: Protestant. Seniority: 166.

6 **Petri** (**R**)—May 28, 1940. Occupation: lawyer. Religion: Lutheran. Seniority: 74.

7 **Obey** (**D**)—October 3, 1938. Occupation: real estate broker. Religion: Roman Catholic. Seniority: 46.

8 **Roth** (**R**)—October 10, 1938. Occupation: real estate broker. Religion: Roman Catholic. Seniority: 54.

9 **Sensenbrenner** (**R**)—June 14, 1943. Occupation: lawyer. Religion: Episcopalian. Seniority: 54.

WYOMING

AL **Cheney** (**R**)—January 30, 1941. Occupation: financial consultant. Religion: Methodist. Seniority: 54.

Appendix B

Seniority in the 100th Congress

Senate Seniority

Senate rank generally is determined according to the official date of the beginning of a member's service, except in the case of new members sworn in at times other than the beginning of a Congress. For those appointed or elected to fill unexpired terms, the date of the appointment, certification, or swearing-in determines the senator's rank.

When members are sworn in on the same day, custom decrees that those with prior political experience take precedence. Counted as political experience, in order of importance, is senatorial, House, and gubernatorial service. Information on prior experience is given where applicable to seniority ranking. The dates following senators' names refer to the beginning of their present service.

DEMOCRATS

1. Stennis—November 5, 1947
2. Proxmire—August 28, 1957
3. Byrd—January 3, 1959
4. Burdick—August 8, 1960
5. Pell—January 3, 1961
6. Kennedy—November 7, 1962
7. Inouye—January 3, 1963
8. Hollings—November 9, 1966
9. Cranston—January 3, 1969
10. Bentsen (ex-representative)—January 3, 1971
11. Chiles—January 3, 1971
12. Nunn—November 8, 1972
13. Johnston—November 14, 1972
14. Biden—January 3, 1973
15. Glenn—December 24, 1974
16. Ford—December 28, 1974
17. Bumpers (ex-governor)—January 3, 1975
18. Leahy—January 3, 1975
19. Metzenbaum—December 29, 1976
20. Riegle—December 30, 1976
21. Matsunaga (ex-representative, seven House terms)—January 3, 1977
22. Melcher (ex-representative, three and one-half House terms)—January 3, 1977
23. Sarbanes (ex-representative, three House terms)—January 3, 1977
24. DeConcini—January 3, 1977
    Moynihan—January 3, 1977
    Sasser—January 3, 1977
27. Baucus—December 15, 1978
28. Pryor (ex-representative)—January 3, 1979
29. Boren (ex-governor)—January 3, 1979
    Exon (ex-governor)—January 3, 1979

31. Bradley—January 3, 1979
    Heflin—January 3, 1979
    Levin—January 3, 1979
34. Mitchell—May 19, 1980
35. Dodd (ex-representative)—January 3, 1981
36. Dixon—January 3, 1981
37. Lautenberg—December 27, 1982
38. Bingaman—January 3, 1983
39. Kerry—January 2, 1985
40. Harkin (ex-representative, five House terms)—January 3, 1985
    Simon (ex-representative, five House terms)—January 3, 1985
42. Gore (ex-representative, four House terms)—January 3, 1985
43. Rockefeller—January 15, 1985
44. Sanford—November 5, 1986
45. Breaux (ex-representative, seven House terms)—January 6, 1987
46. Adams (ex-representative, six House terms)—January 6, 1987
    Wirth (ex-representative, six House terms)—January 6, 1987
48. Fowler (ex-representative, five House terms)—January 6, 1987
    Mikulski (ex-representative, five House terms)—January 6, 1987
50. Daschle (ex-representative, four House terms)—January 6, 1987
    Shelby (ex-representative, four House terms)—January 6, 1987
52. Reid (ex-representative, two House terms)—January 6, 1987
53. Graham (ex-governor)—January 6, 1987
54. Conrad—January 6, 1987

REPUBLICANS

1. Thurmond—November 7, 1956*
2. Hatfield—January 10, 1967
3. Stevens—December 24, 1968
4. Dole (ex-representative)—January 3, 1969
5. Packwood—January 3, 1969
6. Roth—January 1, 1971
7. Weicker—January 3, 1971
8. Stafford—September 16, 1971
9. McClure (ex-representative)—January 3, 1973
10. Helms—January 3, 1973
    Domenici—January 3, 1973
12. Garn—December 21, 1974
13. Danforth—December 27, 1976
14. Chafee—December 29, 1976
15. Heinz (ex-representative)—January 3, 1977
16. Hatch—January 3, 1977
    Lugar—January 3, 1977
    Wallop—January 3, 1977
19. Durenberger—November 8, 1978
20. Kassebaum—December 23, 1978
21. Cochran—December 27, 1978
22. Boschwitz—December 30, 1978
23. Simpson—January 1, 1979
24. Warner—January 2, 1979
25. Armstrong (ex-representative, three House terms)—January 3, 1979
    Cohen (ex-representative, three House terms)—January 3, 1979
27. Pressler (ex-representative, two House terms)—January 3, 1979
28. Humphrey—January 3, 1979
29. Rudman—December 29, 1980
30. Symms (ex-representative, four House terms)—January 3, 1981
31. Grassley (ex-representative, three House terms)—January 3, 1981
32. Kasten (ex-representative, two House terms)—January 3, 1981
    Quayle (ex-representative, two House terms)—January 3, 1981
34. D'Amato—January 3, 1981
    Murkowski—January 3, 1981
    Nickles—January 3, 1981
    Specter—January 3, 1981
38. Trible (ex-representative)—January 3, 1983
39. Hecht—January 3, 1983
    Wilson—January 3, 1983
41. Evans—September 12, 1983

42. Gramm (ex-representative)—January 3, 1985
43. McConnell—January 3, 1985
44. McCain (ex-representative)—January 6, 1987
45. Bond (ex-governor)—January 6, 1987
46. Karnes—March 13, 1987

** Thurmond began his Senate service November 7, 1956, as a Democrat. He became a Republican September 16, 1964. The Republican Conference allowed his seniority to count from his 1956 election to the Senate.*

House Seniority

House rank generally is determined according to the official date of the beginning of a member's service, except in the case of members elected to fill vacancies, in which instance the date of election determines rank.

When members enter the House on the same day, those with prior House experience take precedence, starting with those with the longest consecutive service. Experience as a senator or governor is disregarded. Prior experience is given where applicable to seniority ranking. The dates following members' names refer to the beginning of their present service.

DEMOCRATS

1. Whitten (Miss.)—November 4, 1941
2. Price (Ill.)—January 3, 1945
3. Bennett (Fla.)—January 3, 1949
   Rodino (N.J.)—January 3, 1949
5. Boland (Mass.)—January 3, 1953
   Brooks (Texas)—January 3, 1953
7. Natcher (Ky.)—August 1, 1953
8. Fascell (Fla.)—January 3, 1955
   Wright (Texas)—January 3, 1955
10. Dingell (Mich.)—December 13, 1955
11. Kastenmeier (Wis.)—December 13, 1959
12. Rostenkowski (Ill.)—January 3, 1959
    Smith (Iowa)—January 3, 1959
    Stratton (N.Y.)—January 3, 1959
15. St Germain (R.I.)—January 3, 1961
16. Udall (Ariz.)—May 2, 1961
17. Gonzalez (Texas)—November 4, 1961
18. Edwards (Calif.)—January 3, 1963
    Gibbons (Fla.)—January 3, 1963
    Hawkins (Calif.)—January 3, 1963
    Pepper (Fla.)—January 3, 1963
    Roybal (Calif.)—January 3, 1963
23. Pickle (Texas)—December 21, 1963
24. Yates (Ill.) (seven terms previously)—January 3, 1965
25. Annunzio (Ill.)—January 3, 1965
    Conyers (Mich.)—January 3, 1965
    de la Garza (Texas)—January 3, 1965
    Foley (Wash.)—January 3, 1965
    Ford (Mich.)—January 3, 1965
    Hamilton (Ind.)—January 3, 1965
    Howard (N.J.)—January 3, 1965
32. Jones (N.C.)—February 5, 1966
33. Bevill (Ala.)—January 3, 1967
    Montgomery (Miss.)—January 3, 1967
    Nichols (Ala.)—January 3, 1967
36. Gaydos (Pa.)—November 5, 1968
37. Alexander (Ark.)—January 3, 1969
    Anderson (Calif.)—January 3, 1969
    Biaggi (N.Y.)—January 3, 1969
    Chappell (Fla.)—January 3, 1969
    Clay (Mo.)—January 3, 1969
    Daniel (Va.)—January 3, 1969
    Stokes (Ohio)—January 3, 1969
    Yatron (Pa.)—January 3, 1969
45. Jones (Tenn.)—March 25, 1969
46. Obey (Wis.)—April 1, 1969
47. Roe (N.J.)—November 4, 1969
48. Aspin (Wis.)—January 3, 1971
    Dellums (Calif.)—January 3, 1971
    Mazzoli (Ky.)—January 3, 1971
    Rangel (N.Y.)—January 3, 1971
52. Brown (Calif.) (four terms previously)—January 3, 1973

53. Lehman (Fla.)—January 3, 1973
Moakley (Mass.)—January 3, 1973
Rose (N.C.)—January 3, 1973
Schroeder (Colo.)—January 3, 1973
Stark (Calif.)—January 3, 1973
Studds (Mass.)—January 3, 1973
Wilson (Texas)—January 3, 1973
60. Boggs (La.)—March 20, 1973
61. Collins (Ill.)—June 5, 1973
62. Murtha (Pa.)—February 5, 1974
63. Traxler (Mich.)—April 16, 1974
64. Jacobs (Ind.) (four terms previously)—January 3, 1975
Scheuer (N.Y.) (four terms previously)—January 3, 1975
66. AuCoin (Ore.)—January 3, 1975
Bonker (Wash.)—January 3, 1975
Derrick (S.C.)—January 3, 1975
Downey (N.Y.)—January 3, 1975
Early (Mass.)—January 3, 1975
English (Okla.)—January 3, 1975
Florio (N.J.)—January 3, 1975
Ford (Tenn.)—January 3, 1975
Hefner (N.C.)—January 3, 1975
Hubbard (Ky.)—January 3, 1975
Hughes (N.J.)—January 3, 1975
LaFalce (N.Y.)—January 3, 1975
Lloyd (Tenn.)—January 3, 1975
McHugh (N.Y.)—January 3, 1975
Miller (Calif.)—January 3, 1975
Mineta (Calif.)—January 3, 1975
Neal (N.C.)—January 3, 1975
Nowak (N.Y.)—January 3, 1975
Oberstar (Minn.)—January 3, 1975
Russo (Ill.)—January 3, 1975
Sharp (Ind.)—January 3, 1975
Solarz (N.Y.)—January 3, 1975
Waxman (Calif.)—January 3, 1975
89. Markey (Mass.)—November 2, 1976
90. Luken (Ohio) (one term previously)—January 3, 1977
91. Akaka (Hawaii)—January 3, 1977
Applegate (Ohio)—January 3, 1977
Barnard (Ga.)—January 3, 1977
Beilenson (Calif.)—January 3, 1977
Bonior (Mich.)—January 3, 1977
Dicks (Wash.)—January 3, 1977
Flippo (Ala.)—January 3, 1977
Gephardt (Mo.)—January 3, 1977
Glickman (Kan.)—January 3, 1977
Huckaby (La.)—January 3, 1977
Jenkins (Ga.)—January 3, 1977
Kildee (Mich.)—January 3, 1977
Murphy (Pa.)—January 3, 1977
Oakar (Ohio)—January 3, 1977
Panetta (Calif.)—January 3, 1977
Pease (Ohio)—January 3, 1977
Rahall (W.Va.)—January 3, 1977
Skelton (Mo.)—January 3, 1977
Vento (Minn.)—January 3, 1977
Volkmer (Mo.)—January 3, 1977
Walgren (Pa.)—January 3, 1977
Watkins (Okla.)—January 3, 1977
Weiss (N.Y.)—January 3, 1977
114. Garcia (N.Y.)—February 14, 1978
115. Anthony (Ark.)—January 3, 1979
Boner (Tenn.)—January 3, 1979
Byron (Md.)—January 3, 1979
Coelho (Calif.)—January 3, 1979
Dixon (Calif.)—January 3, 1979
Donnelly (Mass.)—January 3, 1979
Fazio (Calif.)—January 3, 1979
Frost (Texas)—January 3, 1979
Gray (Pa.)—January 3, 1979
Guarini (N.J.)—January 3, 1979
Hall (Ohio)—January 3, 1979
Hutto (Fla.)—January 3, 1979
Leath (Texas)—January 3, 1979
Leland (Texas)—January 3, 1979
Lowry (Wash.)—January 3, 1979
Matsui (Calif.)—January 3, 1979
Mavroules (Mass.)—January 3, 1979
Mica (Fla.)—January 3, 1979
Nelson (Fla.)—January 3, 1979
Sabo (Minn.)—January 3, 1979
Stenholm (Texas)—January 3, 1979
Swift (Wash.)—January 3, 1979
Synar (Okla.)—January 3, 1979
Williams (Mont.)—January 3, 1979
Wolpe (Mich.)—January 3, 1979
140. Tauzin (La.)—May 17, 1980
141. Crockett (Mich.)—November 4, 1980

142. Coyne (Pa.)—January 3, 1981
Dorgan (N.D.)—January 3, 1981
Dwyer (N.J.)—January 3, 1981
Dymally (Calif.)—January 3, 1981
Dyson (Md.)—January 3, 1981
Eckart (Ohio)—January 3, 1981
Foglietta (Pa.)—January 3, 1981
Frank (Mass.)—January 3, 1981
Gejdenson (Conn.)—January 3, 1981
Hall (Texas)—January 3, 1981
Hatcher (Ga.)—January 3, 1981
Hertel (Mich.)—January 3, 1981
Lantos (Calif.)—January 3, 1981
McCurdy (Okla.)—January 3, 1981
Roemer (La.)—January 3, 1981
Savage (Ill.)—January 3, 1981
Schumer (N.Y.)—January 3, 1981
Wyden (Ore.)—January 3, 1981
160. Hoyer (Md.)—May 19, 1981
161. Dowdy (Miss.)—July 7, 1981
162. Kennelly (Conn.)—January 12, 1982
163. Martinez (Calif.)—July 13, 1982
164. Carr (Mich.) (three terms previously)—January 3, 1983
165. Kostmayer (Pa.) (two terms previously)—January 3, 1983
166. Andrews (Texas)—January 3, 1983
Bates (Calif.)—January 3, 1983
Berman (Calif.)—January 3, 1983
Borski (Pa.)—January 3, 1983
Bosco (Calif.)—January 3, 1983
Boucher (Va.)—January 3, 1983
Boxer (Calif.)—January 3, 1983
Bryant (Texas)—January 3, 1983
Carper (Del.)—January 3, 1983
Coleman (Texas)—January 3, 1983
Cooper (Tenn.)—January 3, 1983
Durbin (Ill.)—January 3, 1983
Erdreich (Ala.)—January 3, 1983
Evans (Ill.)—January 3, 1983
Feighan (Ohio)—January 3, 1983
Kaptur (Ohio)—January 3, 1983
Kolter (Pa.)—January 3, 1983
Lehman (Calif.)—January 3, 1983
Levin (Mich.)—January 3, 1983
Levine (Calif.)—January 3, 1983
Lipinski (Ill.)—January 3, 1983
MacKay (Fla.)—January 3, 1983
McCloskey (Ind.)—January 3, 1983
Mollohan (W.Va.)—January 3, 1983
Moody (Wis.)—January 3, 1983
Morrison (Conn.)—January 3, 1983
Mrazek (N.Y.)—January 3, 1983
Olin (Va.)—January 3, 1983
Ortiz (Texas)—January 3, 1983
Owens (N.Y.)—January 3, 1983
Penny (Minn.)—January 3, 1983
Ray (Ga.)—January 3, 1983
Richardson (N.M.)—January 3, 1983
Rowland (Ga.)—January 3, 1983
Sikorski (Minn.)—January 3, 1983
Sisisky (Va.)—January 3, 1983
Slattery (Kan.)—January 3, 1983
Smith (Fla.)—January 3, 1983
Spratt (S.C.)—January 3, 1983
Staggers (W.Va.)—January 3, 1983
Tallon (S.C.)—January 3, 1983
Thomas (Ga.)—January 3, 1983
Torres (Calif.)—January 3, 1983
Torricelli (N.J.)—January 3, 1983
Towns (N.Y.)—January 3, 1983
Valentine (N.C.)—January 3, 1983
Wheat (Mo.)—January 3, 1983
Wise (W.Va.)—January 3, 1983
214. Ackerman (N.Y.)—March 1, 1983
215. Hayes (Ill.)—August 23, 1983
216. Darden (Ga.)—November 8, 1983
217. Kleczka (Wis.)—April 3, 1984
218. Perkins (Ky.)—November 6, 1984
219. Gray (Ill.) (10 terms previously)—January 3, 1985
220. Atkins (Mass.)—January 3, 1985
Bruce (Ill.)—January 3, 1985
Bustamante (Texas)—January 3, 1985
Gordon (Tenn.)—January 3, 1985
Kanjorski (Pa.)—January 3, 1985
Manton (N.Y.)—January 3, 1985
Robinson (Ark.)—January 3, 1985
Stallings (Idaho)—January 3, 1985
Traficant (Ohio)—January 3, 1985
Visclosky (Ind.)—January 3, 1985
230. Chapman (Texas)—September 4,

1985

231. Clarke (N.C.) (one term previously)—January 6, 1987
Owens (Utah) (one term previously)—January 6, 1987

233. Bilbray (Nev.)—January 6, 1987
Campbell (Colo.)—January 6, 1987
Cardin (Md.)—January 6, 1987
DeFazio (Ore.)—January 6, 1987
Espy (Miss.)—January 6, 1987
Flake (N.Y.)—January 6, 1987
Grant (Fla.)—January 6, 1987
Harris (Ala.)—January 6, 1987
Hayes (La.)—January 6, 1987
Hochbrueckner (N.Y.)—January 6, 1987
Johnson (S.D.)—January 6, 1987
Jontz (Ind.)—January 6, 1987
Kennedy (Mass.)—January 6, 1987
Lancaster (N.C.)—January 6, 1987
Lewis (Ga.)—January 6, 1987
McMillen (Md.)—January 6, 1987
Mfume (Md.)—January 6, 1987
Nagle (Iowa)—January 6, 1987
Patterson (S.C.)—January 6, 1987
Pickett (Va.)—January 6, 1987
Price (N.C.)—January 6, 1987
Sawyer (Ohio)—January 6, 1987
Skaggs (Colo.)—January 6, 1987
Slaughter (N.Y.)—January 6, 1987

257. Brennan (Maine)—January 8, 1987

REPUBLICANS

1. Broomfield (Mich.)—January 3, 1957
Michel (Ill.)—January 3, 1957

3. Conte (Mass.)—January 3, 1959
Latta (Ohio)—January 3, 1959

5. Horton (N.Y.)—January 3, 1963
McDade (Pa.)—January 3, 1963
Quillen (Tenn.)—January 3, 1963

8. Dickinson (Ala.)—January 3, 1965
Duncan (Tenn.)—January 3, 1965

10. Vander Jagt (Mich.)—November 8, 1966

11. Hammerschmidt (Ark.)—January 3, 1967
Miller (Ohio)—January 3, 1967
Myers (Ind.)—January 3, 1967
Wylie (Ohio)—January 3, 1967

15. Coughlin (Pa.)—January 3, 1969
Fish (N.Y.)—January 3, 1969
Lujan (N.M.)—January 3, 1969

18. Crane (Ill.)—November 25, 1969

19. Archer (Texas)—January 3, 1971
Frenzel (Minn.)—January 3, 1971
Kemp (N.Y.)—January 3, 1971
Lent (N.Y.)—January 3, 1971
McKinney (Conn.)—January 3, 1971
Spence (S.C.)—January 3, 1971
Young (Fla.)—January 3, 1971

26. Gilman (N.Y.)—January 3, 1973
Lott (Miss.)—January 3, 1973
Madigan (Ill.)—January 3, 1973
Moorhead (Calif.)—January 3, 1973
Regula (Ohio)—January 3, 1973
Rinaldo (N.J.)—January 3, 1973
Shuster (Pa.)—January 3, 1973
Taylor (Mo.)—January 3, 1973

34. Young (Alaska)—March 6, 1973

35. Lagomarsino (Calif.)—March 5, 1974

36. Goodling (Pa.)—January 3, 1975
Gradison (Ohio)—January 3, 1975
Hyde (Ill.)—January 3, 1975
Jeffords (Vt.)—January 3, 1975
Schulze (Pa.)—January 3, 1975
Smith (Neb.)—January 3, 1975

42. Coleman (Mo.)—November 2, 1976

43. Badham (Calif.)—January 3, 1977
Edwards (Okla.)—January 3, 1977
Ireland (Fla.)—January 3, 1977*
Leach (Iowa)—January 3, 1977
Marlenee (Mont.)—January 3, 1977
Pursell (Mich.)—January 3, 1977
Stump (Ariz.)—January 3, 1977*
Walker (Pa.)—January 3, 1977

51. Stangeland (Minn.)—February 22, 1977

52. Livingston (La.)—August 27, 1977

53. Green (N.Y.)—February 14, 1978

54. Bereuter (Neb.)—January 3, 1979
Cheney (Wyo.)—January 3, 1979
Clinger (Pa.)—January 3, 1979

Courter (N.J.)—January 3, 1979
Dannemeyer (Calif.)—January 3, 1979
Davis (Mich.)—January 3, 1979
Gingrich (Ga.)—January 3, 1979
Hopkins (Ky.)—January 3, 1979
Lewis (Calif.)—January 3, 1979
Lungren (Calif.)—January 3, 1979
Pashayan (Calif.)—January 3, 1979
Ritter (Pa.)—January 3, 1979
Roth (Wis.)—January 3, 1979
Sensenbrenner (Wis.)—January 3, 1979
Shumway (Calif.)—January 3, 1979
Snowe (Maine)—January 3, 1979
Solomon (N.Y.)—January 3, 1979
Tauke (Iowa)—January 3, 1979
Thomas (Calif.)—January 3, 1979
Whittaker (Kan.)—January 3, 1979

74. Petri (Wis.)—April 3, 1979
75. Porter (Ill.)—January 22, 1980
76. Parris (Va.) (one term previously)—January 3, 1981
77. Bliley (Va.)—January 3, 1981

Brown (Colo.)—January 3, 1981
Coats (Ind.)—January 3, 1981
Craig (Idaho)—January 3, 1981
Daub (Neb.)—January 3, 1981
Dreier (Calif.)—January 3, 1981
Emerson (Mo.)—January 3, 1981
Fields (Texas)—January 3, 1981
Gregg (N.H.)—January 3, 1981
Gunderson (Wis.)—January 3, 1981
Hansen (Utah)—January 3, 1981
Hiler (Ind.)—January 3, 1981
Hunter (Calif.)—January 3, 1981
Lowery (Calif.)—January 3, 1981
Martin (Ill.)—January 3, 1981
Martin (N.Y.)—January 3, 1981
McCollum (Fla.)—January 3, 1981
McEwen (Ohio)—January 3, 1981
McGrath (N.Y.)—January 3, 1981
Molinari (N.Y.)—January 3, 1981
Morrison (Wash.)—January 3, 1981
Roberts (Kan.)—January 3, 1981
Rogers (Ky.)—January 3, 1981
Roukema (N.J.)—January 3, 1981
Schneider (R.I.)—January 3, 1981
Shaw (Fla.)—January 3, 1981
Skeen (N.M.)—January 3, 1981
Smith (N.J.)—January 3, 1981
Smith, Denny (Ore.)—January 3, 1981
Weber (Minn.)—January 3, 1981
Wolf (Va.)—January 3, 1981
Wortley (N.Y.)—January 3, 1981

109. Oxley (Ohio)—June 25, 1981
110. Bartlett (Texas)—January 3, 1983

Bateman (Va.)—January 3, 1983
Bilirakis (Fla.)—January 3, 1983
Boehlert (N.Y.)—January 3, 1983
Burton (Ind.)—January 3, 1983
Chandler (Wash.)—January 3, 1983
DeWine (Ohio)—January 3, 1983
Gekas (Pa.)—January 3, 1983
Johnson (Conn.)—January 3, 1983
Kasich (Ohio)—January 3, 1983
Lewis (Fla.)—January 3, 1983
Mack (Fla.)—January 3, 1983
McCandless (Calif.)—January 3, 1983
Nielson (Utah)—January 3, 1983
Packard (Calif.)—January 3, 1983
Ridge (Pa.)—January 3, 1983
Smith, Robert F. (Ore.)—January 3, 1983
Sundquist (Tenn.)—January 3, 1983
Vucanovich (Nev.)—January 3, 1983

129. Schaefer (Colo.)—March 29, 1983
130. Saxton (N.J.)—November 6, 1984
131. Dornan (Calif.) (three terms previously)—January 3, 1985
132. Armey (Texas)—January 3, 1985

Barton (Texas)—January 3, 1985
Bentley (Md.)—January 3, 1985
Boulter (Texas)—January 3, 1985
Callahan (Ala.)—January 3, 1985
Coble (N.C.)—January 3, 1985
Combest (Texas)—January 3, 1985
DeLay (Texas)—January 3, 1985
DioGuardi (N.Y.)—January 3, 1985
Fawell (Ill.)—January 3, 1985

Gallo (N.J.)—January 3, 1985
Henry (Mich.)—January 3, 1985
Kolbe (Ariz.)—January 3, 1985
Lightfoot (Iowa)—January 3, 1985
McMillan (N.C.)—January 3, 1985
Meyers (Kan.)—January 3, 1985
Miller (Wash.)—January 3, 1985
Rowland (Conn.)—January 3, 1985
Schuette (Mich.)—January 3, 1985
Slaughter (Va.)—January 3, 1985
Smith (N.H.)—January 3, 1985
Sweeney (Texas)—January 3, 1985
Swindall (Ga.)—January 3, 1985

155. Ballenger (N.C.)—November 4, 1986
156. Lukens (Ohio) (two terms previously)—January 6, 1987
157. Baker (La.)—January 6, 1987
Buechner (Mo.)—January 6, 1987
Bunning (Ky.)—January 6, 1987
Davis (Ill.)—January 6, 1987
Gallegly (Calif.)—January 6, 1987
Grandy (Iowa)—January 6, 1987
Hastert (Ill.)—January 6, 1987
Hefley (Colo.)—January 6, 1987
Herger (Calif.)—January 6, 1987
Holloway (La.)—January 6, 1987
Houghton (N.Y.)—January 6, 1987
Inhofe (Okla.)—January 6, 1987
Konnyu (Calif.)—January 6, 1987
Kyl (Ariz.)—January 6, 1987
Morella (Md.)—January 6, 1987
Ravenel (S.C.)—January 6, 1987
Rhodes (Ariz.)—January 6, 1987
Saiki (Hawaii)—January 6, 1987
Smith (Texas)—January 6, 1987
Upton (Mich.)—January 6, 1987
Weldon (Pa.)—January 6, 1987

* *Ireland and Stump began House service January 3, 1977, as Democrats, and later switched parties. The Republican Conference let their seniority count from 1977.*

Appendix C

Congressional Powers

The authors of the Constitution recognized that the new government needed an executive to carry out the laws and a judiciary to resolve conflicts in them. But Congress would be the heart of the new republic. The House of Representatives was the only part of the federal government originally elected by the people; consequently, Congress was the branch of government expected to respond directly to their needs.

It was thus to the national legislature that the framers entrusted most of the power necessary to govern the new nation. To Congress the Constitution granted "all legislative Powers." These included the power to tax, regulate commerce, declare war, approve treaties, and raise and maintain armies.

The framers also gave Congress some authority over the other two branches. Congress was granted the power to establish whatever federal judicial system below the Supreme Court seemed desirable and to impeach and convict the president, federal judges, and other federal officers for treason, bribery, or other high crimes and misdemeanors. Each chamber has authority to seat and discipline its own members.

The exercise of these powers is subject to some limitation. The Constitution specifically prevents Congress from singling out individuals for punishment and from imposing a direct tax that is unapportioned or an indirect tax that is not uniform. The most significant constitutional limitations may be those added by the First Amendment, prohibiting Congress from interfering with the free exercise of speech, the press, assembly, or religion, and the Fifth Amendment, prohibiting the taking of life, liberty, or property without due process of law.

Fiscal Powers

Perhaps the most important of the constitutional prerogatives granted to Congress are the powers to tax and to spend. Congress may use its power to tax both to raise revenue to run the country and as a regulatory device. The power to spend allows Congress to determine policy on almost every matter that affects daily life in the United States.

Taxation

Taxes on the income and profits of individuals and corporations have become the federal government's basic sources of revenue since the Sixteenth Amendment permitting a general income tax was ratified in 1913. In addition, Congress has imposed an excess profits tax on corporations during wartime, levied a variety of excise taxes, authorized estate and gift taxes, and imposed payroll taxes to underpin the old-age insurance and unemployment compensation systems.

Tax legislation must, under a constitutional provision, originate in the House of Representatives. Tax and tariff bills are handled there by the Ways and Means Committee. After the House acts, such bills go to the Senate where they are referred to the Finance Committee. Because that committee and the full Senate may amend the House version of a tax bill, the Senate plays an influential role in the consideration and adoption of tax legislation. In a departure from tradition and constitutional dictates, the Senate initiated a major tax bill in 1982. It was enacted, although some House members challenged the constitutionality of the legislation.

In the post-World War II era, initiatives on raising, lowering, or enacting new taxes generally have been taken by the executive branch; it has prepared the initial recommendations and Congress has acted on them. But there is no requirement that the executive initiate tax changes. Congress itself generated a major tax reform bill in 1969 and a wide-ranging tax revision bill in 1976.

Appropriations

Revenue raised through taxation is not available in the Treasury to be disbursed by the executive branch to meet governmental needs simply as agency officials see fit. The Constitution gives to Congress the sole authority to determine how monies collected shall be spent and requires a regular statement of expenditures.

This appropriations procedure works in two steps after the president presents his annual budget requests to Congress. First, the various congressional committees consider the parts of the request that fall under their jurisdictions and report out bills authorizing expenditures and setting a ceiling on the amount of funds that can be spent for the programs. After the authorization becomes law, Congress actually provides (appropriates) the money to fund the programs. The amount of money appropriated often is less than the maximum amount specified in the authorization for the program.

Although the Constitution does not require it, appropriations traditionally originate in the House. Appropriations initially are considered by the relevant subcommittee of the House Appropriations Committee where the bulk of basic spending decisions are made, although both the full committee and the House may amend a bill before it is passed and sent to the Senate. What the Senate does in effect is to review the House action and hear appeals from agencies seeking changes in the allotments accorded them by the House.

Budget Control

Congress, having long treated its taxing and spending powers separately, in 1974 enacted the Congressional Budget and Impoundment Control Act (PL 93-344) to provide a method of setting overall fiscal policy for the federal government, and in some respects constrain congressional committees from acting against the goals espoused in the budget.

The budget law set up House and Senate Budget committees to write annual budgets and keep track of Congress's performance in adhering to them, and it created a Congressional Budget Office to provide technical information about the economy and the budget that previously was available only from the president's budget agency, the Office of Management and Budget.

In December 1985 the perceived failure of the 1974 law to prevent steadily increasing, multibillion-dollar deficits led Congress to make radical changes in budget procedures that presumably would force a balanced budget by October 1990. The new law, known as Gramm-Rudman-Hollings (PL 99-177) for its Senate sponsors, set maximum annual allowable deficits for the years 1986-1991, and mandated automatic, across-the-board spending cuts if Congress failed to meet those goals.

Aside from a legal challenge to a key element of the process making the automatic cuts, the law was seen by many observers as a significant political step for a Congress previously unwilling to address huge deficits.

However, legislating under the lash of the 1985 Gramm-Rudman-Hollings antideficit law did not turn out quite the way it was advertised when the law was enacted in December 1985.

The first hitch came in early February 1986, when President Reagan submitted a fiscal 1987 budget that, according to the Congressional Budget Office (CBO), exceeded the Gramm-Rudman deficit target of $144 billion by some $16 billion in understated defense spending. Administration officials contested the CBO finding, although months later they acknowledged that fiscal 1986 defense outlays were running at least $5 billion ahead of their February estimate.

The same week as the president's budget request, a special federal court found the key feature of Gramm-Rudman—its automatic spending cut mechanism—to be unconstitutional. The mechanism was to be activated in mid-August each year if deficit re-estimates showed Congress and the president had not managed through conventional legislation to hold deficits below targets set by the statute.

Absent the automatic device, the deficit re-estimates would still be made but any spending cuts necessitated by those estimates would take effect only if approved by Congress and the president.

The Supreme Court upheld the lower court ruling that the automatic mechanism violated the separation-of-powers doctrine, because it was assigned executive-type responsibilities to the General Accounting Office, which the court found to be an entity under the legislative branch.

The ruling brought firm assurances from sponsors of the antideficit law that its remaining procedure requiring congressional and presidential approval of spending cuts would work. Yet almost immediately, Sen. Phil Gramm, R-Texas, and his original cosponsors began pushing a revised version of the automatic procedure device which, Gramm said, was needed to eliminate "uncertainty" in deficit cutting.

The Senate July 30 added what became known as Gramm-Rudman-Hollings II, which would allow the Office of Management and Budget to determine the final shape of automatic spending cuts, to legislation (H J Res 668) raising the ceiling on the federal debt.

The debt-limit measure, which became stalled in the Senate by unrelated fights, was passed August 9. But House hostility to the Gramm-Rudman amendment left its future—and that of the debt-limit increase—in considerable doubt.

Meanwhile, the Senate tried unsuccessfully to get the House to swallow a version of the Gramm-Rudman fix as part of a short-term, emergency debt-limit increase, designed to keep the government operating into September. The failed Gramm-Rudman fix would have been in effect for fiscal 1987 only.

Commerce Powers

Nearly as important as the powers to tax and spend is the power to regulate interstate and foreign commerce. Congress's exercise of its virtually exclusive authority in these areas has produced extensive government regulation not only of the actual transport of goods but also of their manufacture, sale, and, in many cases, their purity and safety.

The Constitution gave Congress a broad and positive grant of power to regulate interstate and foreign commerce but left interpretation of the extent of the power to precedent and judicial determination. Although the Supreme Court initially gave Congress almost complete control over interstate commerce, the legislative branch seldom exercised its power. But with the passage of the Interstate Commerce Act of 1887, Congress moved decisively into the area of domestic regulation. The act, prompted by the individual states' inability to curb increasing abuses by railroads, ultimately was broadened to include regulation of trucking companies, bus lines, foreign forwarders, water carriers, oil pipelines, transportation brokers, and express agencies. The act, which established the Interstate Commerce Commission as the first regulatory agency, also led to creation of several other agencies that regulate various aspects of commercial transactions in the United States, as well as entire industries, such as communications and energy.

In 1890 Congress moved into federal regulation of commercial enterprise with enactment of the Sherman Antitrust Act "to protect commerce against unlawful restraints and monopolies." With the turn of the century, Congress began to regulate interstate commerce to protect the health and morals of the general populace. To this end, Congress banned interstate shipment of such items as lottery tickets, impure food, and drugs.

Although the Supreme Court sanctioned most new uses of the interstate commerce power, it balked at certain regulations, such as the congressional attempt in 1916 to outlaw child labor by barring the shipment of goods made by children. It was this narrower view of the commerce power that prevailed when the Supreme Court reviewed and declared unconstitutional many of the early New Deal economic recovery programs. The confrontation resulted in the Court's recognition of Congress's authority to regulate virtually all aspects of business and manufacture affecting interstate commerce.

Only once since 1937 has the Court found an exercise of the commerce clause to be unconstitutional. In that same period it has sanctioned broadened uses of the commerce power. In the Civil Rights Act of 1964, Congress found justification in the commerce clause and the "equal protection" clause of the Fourteenth Amendment for a ban on racial discrimination in most public accommodations. Congress used the commerce clause in 1968 as the basis for legislation making it a federal crime to travel in interstate commerce for the purpose of inciting or participating in a riot. The commerce clause is also the basis for the far-reaching federal clean air and water laws.

Policy Powers

While the president generally takes the initiative in foreign relations, Congress possesses several constitutionally granted powers that are indispensable to the success of the president's policies. These include the powers to raise taxes (to finance wars), create and maintain an armed force, regulate foreign commerce, and ratify treaties. Except for votes on the Vietnam War in the 1970s, and Lebanon and Central America in the 1980s, Congress in the twentieth century has chosen to use its powers to support the president in these matters rather than to challenge him.

While the Constitution gives Congress

the power to declar war and "provide for the common Defence," both the initiation and conduct of war have come to be almost entirely directed by the president. In November 1973 Congress sought to restore some of its control over war efforts when it enacted, over President Nixon's veto, the War Powers Resolution (PL 93-148). In addition to certain reporting requirements, the measure set a sixty-day limit on any presidential commitment of U.S. troops abroad without specific congressional authorization, unless troops were sent to respond to an "attack upon the United States, its territories or possessions, or its armed forces." Unauthorized commitments could be terminated prior to the sixty-day deadline through congressional passage of a concurrent resolution—a measure that does not require the president's signature to take effect.

Although Congress had never used that "legislative veto" authority to force a president to withdraw troops, the threat of a veto may have forced chief executives to consult more closely with Congress in taking military actions abroad. The Supreme Court's June 1983 ruling that legislative vetoes were unconstitutional dealt a blow to congressional influence over such commitments by nullifying that provision of the War Powers Resolution. In the wake of that ruling Congress wrestled with ways to develop an alternative method of influencing decisions. After the April 14, 1986, bombing of Libya, Congress again addressed the question of presidential prerogative. This time the debate centered on if and when the president should consult Congress in cases involving a U.S. response to terrorism.

Another area in which the Supreme Court's ruling could have a potentially far-reaching impact is congressional control of arms sales. In 1976 Congress enacted the Arms Export Control Act (PL 94-329), substantially expanding its power to veto arms sales to foreign countries through adoption of a concurrent resolution. Again, although most arms sales have raised little controversy, Congress has repeatedly challenged the president's judgment on specific sales to countries, particularly those in the volatile Middle East. As with the War Powers Resolution, Congress never has actually vetoed a proposed arms sale, but the possibility forced Presidents Jimmy Carter and Ronald Reagan to make compromises.

In spite of the Supreme Court's legislative veto ruling, congressional power over some other aspects of foreign policy has increased substantially. Legislative authority over the massive post-World War II foreign aid and military assistance programs is an example. The programs have required specific congressional authorizations and repeated congressional appropriations. Frequently Congress has disagreed with the president over the amounts and allocations for these programs, making its views known either through directives in the authorizing legislation, or by changing funding requests in appropriations bills.

The Constitution gives the president authority to make treaties with other countries if two-thirds of the Senate concur. For years this power served as a cornerstone of American foreign policy. Treaties forged peace agreements with other nations, supported U.S. territorial expansion, established national boundaries, protected U.S. commerce, and regulated government affairs with Indian tribes.

Except for rejection of the Versailles Treaty after World War I, Senate action on treaties has not been a major factor in foreign policy. Although the Senate has killed several treaties by inaction, it had by the end of 1985 rejected only twenty treaties since 1789. However, the lengthy debates on the Panama Canal and U.S.-Soviet strategic arms limitation talks (SALT II) treaties in 1978 and 1979, respectively, were seen as Senate moves to expand its power in the foreign policy field.

In recent years the Senate's role has been eroded somewhat by the use of executive agreements instead of treaties with foreign countries; such agreements do not require Senate approval.

Confirmation of Nominations

Under the Constitution the Senate must approve all presidential nominations of federal officers. Most nominations involve promotions of military officers and Senate action is only a formality. But each year several hundred major nominations are subjected to varying degrees of Senate scrutiny. These include nominations to Cabinet and sub-Cabinet positions, independent boards and regulatory agencies, major diplomatic and military posts, and the federal judiciary.

The Senate role in Supreme Court appointments has proved particularly important. It may not be able to dictate Supreme Court nominees, but historically the Senate has not been afraid to reject them. Slightly more than one-fifth of all Supreme Court nominations have failed to win Senate confirmation.

Appointments to lower federal courts are another matter. Traditionally the president has used this power—particularly those at the district court level—to please members of both chambers. Generally the president names as district court judge the person recommended by the House member of Congress from that district. These lower court appointments thus provide the president with his important patronage power—the opportunity to win the good will of a member of Congress or a vote on a crucial issue.

The Senate carefully considers nominations of Cabinet officers, but such officers usually are confirmed with little difficulty on the theory that the president should have great leeway in choosing the members of his official "family." There have been exceptions though. President Reagan first nominated Edwin Meese to be attorney general in January 1984. After thirteen months—longer than any other Cabinet nominee in recent history—he was confirmed.

Presidential appointments to independent boards and commissions present a somewhat different situation. These agencies are created by Congress and are not subordinate to the executive branch. Congress expects these agencies to implement congressional goals and therefore it plays a large role in the selection process. Contests over these nominations have been frequent, although few nominees actually have been rejected.

Impeachment

Impeachment of federal officers is perhaps the most awesome, though the least used, power of Congress. The Constitution specifies that the House shall impeach (indict) federal officials that it believes guilty of treason, bribery, or high crimes and misdemeanors. The charges are drawn up in an impeachment resolution, usually reported by the House Judiciary Committee. If the House adopts the resolution, the Senate holds a trial, with House members acting as prosecutors. If a president is impeached the chief justice presides at the Senate trial. Conviction requires two-thirds approval of the senators present. Punishment is limited to removal from office and disqualification for further federal office. There is no appeal.

The two most famous cases of impeachment resulted in acquittal after sensational trials. They involved President Andrew Johnson, accused of violating the Tenure of Office Act, and Supreme Court Justice Samuel Chase, accused of partisan conduct on the bench. Since 1789 only fourteen federal officials have been impeached by the House. Of the thirteen cases that went to Senate trial, two were dismissed before trial after the person impeached left office, six resulted in acquittal, and five ended in conviction. President Nixon's resignation on August 9, 1974, foreclosed House action on impeachment charges approved by the Judiciary Committee. U.S. District Judge Harry E. Claiborne was removed from office October 9, 1986, for tax fraud. He was the first official to be removed from office in fifty years and the fifth in the history of the nation.

Constitutional Amendments

Congress shares with the states the power to propose amendments to the Constitution. Amendments may be offered by two-thirds of both chambers of Congress or by a convention called by Congress at the request of the legislatures of two-thirds of the states. Amendments must be ratified by the legislatures or conventions of three-fourths of the states. Congress has always specified ratification by the state legislatures, except for the Twenty-first Amendment.

Although these constitutional provisions anticipated a substantial role for the states, Congress has dominated the amendment process. Not once have the states been successful in calling for a convention to propose an amendment to the Constitution. The states fell one short in 1969 when thirty-three of them called for a convention to write an amendment overturning the Supreme Court's "one person, one vote" decisions. As of 1985 the states were two short of the two-thirds required to call a constitutional convention to draft an amendment requiring a balanced federal budget.

Restrained use of the amendment procedure has enabled the Constitution to remain the fundamental law of the land even though the United States has been transformed beyond recognition since the Constitution was drafted. The states have ratified only twenty-six amendments. Included among those are the ten amendments comprising the Bill of Rights, extension of the right to vote to blacks and women, and the guarantees of equal protection and due process of the law against them.

Altogether, Congress has submitted to the states only thirty-three amendments. The states failed to ratify seven of these, including a proposal to give the District of Columbia voting representation in Congress. The proposed amendment, approved by Congress in 1978, failed to win ratification by its 1985 deadline.

The Equal Rights Amendment, approved in 1972 by Congress, failed to win ratification by the extended deadline of June 30, 1982. Despite a massive lobby effort, only thirty-five states had approved the proposal, three short of the necessary thirty-eight. The congressionally approved extension and efforts by five states to rescind their ratification raised constitutional questions about the amendment procedure.

Election of the President

Congress under the Constitution has two key responsibilities relating to the election of the president and vice president. First it must receive and in joint session count the electoral votes certified by the states. Second, if no candidate has a majority of the electoral vote, the House must elect the president and the Senate the vice president.

In modern times the formal counting of electoral votes has been largely a ceremonial function. The House actually has chosen the president only twice, in 1801 and 1825. In the course of the nation's history, however, a number of campaigns deliberately have been designed to throw elections into the House. Apprehension over this has nurtured many electoral reform efforts. The most recent attempt came in 1979 when the Senate rejected a proposed constitutional amendment that would have abolished the electoral college system and replaced it with direct popular election of the president.

The Twentieth and Twenty-fifth Amendments authorize Congress to settle problems arising from the death of a president-elect or candidate or the disability of a president. The Twenty-fifth Amendment, ratified in 1967 to cover what its authors assumed would be rare occurrences, was applied twice in twelve months and gave rise to executive leadership unique in the nation's history. The amendment provides that whenever the office of vice president becomes vacant, the president shall appoint a replacement, subject to confirmation by Congress.

Gerald R. Ford was the first vice president to take office under the amendment. He was sworn in December 6, 1973, to replace Spiro T. Agnew, who had resigned after pleading no contest to a charge of federal income tax evasion. A year later, Nelson A. Rockefeller was sworn in December 19, 1974, to succeed Ford. Ford had become president upon the August 9, 1974, resignation of President Nixon. Thus neither of the nation's two chief officials in 1975 and 1976 was elected by the people.

Congressional Ethics

The Constitution empowers each chamber of Congress to seat, unseat, and punish its own members. The House and Senate have the power to determine whether a member fulfills the constitutional requirements for service, to settle contested elections, and to censure members for misconduct. Some of these powers come into conflict with the right of voters to decide who will represent them. As a result Congress has been cautious in using its authority. While it has acted often to determine the winner in contested elections, it has rejected the clear choice of the voters, for lack of the requisite qualification, in fewer than twenty cases since 1789.

Censure Proceedings

Congress has shown like restraint in expelling or punishing members for disorderly or improper conduct. Expulsions have numbered fifteen in the Senate and four in the House, including the expulsion of Rep. Michael "Ozzie" Myers, D-Pa., in the fall of 1980. Seven senators, twenty-two representatives and one territorial delegate have been formally censured by their colleagues. In 1979-1980 the House censured Charles C. Diggs, Jr., a Michigan Democrat who resigned in June 1980, and Charles H. Wilson, D-Calif., both for financial misconduct. In July 1983 Reps. Daniel B. Crane, R-Ill., and Gerry E. Studds, D-Mass., were censured for sexual misconduct with teenage congressional pages.

One historical reason for the comparatively few instances of congressional punishment of its members had been the difficulty in determining what constitutes conflict of interest and misuse of power. But an increasing incidence of scandals in the 1960s led to creation of ethics committees in both houses to oversee members' conduct.

By the mid-1970s Congress's reputation suffered as a number of current and former members were accused of criminal or unethical behavior. In 1976 Rep. Wayne L. Hays, D-Ohio, was forced to resign under threat of a House probe into charges that he kept a mistress on the public payroll. The same year the House voted to reprimand Robert L. F. Sikes, D-Fla., for financial misconduct.

Shortly after Congress convened in 1977, special committees in both the House and Senate began drawing up new codes of ethics adopted by both chambers in March. The new rules were codified into law and extended to top officials in the executive and legislative branches in 1978.

Still more scandal was unveiled in 1980 through a government undercover investigation of political corruption—known as "Abscam"—in which law enforcement agents, posing as businessmen or wealthy Arabs, attempted to induce some members of Congress and other elected officials to use their influence, for pay, for such things as helping Arabs obtain U.S. residency, get federal grants, and arrange real estate transactions.

The expulsion of Ozzie Myers, which resulted from his Abscam conviction, was a milestone for a House that had long been the butt of derisive jokes about lax punishment of wayward members. The other congressmen involved in the scandal escaped expulsion. Two of the convicted House members resigned: John W. Jenrette, Jr., D-S.C., on December 19, 1980, and Raymond F. Lederer, D-Pa., on May 5, 1981. Three others were defeated for reelection: Richard Kelly, R-Fla., John M. Murphy, D-N.Y., and Frank Thompson, Jr., D-N.J.

The lone senator convicted in the Abscam scandal, Harrison A. Williams, Jr., D-N.J., resigned on March 11, 1982, hours before the Senate was expected to vote on his expulsion.

In the wake of the Abscam convictions, both the House and Senate ethics committees considered revising their codes of conduct.

Power of Investigation

The power of Congress to undertake investigations—perhaps its most controversial of legislative branch power—is not specified in the Constitution. It is based instead on tradition and the belief that investigations are indispensable to the legislative process. Yet, the Supreme Court never has questioned the right of Congress to conduct investigations.

No period of American history has been without congressional investigation. The first was held in 1792, to investigate the massacre of U.S. soldiers in Indian territory. Since then, congressional probes have gathered information on the need for possible future legislation, tested the effectiveness of past legislative action, questioned executive branch actions, and laid the groundwork for impeachment proceedings. Investigations have elevated comparatively minor political figures to national fame, broken the careers of important public men and women, and captured the attention of millions of newspaper readers and television viewers.

Members' Pay

A very ticklish power held by Congress is that of setting members' salaries. Although Congress traditionally has tried to bury its own salary increases in general pay raises for federal workers, increases nevertheless have led to public criticism.

In December 1982, in a break with nearly two centuries of tradition, Congress decided to pay House members more than senators, while the latter could earn unlimited amounts in outside income, including honoraria.

Effective December 18, 1982, House members' salaries were raised to $69,800. Salaries for senators remained at $60,662.50, but they were allowed to earn as much as they chose in outside honoraria. Outside earnings for representatives continued to be limited by the House rules to 30 percent of members' salaries. A limit on outside earnings for senators equal to 15 percent of their congressional salaries, or about $9,100, would have gone into effect January 1, 1983, if the Senate had not acted to change its own rules.

The Senate voted to raise members' salaries to the House level of $69,800 in June 1983. But amid public criticism of senators' outside income, they agreed to place a cap on Senate honoraria that was equal to the House limit.

In 1985 the annual 3.5 percent pay increase came on top of a 4 percent raise that federal white-collar employees and Congress received in 1984. The 1985 raise boosted the salaries of senators and representatives from $72,600 to $75,100.

In 1987 careful machinations allowed members of Congress to go on record against a proposed $12,100 annual pay raise and yet pocket the increase. On February 4, 1987, the House followed the Senate's lead in rejecting salary increases for members. However, the House cleared the measure one day *after* a thirty-day deadline set in law for disapproving pay proposals.

Index